Essex County, Virginia

Guardianship and Orphans Records

1707-1888

A Descriptive Index

Wesley E. Pippenger

HERITAGE BOOKS
2018

HERITAGE BOOKS

AN IMPRINT OF HERITAGE BOOKS, INC.

Books, CDs, and more—Worldwide

For our listing of thousands of titles see our website
at
www.HeritageBooks.com

Published 2018 by
HERITAGE BOOKS, INC.
Publishing Division
5810 Ruatan Street
Berwyn Heights, Md. 20740

International Standard Book Number
Paperbound: 978-0-7884-5814-9

TABLE OF CONTENTS

INTRODUCTION

For this work, I have reviewed microfilm copies of a number of guardians accounts or records books for the period 1707-1888 in Essex County, Virginia. The problem that users often face with using this type of original record is that the court indexes to the guardianship records usually refer to the person bonded or the guardian, and NOT the ward who is the primary interest for genealogical research.

Most of the entries here are from sources that actually have "Guardians" on the spine of the original record book. Also, particularly for the early years, guardianship records (mainly bonds) may be found in Will Books. The index that is created here frequently presents the name of the ward, the name of a deceased or living parent, and the name of the guardian. Since public birth records do not begin in Essex County until 1856 and are rather incomplete for many years thereafter, the guardianship records supplement that void by frequently showing a parent-to-child relationship. Sadly, the earliest guardian bonds rarely give the name of the parent of the orphan.

The filing date is indexed here for most records except bonds wherein the date the bond was executed is used. Oftentimes a guardian account is presented to the court earlier than the date it is finally recorded, as it frequently sat in "limbo" for one or more months pending any exceptions presented. As time goes on, one will find that a certificate may be recorded for a minor over the age of 14 years who has chosen a guardian. A corresponding bond may list additional minors in the same family group who are under the age of 14 years.

Wesley E. Pippenger
Little Egypt
Tappahannock, Virginia

ABBREVIATIONS AND CODES

Abbreviation	Description		
Bond C.	Curator or Committee Bond	Dr.	Doctor
(C)	colored	fr.	from
c/o	child of	h/o	heir of
Co.	county	Ref.	Reference to
Col.	Colonel	s/o	son of
d/o	daughter of	w/o	wife of
dec.	deceased	wid/o	widow of

Code	Source Material
1731	Orphans Accounts (and Bonds) No. 1, 1731-1760, 261 pages, index. Note: *The original was restored in 1947 by the Newport News Chapter of the National Society, Daughters of the American Revolution, in honor of Mrs. John Addison Willett, Sr. (Elizabeth Austin), Treasurer 1927.* [LVA Reel 104; LDS Reels 31170, 31273, 1929895]
1761	Guardians Book No. 2, 1761-1796, 228 pages, index (damaged). Note: *In Memory of Mrs. E. Fenno Heath (Evelyn Wardwell), March 1, 1868-April 1, 1940, Historian, March 15, 1940-April 1, 1940. This Volume was Restored by Chanco Chapter, National Society, Daughters of the American Revolution, 1941.* [LVA Reel 104; LDS Reels 31274, 1929895]
1796	Guardian Book No. 3, 1796-1811, 262 pages, index [LVA Reel 104; LDS Reels 31204, 1929895]
1811	Guardian Book No. 4, 1811-1821, 253 pages, index [LVA Reel 105; LDS Reels 31204, 1929895]
1825	Guardian Book No. 5, 1825-1829, 317 pages, index [LVA Reel 105; LDS Reels 31205, 1929895, 1929896]
1831	Guardians Book No. 6, 1831-1837, 508 pages, index [LVA Reel 105; LDS Reels 31205, 1929896]
1838	Guardians Book No. 7, 1838-1844, 373 pages, index [LVA Reel 106; LDS Reels 31206, 1929896]
1844	Guardians Book No. 8, 1844-1851, 544 pages, index [LVA Reel 106; LDS Reels 31206, 1929896]
1851	Guardians Book No. 9, 1851-1857, 455 pages, index [LVA Reel 107; LDS Reels 31207, 1929923 item 5]
1857	Guardians Book No. 10, 1858-1867, 435 pages, index [LVA Reel 107; LDS Reels 31207, 1929923 item 6, 1929924 item 1]
1867	Guardians Book No. 11, 1867-1888, 600 pages, index [LVA Reel 123; LDS Reel 1929924 item 2]
CCW	Circuit Superior Court of Law and Chancery Bonds, Wills, Inventories and Accounts, 1834-1902, 173 pages, index [LVA Reel 64; LDS Reel 31264 item 1]
D&W12	Deeds and Wills No. 12, 1704-1707, 444 pages, index [LVA Reel 4; LDS Reel 1929931]
D&W13	Deeds and Wills No. 13, 1707-1711, 440 pages, no index. [LVA Reel 5; LDS Reel 1929932]
D&W14	Deeds and Wills No. 14, 1711-1716, 733 pages, no index [LVA Reel 6; LDS Reels 1929932, 1929933]
D&W15	Deeds and Wills No. 15, 1716-1717, 266 pages, index [LVA Reel 7; LDS Reel 1929933]

F	List of Fiduciaries, 1870-1956, unpaged, no index [LVA Reel 138; LDS Reel 1929921 item 3]
WB3	Wills, Inventories and Settlements of Estates No. 3, 1717-1721, 328 pages, index [LVA Reel 40; LDS Reel 1929900]
WB4	Wills, Bonds, Inventories, Etc. No. 4, 1722-1730, 414 pages, index [LVA Reel 40; LDS Reel 1929900]
WB5	Will Book No. 5, 1730-1735, 428 pages, index [LVA Reel 41; LDS Reels 1929900 and 1929901]
WB6	Will Book No. 6, 1735-1743, 443 pages, index [LVA Reel 42; LDS Reel 1929901]
WB7	Will Book No. 7, 1743-1747, 533 pages, index [LVA Reel 43; LDS Reel 1929901]
WB8	Will Book No. 8, 1747-1750/1, 430 pages, index [LVA Reel 44; LDS Reel 1929902]
WB9	Will Book No. 9, 1750/1-1754 pages 9-345, index [LVA Reel 45; LDS Reel 1929902]
WB10	Will Book No. 10, 1754-1756 165 pages, index [LVA Reel 45; LDS Reel 1929902]
WB11	Will Book No. 11, 1756-1762, 434 pages, index [LVA Reel 46; LDS Reel 1929903]
WB12	Will Book No. 12, 1762-1775, 625 pages, index [LVA Reel 47; LDS Reel 1929903]
WB13	Will Book No. 13, 1775-1785, 532 pages, index [LVA Reel 48; LDS Reel 1929904]
WB14	Will Book No. 14, 1786-1792, 357 pages, index [LVA Reel 48; LDS Reel 1929904]
WB15	Will Book No. 15, 1792-1800, 555 pages, index [LVA Reel 49; LDS Reels 1929904 and 1929905]

Note: Will Books No. 15 through 28, for the period 1800-1865, were also indexed in Wesley E. Pippenger, *Index to Virginia Estates, 1800-1865*, Volume 10 (Richmond, Va.: The Virginia Genealogical Society, 2010). Guardianship items were found in Will Books 19, 22, 23, 24, 25, and 27 only.

WB19	Will Book 19, 1816-1823, 428 pages, index [LVA Reel 53; LDS Reel 1929906]
WB22	Will Book 22, 1829-1832, 509 pages, index [LVA Reel 56; LDS Reel 1929907]
WB23	Will Book 23, 1832-1836, 471 pages, index [LVA Reel 57; LDS Reel 1929908]
WB24	Will Book 24, 1836-1842, 722 pages, index [LVA Reel 58; LDS Reel 1929908]
WB25	Will Book 25, 1842-1846, 515 pages, index [LVA Reel 59; LDS Reel 1929909]
WB27	Will Book 27, 1851-1858, 805 pages, index [LVA Reel 61; LDS Reel 1929910]

The original record book is not listed if it did not contain any guardianship records.

Know all Men by these p'sents that we William Covington, Francis Gouldman, & Thomas Bryant are held & firmly bound unto William Daingerfield, Thomas Waring, Robert Brookes, James Garnett, Nicholas Smith, Alexander Parker, Richard Tyler j'r & Thomas Shurshly jun'r Gentlemen Justices of the County of Essex their heirs & Successors in the Sum of One thousand pounds sterl to the which payment well and truly to be made we bind our selves our heirs Ex'rs, and Adm'rs Jointly and severally firmly by these p'sents Witness our hand & seal this 18'th day of August Anno Dm 1730 ———

The Condition of the above Obligation is Such that if the above bound William Covington Guardian of Robert Spilsby Coleman his heirs, Executors & Adm'rs do & Shall well and truly pay or cause to be paid unto the s'd Orphan all Such Estate and Estates as now is or hereafter Shall come to the hands of the s'd William Covington as Soon as the s'd Orphan Shall Attain to lawfull Age or when thereunto required by the Justices of the Peace for the County of Essex as also to Save and keep harmless the s'd Justices their heirs, and Successors from all trouble and damage that Shall or May arise about the s'd Estate then this Obligation to be Null Void and of none Effect Else to be & remain in full force power and Virtue ———

Sealed & delivered
in p'sence of ———

W'm Covington (Seal)

Fran's Gouldman (Seal)

Tho' Bryan — (Seal)

At a Court held for Essex County on the 18'th day of August 1730 W'm Covington, Francis Gouldman & Thomas Bryant acknowledged this bond to be their Act & deed which is Ordered to be recorded ———

Test M Beverley Clk

Sample 1 - Robert Spilsby Coleman to William Covington, 18 AUG 1730

Know all men by these presents that we Otway Rennolds and Arthur F Rennolds are held and firmly bound unto Archibald Ritchie Edmund P Nall, Jones C Clopton and Hubbard T Minor Gentlemen Justices of the Court of Essex County now sitting in the sum of One thousand Dollars to the payment whereof well and truly to be made to the said Justices and their successors, we bind ourselves and each of us and each of our heirs executors and administrators jointly and severally firmly by these presents. Sealed with our Seals and dated this 18" day of June 1832 in the 56th year of the Commonwealth. — The Condition of the above obligation is such that if the above bound Otway Rennolds his Executors and administrators shall well and truly pay and deliver or cause to be paid and delivered unto Otway H. Berryman child of Newton Berryman all such estate or estates as is or are or hereafter shall appear to be due to the said Orphan when and as soon as he shall attain to lawful age or when thereto required by the Justices of the said County Court as also keep harmless the above named Justices their and every of their heirs executors and administrators from all trouble and damages that shall or may arise about the said Estate — then the above obligation to be void, otherwise ~~and~~ to remain in full force —

Sealed and delivered

in the presence of

Essex County Court and Ordered to be recorded. —

Otway Rennolds (Seal)
Arthur F Rennolds (Seal)

Teste — James Roy Micou Jr Clk

Examined

Know all men by these Presents, That we
Robert Williamson and Zebulon On [?] Waters are held
and firmly bound unto the Commonwealth of Virginia,
in the sum of Fifty Dollars, to the Payment whereof
well and truly to be made to the said Commonwealth
of Virginia, we bind ourselves and each of us, our and each
of our heirs, executors and administrators, jointly and severally, firmly by these Presents. Sealed with our seals, and
dated this 21st day of December Anno Domini one thousand eight hundred and forty six and in the 71st year
of the Commonwealth.

The Condition of the above obligation is
such, That if the above bound Robert Williamson his
executors and administrators, shall well and truly pay and
deliver, or cause to be paid and delivered, unto Mary Brooks
Orphan of Dabney Brooks deceased, all such estate or
estates, as now is, or are, or hereafter shall appear to be
due to the said Orphan, when and as soon as she shall
attain the lawful age, or when thereto required by the
Justices of the County Court of Essex, as also to keep
harmless the Justices now sitting, their and every of their
heirs, executors and administrators from all trouble and
damages that shall or may arise about the said estate,
then the above obligation to be void; otherwise to remain in full force.

Sealed and delivered   Robert his
in the Presence of Essex   x   Williamson   (Seal)
County Court and Or-   Dabney mark his
dered to be Recorded.   x   Brooks   (Seal)
Teste—   mark

James Roy Micou C.C.

Sample 3 - Mary Brooks, orphan of Dabney Brooks, to Robert Williamson [future husband], 21 DEC 1846

xi

Ward or Subject (and Parent, Guardian or Other)	Record Type	Date	Reference(s)
A			
Acres, William O., c/o James to Joseph Durham	Bond	17 NOV 1862	1857:296
Acrey, Thomas, c/o Arthur T to Catharine Minter	Bond	20 SEP 1852	1851:130
Adcocke, Joseph to Robert Shepard	Bond	21 JAN 1723/4	WB4:044
Addison, Addison, by James Allen	Allotment	19 DEC 1825	1825:073
Alexander, Mehaley, c/o Aris to Richard L. Haile	Bond	16 DEC 1816	1811:128
Allen, Addison, c/o Thomas to James Allen, Jr.	Bond	21 DEC 1813	1811:049
Allen, Andrew, c/o Philip to Spencer Brooke	Bond	21 MAY 1810	1796:230
Allen, Andrew, from Spencer Brooke	Receipt	19 SEP 1825	1825:006
Allen, Arabella, under 14, c/o Robert to Thomas J. Hundley	Bond	15 JUL 1867	1857:432
Allen, Arabella, by Thomas J. Hundley	Account	15 SEP 1873	1867:219
Allen, Arabella M., above 14, c/o Robert to James E. Tune	Bond	16 AUG 1875	1867:324
Allen, Arthur F., c/o William R to James A. Dunn	Bond	19 APR 1847	1844:209
Allen, Arthur F., by James A. Dunn	Account	19 MAR 1849	1844:344
Allen, Arthur F., by James A. Dunn	Account	15 APR 1850	1844:424
Allen, Arthur F., by James A. Dunn	Account	18 MAR 1851	1844:507
Allen, Arthur F., by James A. Dunn	Account	17 MAY 1852	1851:084
Allen, Arthur F., by James A. Dunn	Account	16 MAY 1853	1851:176
Allen, Arthur F., by James A. Dunn	Account	17 JUL 1854	1851:241
Allen, Arthur F., by James A. Dunn	Account	16 JUL 1855	1851:311
Allen, Arthur F., by James A. Dunn	Account	16 JUN 1856	1851:349
Allen, Arthur F., by James A. Dunn	Account	20 JUL 1857	1851:451
Allen, Arthur F., by James A. Dunn	Account	20 DEC 1858	1857:107
Allen, Arthur F., by James A. Dunn	Account	19 SEP 1859	1857:157
Allen, Arthur F., by James A. Dunn	Account	17 SEP 1860	1857:223
Allen, Arthur F., by James A. Dunn	Account	20 JAN 1862	1857:279
Allen, Arthur F., by James A. Dunn	Account	16 JUL 1866	1857:402
Allen, Betsey, c/o Philip to James Dunn	Bond	15 JUN 1812	1811:012
Allen, Betsey now Brizendine, from James Dunn	Receipt	17 OCT 1825	1825:052
Allen, Catharine, Miss, c/o Henry, by Ambrose Greenhill	Account	20 SEP 1790	1761:170
Allen, Dorothy, Miss, c/o Henry, by Ambrose Greenhill	Account	20 SEP 1790	1761:168
Allen, Fanny, c/o Andrew, by Hannah Allen	Account	18 SEP 1809	1796:219
Allen, Henry to Eliza Allen	Bond	20 MAR 1750/1	WB8:427
Allen, James to Eliza Allen	Bond	20 MAR 1750/1	WB8:427
Allen, James, c/o James to Thomas L. Latane	Bond	18 DEC 1815	1811:112
Allen, Jere, who *has no estate whatever*, by Wm. Garnett	Report	19 SEP 1825	1825:020
Allen, Jeremiah, c/o Silvanus to Wm. Garnett	Bond	18 JAN 1819	1811:168
Allen, Leah, c/o Andrew, by Hannah Allen	Account	18 SEP 1809	1796:218
Allen, Mary, Miss, c/o Henry, by Ambrose Greenhill	Account	20 SEP 1790	1761:169
Allen, Patsey, c/o Andrew, by Hannah Allen	Account	18 SEP 1809	1796:219
Allen, Philip, c/o Andrew, by Hannah Allen	Account	18 SEP 1809	1796:218
Allen, Polly, c/o Philip to James Dunn	Bond	15 JUN 1812	1811:012
Allen, Polly now Boughton, from James Dunn	Receipt	17 OCT 1825	1825:052
Allen, Rachel, c/o Andrew, by Hannah Allen	Account	18 SEP 1809	1796:219
Allen, Susanna, c/o James to Thomas L. Latane	Bond	18 DEC 1815	1811:112
Allen, Tamzon to Eliza Allen	Bond	20 MAR 1750/1	WB8:427
Allen, Thomas to Eliza Allen	Bond	20 MAR 1750/1	WB8:427
Allen, Thomas to Thomas Burke	Bond	16 OCT 1750	WB8:374

Ward or Subject (and Parent, Guardian or Other)	Record Type	Date	Reference(s)
Anderson, Jamima to Elizabeth Anderson	Bond	21 MAR 1737/8	WB6:116
Andrews, Ann, c/o Thomas to Thomas Wright	Bond	21 JUL 1806	1796:182
Andrews, Ann, c/o Mark to James Atkinson	Bond	19 JAN 1818	1811:141
Andrews, Ann C., c/o James to her father	Bond	18 AUG 1834	1831:280
Andrews, Archibald, c/o Thomas to Thomas Wright	Bond	21 JUL 1806	1796:180
Andrews, Arena B., c/o James to her father	Bond	18 AUG 1834	1831:280
Andrews, Edwin, c/o Mark to James Andrews	Bond	19 FEB 1821	1811:248
Andrews, Edwin G., from James Andrews	Receipt	17 MAR 1834	1831:247
Andrews, Elizabeth, c/o Mark to James Clarke	Bond	18 DEC 1815	1811:107
Andrews, George F., c/o James to Mary J. Andrews	Bond	21 SEP 1868	1867:044
Andrews, Harriott, c/o Mark to John Beazley	Bond	19 FEB 1821	1811:245
Andrews, Leonard, c/o Mark to Ann Andrews	Bond	17 JUN 1816	1811:118
Andrews, Leonard, by Ann Andrews	Account	21 NOV 1825	1825:055
Andrews, Leonard, by Ann Andrews	Account	21 SEP 1829	1825:310
Andrews, Martha L., c/o James to by her father	Bond	18 AUG 1834	1831:280
Andrews, Mary J., c/o James to her father	Bond	18 AUG 1834	1831:280
Andrews, Robert Pitts, c/o Thomas to Thomas Wright	Bond	21 JUL 1806	1796:180
Andrews, Sally, c/o Mark to Ann Andrews	Bond	17 JUN 1816	1811:118
Armstrong, Elizabeth to George Wright	Bond	19 MAR 1750/1	WB8:423
Armstrong, John to Mary Dix	Bond	21 MAR 1748/9	WB8:206
Armstrong, John to George Wright	Bond	19 MAR 1750/1	WB8:423
Armstrong, John F., c/o John T. to Leonard Henley	Bond	20 FEB 1860	1857:192
Armstrong, Margaret to George Wright	Bond	19 MAR 1750/1	WB8:423
Armstrong, Martha A., c/o John T. to Leonard Henley	Bond	20 FEB 1860	1857:192
Armstrong, Rachol to George Wright	Bond	19 MAR 1750/1	WB8:423
Armstrong, Ursula to George Wright	Bond	19 MAR 1750/1	WB8:423
Armstrong, William to Richard Armstrong	Bond	21 JUL 1741	WB6:328
Arnold, Thomas T., K.G. Co., to William A. Brockenbrough	P. of Atty.	19 OCT 1874	1867:284
Atkins, Elizabeth, c/o Thomas to Muscoe Garnett	Bond	21 OCT 1844	1838:373
Atkins, Elizabeth, by Muscoe Garnett	Account	17 AUG 1846	1844:174
Atkins, Lallie to Edward Brown	Bond	20 APR 1885	1867:562
Atkins, Lille, over 14, to Edward Brown	Certificate	20 APR 1885	1867:563
Atkins, Thomas O., c/o Thomas to Muscoe Garnett	Bond	21 OCT 1844	1838:373
Atkins, Thomas, by Muscoe Garnett	Account	16 FEB 1852	1851:044
Atkinson, Caroline, over 14, c/o Richard H. to Henry Graves	Bond	19 JUN 1882	1867:489
Atkinson, Elizabeth, c/o James to her father	Bond	19 DEC 1825	1825:070
Atkinson, Fanny O., over 14, c/o Rich. H. to Henry Graves	Bond	19 JUN 1882	1867:489
Atkinson, John, dec., by Charles Atkinson, Admr.	Account	16 APR 1751	1731:126
Atkinson, John, by Charles Atkinson	Account	17 OCT 1752	1731:150
Atkinson, John, dec., by Charles Atkinson	Account	19 NOV 1754	1731:185
Atkinson, John, c/o John to Charles Atkinson	Bond	20 JUL 1756	1731:199
Atkinson, John, over 14, c/o Richard H. to Henry Graves	Bond	19 JUN 1882	1867:489
Atkinson, Richard, c/o James to his father	Bond	19 DEC 1825	1825:070
Atkinson, Thomas to Charles Atkinson	Bond	20 MAR 1749/50	WB8:309
Atkinson, Thomas, h/o John, by Charles Atkinson	Account	19 JAN 1756	WB10:084
Atkinson, William, c/o James to his father	Bond	19 DEC 1825	1825:070
Attwood, Salley, c/o Francis	Account	20 DEC 1757	1731:215
Attwood, Sarah, c/o Frances to John Allen	Bond	17 JAN 1748/9	WB8:128
Atwood, Sally to Isaac Scandrett	Bond	16 OCT 1750	WB8:372
Atwood, Sarah, c/o Francis to Joseph Reeves	Bond	15 MAR 1757	1731:210
Ayres, Thomas to Thomas Thorp	Bond	21 APR 1724	WB4:052

Ward or Subject (and Parent, Guardian or Other)	Record Type	Date	Reference(s)
Ayrton, Ann to Henry Woodnot	Bond	8 MAR 1710/1	D&W13:396

B

Baird, Matthew & wife Ophelia [Cauthorn], from Leroy Cauthorn	Receipt	18 JUN 1832	1831:121
Baird, Ophelia late Cauthorn, w/o Matthew, by Leroy Cauthorn	Account	18 JUN 1832	1831:115
Baldwin, Mary to William Watkins	Bond	19 FEB 1744/5	WB7:256
Baldwin, Mary, by William Watkins	Account	21 OCT 1755	WB10:067
Baldwin, Mary, by William Watkins	Account	16 NOV 1756	1731:207
Baldwin, Mary, by William Watkins	Account	20 DEC 1757	1731:213
Baldwin, Mary, c/o John to William Watkins	Bond	22 MAR 1758	1731:221
Ball, Betsey, c/o Curtis to her father	Bond	20 MAR 1815	1811:081
Ball, Sally, c/o Churchill to Edward Barefoot	Bond	16 JAN 1832	1831:085
Ball, William Henry, c/o Harrison to Elzer Fogg	Bond	17 MAR 1856	1851:341
Banks, James William c/o William to Catharine Allen	Bond	20 MAY 1833	1831:182
Banks, James W., from Caty B. Allen	Receipt	16 NOV 1835	1831:351
Banks, Townley, c/o William to Peter B. Davis	Bond	18 JAN 1813	1811:036
Banks, Townley, by P.B. Davis	Account	21 NOV 1814	1811:071
Banks, Townley, by Peter B. Davis	Account	18 SEP 1815	1811:102
Barnes, Mary C. late Haile, by father Robert G. Haile	Account	16 FEB 1829	1825:277
Barnes, Richard M.F., c/o Richard to Moore F. Brockenbrough	Bond	16 OCT 1820	1811:236
Barnes, Richard M.F., by Moore F. Brockenbrough	Account	21 NOV 1827	1825:190
Barnes, Thomas R., by Arthur L. Barnes	Account	20 AUG 1827	1825:171
Barnes, Thomas R., from Arthur L. Barnes	Receipt	21 AUG 1827	1825:176
Barton, Elizabeth, c/o Thomas to Erasmus Jones	Bond	19 JUN 1809	1796:215
Barton, Elizabeth, c/o Thomas to John Jones	Bond	20 APR 1812	1811:007
Barton, Thomas, by Thomas Allen	Account	19 DEC 1785	1761:146
Barton, Thomas, by Thomas Allen	Account	16 OCT 1786	1761:153
Barton, Thomas, by Thomas Allen	Account	15 DEC 1788	1761:160
Basket, James, c/o Abraham to George W. Shelton	Bond	18 JUL 1831	1831:062
Basket, Thomas, orphans of	Bond	22 JUL 1724	WB4:071
Bates, William, from Christopher Kay	Receipt	21 NOV 1825	1825:069
Battaile, Elizabeth to Andrew Harrison	Bond	10 AUG 1708	D&W13:128
Battaile, John to Augustine Smith	Bond	10 NOV 1708	D&W13:165
Battaile, Lawrence to Augustine Smith	Bond	10 FEB 1708/9	D&W13:184
Battaile, Lawrence to John Battaile	Bond	13 AUG 1713	D&W14:151
Bayliss, Betty Ann late Coghill, c/o Smallwood to S.P. Bayliss	Bond	16 JUL 1855	1851:309
Baylor, Alexander, c/o Robert to Alexander Tunstall & others	Bond	16 JAN 1815	1811:072
Baylor, Alexander, c/o Robert to William T. Brooke	Bond	17 JUN 1816	1811:116
Baylor, Alfred G., c/o Alexander T. to John W. Robinson	Bond	16 SEP 1850	1844:470
Baylor, Alfred G., by John W. Robinson	Account	21 JUN 1852	1851:112
Baylor, Alfred G., by John W. Robinson	Account	21 NOV 1853	1851:217
Baylor, Alfred G., by John W. Robinson	Account	19 MAR 1855	1851:287
Baylor, Ann, c/o Robert to Alexander Tunstall & others	Bond	16 JAN 1815	1811:072
Baylor, Ann, c/o Robert to William T. Brooke	Bond	17 JUN 1816	1811:116
Baylor, Ann Brooke, c/o Alexander T. to John W. Robinson	Bond	16 SEP 1850	1844:470
Baylor, Ann B., by John W. Robinson	Account	21 JUN 1852	1851:112
Baylor, Ann B., by John W. Robinson	Account	21 NOV 1853	1851:217
Baylor, Ann B., by John W. Robinson	Account	19 MAR 1855	1851:287
Baylor, Ann B., by John W. Robinson	Account	20 DEC 1858	1857:119
Baylor, Ann Brooke, c/o Alexander T. to John W. Robinson	Bond	16 AUG 1858	1857:103
Baylor, Ann B., by John W. Robinson	Account	21 FEB 1859	1857:135

Ward or Subject (and Parent, Guardian or Other)	Record Type	Date	Reference(s)
Baylor, Ann B., by John W. Robinson	Account	21 JAN 1861	1857:243, 244
Baylor, Ann B., chose her uncle John B. Robinson, gdn.	Certificate	20 APR 1863	1857:298
Baylor, Ann B., c/o Alexander T. to John B. Robinson	Bond	20 APR 1863	1857:298
Baylor, Ann B., by John W. Robinson	Account	16 MAY 1864	1857:344
Baylor, Ann Brooke, by John B. Robinson	Account	16 JAN 1865	1857:360
Baylor, Ann Brooke, from John B. Robinson	Receipt	16 JUL 1866	1857:396
Baylor, Ann Brooke, by John B. Robinson	Account	20 AUG 1866	1857:409
Baylor, Ann B., by John W. Robinson	Account	21 SEP 1868	1867:040, 042
Baylor, Baynham, c/o Robert to Alexander Tunstall & others	Bond	16 JAN 1815	1811:072
Baylor, Baynham, c/o Robert to William T. Brooke	Bond	17 JUN 1816	1811:116
Baylor, Catharine B., c/o Richard to Baylor, Waring & Brooke	Bond	19 JAN 1863	1857:297
Baylor, Catharine B., over 14, c/o Richard to Richard Baylor	Bond	17 JUN 1872	1867:184
Baylor, Eliz. P., by R.P. Baylor, W.L. Waring, W.H. Brooke	Account	20 MAY 1867	1857:417
Baylor, Elizabeth P., c/o Richard to Baylor, Waring & Brooke	Bond	19 JAN 1863	1857:297
Baylor, Harriett R., c/o Richard to Baylor, Waring & Brooke	Bond	19 JAN 1863	1857:297
Baylor, Harriett R., by R.P. Baylor, W.L. Waring, W.H. Brooke	Account	20 MAY 1867	1857:422
Baylor, Harriett R., by Robert P. Baylor	Account	19 SEP 1870	1867:125, 132
Baylor, Helen, c/o Richard to Baylor, Waring & Brooke	Bond	19 JAN 1863	1857:297
Baylor, Helen S., by R.P. Baylor, W.L. Waring, W.H. Brooke	Account	20 MAY 1867	1857:418
Baylor, Helen S., by Robert P. Baylor	Account	19 SEP 1870	1867:125, 134
Baylor, Henry L., c/o Richard to Baylor, Waring & Brooke	Bond	19 JAN 1863	1857:297
Baylor, Henry L., by R.P. Baylor, W.L. Waring & Wm. H. Brooke	Account	20 FEB 1865	1857:371
Baylor, Henry L., by R.P. Baylor, W.L. Waring, W.H. Brooke	Account	20 MAY 1867	1857:426
Baylor, Henry L., by Robert P. Baylor	Account	19 SEP 1870	1867:125, 138
Baylor, Henry L., over 14, c/o Richard to Richard Baylor	Bond	17 JUN 1872	1867:184
Baylor, Henry L., by Richard Baylor	Account	15 SEP 1873	1867:218
Baylor, Henry L., by Robert P. Baylor	Account	20 JAN 1873	1867:192
Baylor, Kate B., by R.P. Baylor, W.L. Waring, W.H. Brooke	Account	20 MAY 1867	1857:420
Baylor, Kate B., by Robert P. Baylor	Account	19 SEP 1870	1867:125, 126
Baylor, Kate B., by Richard Baylor	Account	15 SEP 1873	1867:216
Baylor, Mary A., c/o Alexander T. to John W. Robinson	Bond	16 SEP 1850	1844:470
Baylor, Mary A., by John W. Robinson	Account	21 JUN 1852	1851:112
Baylor, Mary A., by John W. Robinson	Account	21 NOV 1853	1851:217
Baylor, Mary A., by John W. Robinson	Account	19 MAR 1855	1851:287
Baylor, Mary, c/o Richard to Baylor, Waring & Brooke	Bond	19 JAN 1863	1857:297
Baylor, Mary, by R.P. Baylor, W.L. Waring, W.H. Brooke	Account	20 MAY 1867	1857:428
Baylor, Richard Wm., c/o Robert to Alexander Tunstall & others	Bond	16 JAN 1815	1811:072
Baylor, Richard, c/o Robert to William T. Brooke	Bond	17 JUN 1816	1811:116
Baylor, Richard, c/o Richard to Baylor, Waring & Brooke	Bond	19 JAN 1863	1857:297
Baylor, Richard, by R.P. Baylor, W.L. Waring & Wm. H. Brook	Account	20 FEB 1865	1857:369
Baylor, Richard, by R.P. Baylor, W.L. Waring, W.H. Brooke	Account	20 MAY 1867	1857:424
Baylor, Robert, c/o Robert to Alexander Tunstall & others	Bond	16 JAN 1815	1811:072
Baylor, Robert, c/o Robert to William T. Brooke	Bond	17 JUN 1816	1811:116
Baylor, William, c/o Robert to William T. Brooke	Bond	17 JUN 1816	1811:116
Baynham, John Man Waring, c/o Dr. Wm. to Alexr. Somervail	Bond	16 JAN 1815	1811:073
Baynham, John Manwaring, c/o Wm., by Alexr. Somervail	Account	15 JUL 1816	1811:119
Baynham, John M., by Alexander Somervail	Account	21 JUL 1817	1811:134
Baynham, John M., by Alexander Somervail	Settlement	21 JUL 1818	1811:154
Baynham, John M., by Alexander Somervail	Settlement	16 AUG 1819	1811:192
Baynham, John M., from Alexander Somervail	Receipt	19 MAR 1832	1831:108
Baynham, John M., from Alexander Somervail	Receipt	20 AUG 1834	1831:280

Ward or Subject (and Parent, Guardian or Other)	Record Type	Date	Reference(s)
Baynham, William Anthony, c/o Wm., by Alexr. Somervail	Account	15 JUL 1816	1811:119
Baynham, William A., by Alexander Somervail	Account	21 JUL 1817	1811:134
Baynham, William A., by Alexander Somervail	Settlement	21 JUL 1818	1811:154
Baynham, William A., by Alexander Somervail	Settlement	16 AUG 1819	1811:192
Baynham, William A., by Alexander Somervail	Account	16 SEP 1833	WB23:128
Baynham, William A., from Alexander Somervail	Receipt	20 OCT 1834	1831:281
Baynham, Wm. Anthony, c/o Dr. Wm. to Alexr. Somervail	Bond	16 JAN 1815	1811:073
Beale, John F., c/o John H. to John Ferguson	Bond	18 OCT 1819	1811:195
Beale, John Ferguson, by John Ferguson	Account	22 MAR 1820	1811:210
Beale, Robert F., c/o John H. to John Ferguson	Bond	18 OCT 1819	1811:195
Beale, Robert Ferguson, by John Ferguson	Account	22 MAR 1820	1811:210
Beasley, Ellis S., by James B. Beasley	Account	16 JUN 1879	1867:411
Beasley, John M., by James B. Beasley	Account	16 JUN 1879	1867:411
Beazley, Ellis, c/o Ellis to Robert Sorrell	Bond	20 SEP 1869	1867:105
Beazley, Ellis A., c/o Ellis A. to James B. Beazley	Bond	20 MAY 1872	1867:182
Beazley, Fanny J. (a.k.a. Teresa J.), by Elzer Fogg	Account	21 JUL 1862	1857:292
Beazley, Fanny J. a.k.a. Teresa J., by Elzer Fogg	Account	16 SEP 1867	1867:008
Beazley, Fanny J. a.k.a. Teresa J., by Elzer Fogg	Account	21 DEC 1868	1867:078
Beazley, James, c/o Ellis to Robert Sorrell	Bond	20 SEP 1869	1867:105
Beazley, John, c/o Ellis to Robert Sorrell	Bond	20 SEP 1869	1867:105
Beazley, John Newton, c/o Ellis A. to James B. Beazley	Bond	20 MAY 1872	1867:181
Beazley, Levinia, c/o Ellis to Robert Sorrell	Bond	20 SEP 1869	1867:105
Beazley, Martha Ellen, c/o William to Elzer Fogg	Bond	16 APR 1855	1851:295
Beazley, Martha E., by Elzer Fogg	Account	15 FEB 1858	1857:055
Beazley, Olivia A., c/o Ellis to Edward B. Blake	Bond	18 OCT 1869	1867:113
Beazley, Richard H., c/o John to Robert Hill	Bond	15 DEC 1828	1825:262
Beazley, Teresa J., under 14, c/o William J. to Elzer Fogg	Bond	20 AUG 1855	1851:311
Beazley, Teresa J. (now Fanny J.), by Elzer Fogg	Account	21 JUL 1862	1857:292
Beazley, William Jackson, inf. of Ephraim, by Warner Lewis	Account	19 JUN 1837	1831:474
Beazley, William Jackson, s/o Ephraim, by Warner Lewis	Account	20 JUN 1842	1838:216
Beazley, William Jackson, by Warner Lewis	Account	24 FEB 1843	1838:238
Beazley, William Jackson, master, by Warner Lewis	Account	19 FEB 1844	1838:309
Beazley, William Jackson, by Warner Lewis	Account	15 JUN 1846	1844:146
Beazley, William Jackson, by Warner Lewis	Account	19 MAR 1849	1844:348
Beazley, William Jackson, by Warner Lewis	Account	15 SEP 1851	1851:018
Beazley, William J., by Warner Lewis	Account	21 JAN 1856	1851:336
Belfield, Anna B., c/o David P. to her father	Bond	19 FEB 1844	1838:303
Belfield, Elizabeth M.B., c/o David P. to her father	Bond	19 FEB 1844	1838:303
Belfield, Mary S., c/o David P. to her father	Bond	19 FEB 1844	1838:303
Berryman, Otway H., c/o Newton to Otway Rennolds	Bond	18 JUN 1832	1831:122
Beverley, Harriet, c/o Robert to Robert Beverley	Bond	16 JUN 1800	1796:059
Beverley, Harriet, c/o Robert to Carter Beverley	Bond	16 JUN 1800	1796:060
Beverley, Harriet, by Carter Beverley	Account	20 FEB 1804	1796:148
Beverley, Harriott, c/o Robert to Carter Beverley	Bond	19 DEC 1803	1796:142
Beverley, Jane Bradshaw, c/o Robert to Carter Beverley	Bond	16 JUN 1800	1796:060
Beverley, Jane Bradshaw, c/o Robert to Robert Beverley	Bond	16 JUN 1800	1796:059
Beverley, Jane R., by Carter Beverley	Account	20 FEB 1804	1796:146
Beverley, McKinzie, c/o Robert to Robert Beverley	Bond	16 JUN 1800	1796:059
Beverley, McKinzie, c/o Robert to Carter Beverley	Bond	16 JUN 1800	1796:060
Beverley, McKinzie, c/o Robert to Carter Beverley	Bond	19 DEC 1803	1796:142
Beverley, McKinzie, by Carter Beverley	Account	20 FEB 1804	1796:149

Ward or Subject (and Parent, Guardian or Other)	Record Type	Date	Reference(s)
Beverley, Peter Randolph, c/o Robert to Carter Beverley	Bond	16 JUN 1800	1796:060
Beverley, Peter Randolph, c/o Robert to Robert Beverley	Bond	16 JUN 1800	1796:059
Beverley, Peter Randolph, c/o Robert to Carter Beverley	Bond	19 DEC 1803	1796:142
Bigger, J. Bell for wife Ann B. Muse, from Peter S. Trible	Receipt	20 MAR 1854	1851:227
Bird, George Anna, over 14, c/o Alexr. to Erastus Edwards	Bond	21 JAN 1878	1867:376
Bird, Richard C., s/o John to his father	Bond	17 JAN 1853	1851:163
Bird, Richard Claybrooke, c/o John to Sarah J. Bird	Bond	20 SEP 1858	1857:105
Bizwell, Ann to Robert Parker	Bond	21 NOV 1732	WB5:113
Bizwell, Mary to William Bizwell	Bond	21 MAR 1731/2	WB5:070
Blackburn, Ada, under 14, c/o Robert L. to Beazley & Anderson	Bond	15 OCT 1866	1857:414
Blackburn, Letitia, under 14, c/o Robert L. to Beazley & Anderson	Bond	15 OCT 1866	1857:414
Blackburn, Mary, c/o Churchill to Phoeby Blackburn	Bond	21 SEP 1835	1831:329
Blackburn, Sarah, c/o Churchill to Phoeby Blackburn	Bond	21 SEP 1835	1831:329
Blackburn, William, c/o Churchill to Phoeby Blackburn	Bond	21 SEP 1835	1831:329
Blackston, Mary, c/o Arguile to Robt. Spilsbee Coleman	Bond	16 MAY 1759	1731:242
Blake, Benjamin R., c/o Benjamin to Austin Brockenbrough	Bond	18 FEB 1839	1838:046
Blake, Benjamin for Wm. A. Dyke, by Larkin Hundley	Account	20 OCT 1845	1844:062
Blake, Catharine A., c/o Benjamin to Austin Brockenbrough	Bond	23 NOV 1831	1831:080
Blake, Catharine A., now Dawson, by Austin Brockenbrough	Account	16 DEC 1833	WB23:174
Blake, Jane Louisa, by Austin Brockenbrough	Account	21 SEP 1840	1838:102
Blake, Jane Louisa, c/o Benjamin to Austin Brockenbrough	Bond	18 DEC 1843	1838:296
Blake, Jane Louisa, by Dr. Austin Brockenbrough	Account	20 MAY 1844	1838:320
Blake, Thomas, c/o Thomas to Benjamin Blake	Bond	19 JUN 1837	1831:474
Bohanan, Ann, by Alexr. Saunders	Account	19 SEP 1774	1761:122
Bohanan, Ann, by Alexander Saunders	Account	19 SEP 1775	1761:124
Bohanan, Elizabeth, to Jonathan Dunn	Bond	16 JUL 1751	WB9:076
Bohanan, Sarah [Burhanan], to Jonathan Dunn	Bond	16 JUL 1751	WB9:076
Bohanan, Sarah, by Alexander Saunders	Account	19 SEP 1775	1761:124
Bohannan, Ambrose, c/o Ambrose, by Ambrose Wright	Account	16 FEB 1767	1761:063
Bohannan, Ambrose, c/o Ambrose, by Ambrose Wright	Account	18 SEP 1769	1761:073, 074
Bohannan, John, orphans of, by Alex. Saunders	Account	16 AUG 1779	1761:137
Bohannan, Joseph, c/o Ambrose, by Ambrose Wright	Account	16 FEB 1767	1761:063
Bohannan, Joseph, c/o Ambrose, by Ambrose Wright	Account	18 SEP 1769	1761:075, 076
Bohannan, Sarah, c/o Ambrose, by Ambrose Wright	Account	20 AUG 1765	1761:055
Bohannan, Sarah, c/o Ambrose, by Ambrose Wright	Account	16 FEB 1767	1761:064
Bohannon, Ambrose, c/o Ambrose, by Ambrose Wright	Account	20 AUG 1765	1761:053
Bohannon, Joseph, c/o Ambrose, by Ambrose Wright	Account	20 AUG 1765	1761:054
Bond, Robert, c/o William, to William Saunders	Bond	21 FEB 1785	WB13:468
Bond, William, by Richard Jeffries	Account	19 JUN 1786	1761:149
Bonds, Robert, by Wm. Saunders	Account	19 JUL 1790	1761:166
Bonds, Walker, by Thomas Johnson	Account	17 OCT 1785	1761:146
Booth, James to Salvator Muscoe	Bond	16 AUG 1715	D&W14:388
Booth, Margaret to Salvator Muscoe	Bond	16 AUG 1715	D&W14:388
Booth, Margaret to James Booth	Bond	20 MAR 1716/7	D&W15:020
Booth, Phebe to James Booth	Bond	21 MAY 1717	D&W15:048
Booth, Phoebe to Salvator Muscoe	Bond	16 AUG 1715	D&W14:388
Booth, William to Salvator Muscoe	Bond	16 AUG 1715	D&W14:388
Booth, William to James Booth	Bond	20 MAR 1716/7	D&W15:019
Booth, William to James Booth	Bond	20 MAR 1716/7	D&W15:019
Boughan, Augustin to William Wortham	Bond	21 SEP 1731	WB5:056
Boughan, Austin, by Henry H. Boughan	Account	17 DEC 1827	1825:196

Ward or Subject (and Parent, Guardian or Other)	Record Type	Date	Reference(s)
Boughan, Austin, from Henry H. Boughan	Receipt	21 MAY 1829	1825:280
Boughan, Benjamin, from Henry H. Boughan	Receipt	20 NOV 1827	1825:216
Boughan, Betty, c/o Augustine, to Hannah Boughan	Bond	21 DEC 1756	WB10:114
Boughan, Cary C., c/o John to Frances Boughan	Bond	15 MAY 1843	1838:249
Boughan, Cary, c/o John to Frances Boughan	Bond	17 FEB 1845	1844:006
Boughan, Cary C., by Frances Boughan	Account	21 JUL 1845	1844:035
Boughan, Catharine, c/o Major to John Boughan	Bond	18 JAN 1813	1811:037
Boughan, Catharine, by Frances Boughan	Account	21 JUL 1845	1844:035
Boughan, Catharine, c/o John to Charles L. Boughan	Bond	18 AUG 1845	1844:055
Boughan, Catharine, c/o John to Frances Boughan	Bond	17 FEB 1845	1844:006
Boughan, Catharine, c/o John to Charles L. Boughan	Bond	16 MAR 1846	1844:100
Boughan, Catharine E., c/o John to Ephraim Beazley	Bond	18 FEB 1850	1844:405
Boughan, Charles L., gdn. for John T., fr. Zebulon M.P. Carter	Receipt	16 MAR 1846	1844:099
Boughan, Elizabeth, c/o Griffing to Washington Banks	Bond	20 JAN 1800	1796:051
Boughan, Elizabeth C., c/o John to Frances Boughan	Bond	15 MAY 1843	1838:249
Boughan, Elizabeth C., by Charles L. Boughan	Account	19 APR 1847	1844:200
Boughan, Elizabeth C., by Charles L. Boughan	Account	20 JAN 1851	1844:503
Boughan, Elizabeth C., by Ephraim Beazley	Account	16 FEB 1852	1851:046
Boughan, Elizabeth C., by Ephraim Beazley	Account	20 NOV 1854	1851:272
Boughan, Frankey, c/o Augustine, to Hannah Boughan	Bond	21 DEC 1756	WB10:114
Boughan, Griffing, c/o Augustine to Francis Waring	Bond	19 OCT 1756	1731:205
Boughan, Henry, c/o Griffing to Washington Banks	Bond	20 JAN 1800	1796:051
Boughan, John T., c/o John to Frances Boughan	Bond	15 MAY 1843	1838:249
Boughan, John T. by Charles L., from Philip Montague	Receipt	15 SEP 1845	1844:059
Boughan, John Thomas, c/o John to Frances Boughan	Bond	17 FEB 1845	1844:006
Boughan, John T., c/o John to Charles L. Boughan	Bond	18 AUG 1845	1844:055
Boughan, John T., by Frances Boughan	Account	21 JUL 1845	1844:035
Boughan, John T., ward of Charles L., fr. Zebulon M.P. Carter	Receipt	16 MAR 1846	1844:099
Boughan, John T., c/o John to Charles L. Boughan	Bond	16 MAR 1846	1844:100
Boughan, John T., by Charles L. Boughan	Account	19 APR 1847	1844:206
Boughan, John T., by Charles L. Boughan	Account	20 JAN 1851	1844:497
Boughan, Kitty, c/o Griffing to Joseph J. Monroe	Bond	23 NOV 1798	1796:089
Boughan, Mary, c/o Augustine, to Hannah Boughan	Bond	21 DEC 1756	WB10:114
Boughan, Thomas, c/o Major to John Boughan	Bond	18 JAN 1813	1811:037
Boughton, Alexander, c/o Thomas to Mary Boughton	Bond	21 DEC 1795	1761:221
Boughton, Alexander, c/o Thomas, by Mrs. Mary Boughton	Account	16 JAN 1809	1796:206
Boughton, Ann, c/o Thomas to Mary Boughton	Bond	21 DEC 1795	1761:221
Boughton, Ann, c/o Thomas to Reuben Simco	Bond	18 JUL 1808	1796:201
Boughton, Ann, c/o Thomas, by Mrs. Mary Boughton	Account	16 JAN 1809	1796:206
Boughton, Ann H., c/o John to Brooks Boughton	Bond	15 AUG 1836	1831:429
Boughton, Ann H., by Brooks Boughton	Account	17 DEC 1838	1838:035
Boughton, Ann H., by Reuben B. Boughton	Account	18 MAY 1840	1838:086
Boughton, Ann H., by Brooks Boughton	Account	15 MAY 1843	1838:260
Boughton, Ann H., by Brooks Boughton	Account	19 APR 1847	1844:202
Boughton, Ann E.B., c/o Brooks to Gabriel H. Dillard	Bond	15 DEC 1862	1857:296
Boughton, Ann E.P., c/o Brooks to Roberta P. Boughton	Bond	17 AUG 1863	1857:300
Boughton, Charles H., c/o John to Reuben B. Boughton	Bond	15 AUG 1836	1831:428
Boughton, Charles H., by Reuben B. Boughton	Account	17 DEC 1838	1838:036
Boughton, Charles H., by Reuben B. Boughton	Account	18 MAY 1840	1838:084
Boughton, Charles H., by Reuben B. Boughton	Account	19 SEP 1842	1838:232
Boughton, Charles H., by Reuben B. Boughton	Account	21 FEB 1842	1838:176

Ward or Subject (and Parent, Guardian or Other)	Record Type	Date	Reference(s)
Boughton, Charles H., by Reuben B. Boughton	Account	18 AUG 1845	1844:056
Boughton, Elizabeth, c/o Thomas to Mary Boughton	Bond	21 DEC 1795	1761:221
Boughton, George, c/o Thomas to Mary Boughton	Bond	21 DEC 1795	1761:221
Boughton, George, c/o Thomas, by Mrs. Mary Boughton	Account	16 JAN 1809	1796:207
Boughton, George W., c/o Brooks to Gabriel H. Dillard	Bond	15 DEC 1862	1857:296
Boughton, George W., c/o Brooks to Roberta P. Boughton	Bond	17 AUG 1863	1857:300
Boughton, Infant, c/o Brooks to Gabriel H. Dillard	Bond	15 DEC 1862	1857:296
Boughton, Joshua L., c/o John to Reuben B. Boughton	Bond	15 AUG 1836	1831:428
Boughton, Joshua L., by Reuben B. Boughton	Account	17 DEC 1838	1838:036
Boughton, Joshua L., by Reuben B. Boughton	Account	18 MAY 1840	1838:082
Boughton, Joshua L., by Reuben B. Boughton	Account	19 SEP 1842	1838:230
Boughton, Joshua L., by Reuben B. Boughton	Account	21 FEB 1842	1838:178
Boughton, Joshua L., by Reuben B. Boughton	Account	16 DEC 1850	1844:495
Boughton, Lala Burt, c/o Brooks to Roberta P. Boughton	Bond	17 AUG 1863	1857:300
Boughton, Lalabert, c/o Brooks to Gabriel H. Dillard	Bond	15 DEC 1862	1857:296
Boughton, Martha, c/o Thomas to Mary Boughton	Bond	21 DEC 1795	1761:221
Boughton, Martha, c/o Thomas, by Mrs. Mary Boughton	Account	16 JAN 1809	1796:205
Boughton, Martha A., c/o Brooks to Gabriel H. Dillard	Bond	15 DEC 1862	1857:296
Boughton, Martha A., c/o Brooks to Roberta P. Boughton	Bond	17 AUG 1863	1857:300
Boughton, Mary C., c/o Brooks to Roberta P. Boughton	Bond	17 AUG 1863	1857:300
Boughton, Philip Carter, c/o Richard to Alexr. S. Boughton	Bond	19 FEB 1816	1811:114
Boughton, Polly, c/o Richard to Alexr. S. Boughton	Bond	19 FEB 1816	1811:114
Boughton, Richard, c/o Richard to Alexr. S. Boughton	Bond	19 FEB 1816	1811:114
Boughton, Robert, c/o Richard to Alexr. S. Boughton	Bond	19 FEB 1816	1811:114
Boughton, Susanna, c/o Thomas to Mary Boughton	Bond	21 DEC 1795	1761:221
Boughton, Thomas & wife Polly Allen, from James Dunn	Receipt	17 OCT 1825	1825:052
Boughton, Washington, c/o Richard to Alexr. S. Boughton	Bond	19 FEB 1816	1811:114
Boulware, Caroline, c/o Thomas to Henry H. Boughan	Bond	15 JAN 1816	1811:113
Boulware, Caroline, from H.H. Boughan	Receipt	19 SEP 1825	1825:024
Boulware, Elizabeth to Robert Parker	Bond	18 SEP 1716	D&W14:646
Boulware, Elizabeth, c/o Thomas to Henry H. Boughan	Bond	15 JAN 1816	1811:113
Boulware, John to John Boulware	Bond	17 MAY 1736	WB6:009
Bowie, Walter and wife Julia Ann Spindle, from Barbee Spindle	Receipt	19 SEP 1825	1825:016
Braxton, Augustine, c/o Carter to Temple Elliott	Bond	16 MAR 1812	1811:006
Braxton, Augustine M., infant, by Temple Elliott	Settlement	18 OCT 1819	1811:202
Braxton, Carter, c/o Carter to Thomas Brockenbrough	Bond	16 DEC 1811	1811:003
Braxton, Elizabeth, c/o Carter to Temple Elliott	Bond	16 MAR 1812	1811:006
Braxton, Judith, c/o Carter to Temple Elliott	Bond	16 MAR 1812	1811:006
Braxton, Judith S., infant, by Temple Elliott	Settlement	18 OCT 1819	1811:200
Braxton, Robert, c/o Carter to Temple Elliott	Bond	16 MAR 1812	1811:006
Braxton, Robert C., infant, by Temple Elliott	Settlement	18 OCT 1819	1811:198
Bray, Betsey, c/o Charles to Elizabeth Bray	Bond	16 JAN 1804	1796:145
Bray, Charles, c/o Charles to Elizabeth Bray	Bond	16 JAN 1804	1796:145
Bray, Charles, c/o Charles to Winter Bray	Bond	18 DEC 1809	1796:223
Bray, Charles, master, by John Collins	Settlement	17 JUL 1815	1811:088
Bray, Charles, from Winter Bray	Receipt	19 FEB 1821	1811:250
Bray, Charles, c/o Winter to John S. Trible	Bond	15 MAY 1854	1851:238
Bray, Charles R., s/o Winter, by John S. Trible	Account	20 AUG 1855	1851:317
Bray, Charles R., by John S. Trible	Account	17 NOV 1856	1851:384
Bray, Charles R., by John S. Trible	Account	20 DEC 1858	1857:115
Bray, Charles R., by John S. Trible	Account	18 JAN 1858	1857:049

Ward or Subject (and Parent, Guardian or Other)	Record Type	Date	Reference(s)
Bray, Charles R., by John S. Trible	Account	21 NOV 1859	1857:189
Bray, Charles R., by John S. Trible	Account	15 OCT 1860	1857:227
Bray, Charles R., by John S. Trible	Account	20 JAN 1862	1857:283
Bray, Charles R., by John S. Trible	Account	18 JAN 1864	1857:304
Bray, Charles R., by John S. Trible	Account	19 OCT 1868	1867:070
Bray, Charles R., c/o Winter to Samuel D. Pilcher	Bond	15 JUN 1868	1867:031
Bray, Elizabeth, c/o Charles to Winter Bray	Bond	18 DEC 1809	1796:223
Bray, Elizabeth, by Winter Bray	Account	15 JUN 1812	1811:015
Bray, Elizabeth, Miss, by John Collins	Account	17 AUG 1812	1811:018
Bray, Mary Ann, c/o Charles to Elizabeth Bray	Bond	16 JAN 1804	1796:145
Bray, Mary Ann, c/o Charles to Winter Bray	Bond	18 DEC 1809	1796:223
Bray, Mary Ann, by John Collins	Settlement	17 JUL 1815	1811:087
Bray, Mary C., c/o Thomas B.W. to John Waring	Bond	19 MAR 1832	1831:107
Bray, Mary C., c/o Charles to Susan Bray	Bond	21 APR 1851	1844:518
Bray, Maryann, by Winter Bray	Account	18 JAN 1819	1811:171
Bray, Polly, c/o Charles to Elizabeth Bray	Bond	16 JAN 1804	1796:145
Bray, Polly, c/o Charles to Winter Bray	Bond	18 DEC 1809	1796:223
Bray, Polly, by John Collins	Settlement	17 JUL 1815	1811:090
Bray, Susanna, c/o Charles to Elizabeth Bray	Bond	16 JAN 1804	1796:144
Bray, William, c/o John, by Jane Bray	Account	19 DEC 1785	1761:147
Bray, William H., c/o Charles to Susan Bray	Bond	21 APR 1851	1844:518
Bray, William H., c/o Charles to Boughan Richards	Bond	19 JUL 1858	1857:071
Bray, William H., by Susan Bray	Account	17 OCT 1859	1857:171
Bray, Winter, c/o Charles to Elizabeth Bray	Bond	16 JAN 1804	1796:144
Bray, Winter, c/o Charles to John Croxton, Jr.	Bond	21 APR 1806	1796:174
Bray, Winter to Charles Bray	Receipt	19 FEB 1821	1811:250
Bray, Winter, c/o Winter to John S. Trible	Bond	15 MAY 1854	1851:238
Bray, Winter, s/o Winter, by John S. Trible	Account	20 AUG 1855	1851:315
Bray, Winter, by John S. Trible	Account	17 NOV 1856	1851:385
Bray, Winter, by John S. Trible	Account	20 DEC 1858	1857:113
Bray, Winter, by John S. Trible	Account	18 JAN 1858	1857:051
Bray, Winter, by John S. Trible	Account	21 NOV 1859	1857:187
Bray, Winter, by John S. Trible	Account	15 OCT 1860	1857:227
Bray, Winter, by John S. Trible	Account	20 JAN 1862	1857:281
Bray, Winter, by John S. Trible	Account	18 JAN 1864	1857:303
Bray, Winter, by John S. Trible	Account	21 OCT 1868	1867:048
Bray, Winter & Charles R., by John S. Trible	Account	19 OCT 1868	1867:057
Breedlove, Isaac, c/o Nathan to John Trible	Bond	17 FEB 1800	1796:055
Britt, John, c/o John to William Ramsey	Bond	15 MAY 1759	1731:241
Brizendine, Biveon & wife Betsey Allen, from James Dunn	Receipt	17 OCT 1825	1825:052
Brizendine, Churchill R., c/o John C. to Martha J. Brizendine	Bond	19 OCT 1857	1857:032
Brizendine, Eliza, c/o Vincent to her father	Bond	20 JUL 1812	1811:017
Brizendine, Emma F., c/o Ferriall & Margaret to R.C. Phillips	Certificate	21 FEB 1876	1867:346
Brizendine, Emma F., over 14, c/o Feriol to Robert C. Phillips	Bond	21 FEB 1876	1867:346
Brizendine, Emma, by R.C. Phillips	Account	19 JAN 1880	1867:418
Brizendine, Emma now Taylor, from R.C. Phillips	Receipt	18 JUL 1887	1867:587
Brizendine, Ewen V., c/o Ewen to William A. Brizendine	Bond	18 JUL 1853	1851:186
Brizendine, Geo. W., c/o Ferriall & Margaret to R.C. Phillips	Certificate	21 FEB 1876	1867:346
Brizendine, George W., over 14, c/o Feriol to Robert C. Phillips	Bond	21 FEB 1876	1867:346
Brizendine, George W., by R.C. Phillips	Account	19 JAN 1880	1867:418
Brizendine, George W., by R.C. Phillips	Account	16 APR 1883	1867:516

Ward or Subject (and Parent, Guardian or Other)	Record Type	Date	Reference(s)
Brizendine, George W., from R.C. Phillips	Receipt	18 JUL 1887	1867:587
Brizendine, Harvey L., by Martha J. Brizendine	Account	21 JAN 1861	1857:249
Brizendine, Harvie L., c/o John C. to Martha J. Brizendine	Bond	19 OCT 1857	1857:032
Brizendine, John Fountaine, c/o John C. to Martha J. Brizendine	Bond	19 OCT 1857	1857:032
Brizendine, John F., by Martha J. Brizendine	Account	21 JAN 1861	1857:248
Brizendine, Ludy, c/o John to John Davis	Bond	16 DEC 1793	1761:197
Brizendine, Margaret J., c/o John C. to Martha J. Brizendine	Bond	19 OCT 1857	1857:032
Brizendine, Marinda, c/o John C. to Leonard Henley	Bond	19 OCT 1857	1857:033
Brizendine, Mary, c/o John C. to Leonard Henley	Bond	19 OCT 1857	1857:033
Brizendine, Mildred, c/o Henry to William G. Newbill	Bond	20 SEP 1847	1844:245
Brizendine, Mildred, by William G. Newbill	Account	18 MAR 1850	1844:422
Brizendine, Nancy, c/o Francis to Randolph Brizendine	Bond	15 OCT 1804	1796:156
Brizendine, Orville, c/o John C. to Leonard Henley	Bond	19 OCT 1857	1857:033
Brizendine, Philip, c/o Vincent to his father	Bond	20 JUL 1812	1811:017
Brizendine, Richard, c/o Vincent to his father	Bond	20 JUL 1812	1811:017
Brizendine, Rosa F., over 14, c/o Feriol to Robert C. Phillips	Bond	21 FEB 1876	1867:346
Brizendine, Rosa F., c/o Ferriall & Margaret to R.C. Phillips	Certificate	21 FEB 1876	1867:346
Brizendine, Rosa, by R.C. Phillips	Account	19 JAN 1880	1867:418
Brizendine, Rosa, by R.C. Phillips	Account	16 APR 1883	1867:514
Brizendine, Rosa F., by R.C. Phillips	Account	18 NOV 1884	1867:559
Brizendine, Susan, c/o Travis to her father	Bond	17 SEP 1827	1825:177
Brizendine, Thomas, by Vincent Ramsey	Account	18 APR 1831	1831:013
Brizendine, Thomas, from Vincent Ramsey	Receipt	18 APR 1831	1831:013
Brizendine, Vass, c/o Travis to his father	Bond	17 SEP 1827	1825:177
Brizendine, Virginia Emily, c/o John C. to Leonard Henley	Bond	19 OCT 1857	1857:033
Broaddus, Mary, over 14, of unknown father, to James Chandler	Bond	21 FEB 1887	1867:584
Broaddus, Richard F., s/o Alexander W. to his father	Bond	16 FEB 1857	1851:398
Brockenbrough, Austin, c/o Austin to Frances Brockenbrough	Bond	17 JAN 1859	1857:122
Brockenbrough, Austin, by Frances Brockenbrough	Account	18 APR 1864	1857:332
Brockenbrough, Austin, by Frances Brockenbrough	Account	18 APR 1864	1857:314, 316
Brockenbrough, Benjamin B., c/o Austin to Frances Brockenbrough	Bond	17 JAN 1859	1857:122
Brockenbrough, Benjamin B., by Frances Brockenbrough	Account	18 APR 1864	1857:318, 320
Brockenbrough, Betty G., by John F. Brockenbrough	Account	19 OCT 1874	1867:255
Brockenbrough, Betty G., to bro. Wm. A. Brockenbrough	P. of Atty.	19 OCT 1874	1867:282, 285
Brockenbrough, Cath. W.G., c/o Wm. A. to John T. Brockenbrough	Bond	17 JAN 1859	1857:123
Brockenbrough, Catharine W.G., c/o Dr. Wm. A. to John T. Brockenbrough	Certificate	17 JAN 1859	1857:122
Brockenbrough, Catharine W.G., c/o Dr. William A., over 14	Certificate	17 JAN 1859	1857:122
Brockenbrough, Catherine W.G., by John F. Brockenbrough	Account	19 OCT 1874	1867:272
Brockenbrough, Gabriella, c/o Austin to Frances Brockenbrough	Bond	17 JAN 1859	1857:122
Brockenbrough, John T., c/o Wm. A. to John T. Brockenbrough	Bond	17 JAN 1859	1857:123
Brockenbrough, John F., Jr., by John F. Brockenbrough	Account	19 OCT 1874	1867:266
Brockenbrough, John F. & Marius C., of San Saba Co., Tex.	P. of Atty.	19 OCT 1874	1867:286
Brockenbrough, Judith Branch, by John F. Brockenbrough	Account	19 OCT 1874	1867:262
Brockenbrough, Kate G., to bro. Wm. A. Brockenbrough	P. of Atty.	19 OCT 1874	1867:282
Brockenbrough, Lettice L., c/o Dr. Wm. A. to John F. Brockenbrough	Certificate	17 JAN 1859	1857:122
Brockenbrough, Lettice L., c/o Wm. A. to John T. Brockenbrough	Bond	17 JAN 1859	1857:123
Brockenbrough, Lettice L., over 14, c/o Dr. William A.	Certificate	17 JAN 1859	1857:122
Brockenbrough, Letty L., by John F. Brockenbrough	Account	19 OCT 1874	1867:276
Brockenbrough, Letty L., to bro. Wm. A. Brockenbrough	P. of Atty.	19 OCT 1874	1867:282
Brockenbrough, Lucy Y., to bro. Wm. A. Brockenbrough	P. of Atty.	19 OCT 1874	1867:282
Brockenbrough, Lucy Yates, by John F. Brockenbrough	Account	19 OCT 1874	1867:252

Ward or Subject (and Parent, Guardian or Other)	Record Type	Date	Reference(s)
Brockenbrough, Marius C., c/o Wm. A. to John T. Brockenbrough	Bond	17 JAN 1859	1857:123
Brockenbrough, Marius C. & John F., of San Saba Co., Tex.	P. of Atty.	19 OCT 1874	1867:286
Brockenbrough, Marius C., by John F. Brockenbrough	Account	19 OCT 1874	1867:248
Brockenbrough, Mary R., by John F. Brockenbrough	Account	19 OCT 1874	1867:258
Brockenbrough, William A., fr. Thomas T. Arnold, K.G. Co.	P. of Atty.	19 OCT 1874	1867:284
Brockenbrough, William A., by John F. Brockenbrough	Account	19 OCT 1874	1867:246
Brockenbrough, William A., children of, by John F. Brockenbrough	Account	19 OCT 1874	1867:230
Brockenbrough, Wm. A., heirs of, Richmond Co.	P. of Atty.	19 OCT 1874	1867:282
Broocke, Elizabeth late Crow, by Sally Crow	Account	17 SEP 1832	1831:135
Broocke, Hezekiah, c/o Philip, Jr. to Leonard Henley	Bond	19 NOV 1849	1844:399
Broocke, Isaac, c/o Philip, Jr. to Leonard Henley	Bond	19 NOV 1849	1844:399
Broocke, James R., c/o Philip, Jr. to Leonard Henley	Bond	19 NOV 1849	1844:399
Broocke, Mary, c/o Philip, Jr. to Leonard Henley	Bond	19 NOV 1849	1844:399
Broocke, Mildred, c/o Philip, Jr. to Leonard Henley	Bond	19 NOV 1849	1844:399
Broocke, Robert, c/o Isaac, by William Broocke	Account	17 AUG 1767	1761:064
Broocke, Robert, c/o Isaac, by William Broocke	Account	21 AUG 1769	1761:068
Broocke, Robert, c/o Isaac, by William Broocke	Account	20 AUG 1770	1761:080
Broocke, Robert, c/o Wm., by William Broocke	Account	21 SEP 1772	1761:088
Broocke, Robert, by William Broocke	Account	18 SEP 1775	1761:127
Broocke, Thomas, c/o Thomas, by William Cheaney	Account	17 AUG 1778	1761:135
Broocke, Thomas, c/o Thomas, by William Cheaney	Account	20 SEP 1779	1761:141
Broocke, William, by Alexr. Saunders	Account	17 SEP 1770	1761:082
Broocke, William, c/o Peter, by Alexander Saunders	Account	19 OCT 1772	1761:089
Broocke, Wm. B., by attorney Chancey G. Griswold	Receipt	15 JUN 1840	1838:092
Broocks, Betsey Ann, c/o Isaac to her father	Bond	17 JUL 1826	1825:118
Broocks, Catharine Louisa, c/o Isaac to her father	Bond	17 JUL 1826	1825:118
Broocks, Mary St. John, c/o Isaac to her father	Bond	17 JUL 1826	1825:118
Broocks, Philip, c/o Richard, by Philip Kidd	Account	19 JUN 1786	WB14:027
Broocks, Richard, orphans of	Account	19 JUN 1786	WB14:027
Brooke, Ann, c/o Christopher to Benjamin Johnson	Bond	18 JUN 1792	1761:180
Brooke, Margaret, c/o Christopher to Spencer Clark	Bond	18 JUN 1792	1761:181
Brooke, Robert, s/o Robert to Robert Brooke	Bond	22 FEB 1758	1731:220
Brooke, Robert, by William Brooke	Account	16 AUG 1773	1761:098
Brooke, Robert, by William Brooke	Account	17 OCT 1774	1761:122
Brooke, Robert, c/o Christopher to Benjamin Johnson	Bond	18 JUN 1792	1761:180
Brooke, Robert, c/o Humphrey B. to Andrew Monroe	Bond	21 MAY 1810	1796:229
Brooke, Suckey, Miss, by Andrew Crawford	Account	16 AUG 1773	1761:095
Brookes, Ann, by Thomas Thorp	Account	17 SEP 1746	1731:097
Brookes, Ann, c/o William, by Thomas Thorp	Account	15 OCT 1751	1731:138
Brookes, William, by Thomas Thorp	Account	17 SEP 1746	1731:095
Brookes, William, c/o William, by Thomas Thorp	Account	15 OCT 1751	1731:138
Brookes, William, dec., orphans of, by Thomas Thorp	Account	15 OCT 1751	1731:138
Brooks, Alberta, c/o Benjamin O. to Burton P. Anderson	Certificate	22 AUG 1882	1867:491
Brooks, Alberta, over 14, c/o Benj. O. to Burton P. Anderson	Bond	22 AUG 1882	1867:491
Brooks, Alexander, c/o Lewis D. to his father	Bond	16 NOV 1835	1831:347
Brooks, Ann to Thomas Thorp	Bond	21 DEC 1742	WB6:412
Brooks, Ann, by Thomas Thorp	Account	17 SEP 1745	1731:083
Brooks, Austin, husband of Mary Ann Bray	Receipt	27 OCT 1818	1811:173
Brooks, Beverley, c/o Lewis D. to his father	Bond	16 NOV 1835	1831:347
Brooks, Elizabeth to Thomas Thorp	Bond	21 DEC 1742	WB6:411
Brooks, Lewis Durham, c/o Lewis to his father	Bond	19 OCT 1801	1796:109

Ward or Subject (and Parent, Guardian or Other)	Record Type	Date	Reference(s)
Brooks, Mary, c/o Dabney to Robert Williamson	Bond	21 DEC 1846	1844:185
Brooks, William, by Thomas Thorp	Account	17 SEP 1745	1731:084
Brooks, William, by Thomas Thorp	Account	20 OCT 1747	1731:109
Brooks, William, by Thomas Thorp	Account	18 OCT 1748	1731:124
Brooks, Willis & wife Elizabeth Jones, from Nancy Jones	Receipt	16 MAR 1835	1831:290
Brookshire, Margaret late Wortham to Thomas Thorp	Bond	19 APR 1757	1731:211
Brown, Andrew C., by William Fleet	Account	19 SEP 1803	1796:136
Brown, Basil, c/o Bennett to William Fleet	Bond	17 JUL 1797	1796:009
Brown, Charles, c/o Bennett to William Fleet	Bond	21 DEC 1795	1761:218
Brown, Charles L., c/o Daniel to Elizabeth Brown	Bond	17 OCT 1825	1825:039
Brown, Charles L.	Suit Ref.	21 NOV 1832	1831:153
Brown, Edward, c/o William to William Brown	Bond	17 FEB 1868	1867:024
Brown, Eliza A., c/o Daniel to Larkin Noel	Bond	20 MAY 1829	1825:280
Brown, Eliza Ann, age about 19, for sale of house & lot	Bond	21 NOV 1832	1831:153
Brown, Eliza A., by Richard Rowzee	Suit Ref.	21 NOV 1832	1831:153
Brown, Elizabeth to Jane Olive	Bond	16 MAY 1716	D&W14:554
Brown, Elizabeth Ann, c/o Daniel to Elizabeth Brown	Bond	17 OCT 1825	1825:039
Brown, Fanny Ann, c/o William to William Brown	Bond	17 FEB 1868	1867:024
Brown, Francis to Jane Mills	Bond	10 MAY 1710	D&W13:324
Brown, John, c/o Daniel, to James Powers	Bond	15 DEC 1828	1825:261
Brown, Joseph B., c/o Edward to Daniel Brown	Bond	16 NOV 1818	1811:163
Brown, Julia C., by James Powers	Account	20 AUG 1832	1831:126
Brown, Julia C., by James Powers	Account	16 SEP 1833	1831:194
Brown, Juliet C., c/o Daniel to Elizabeth Brown	Bond	17 OCT 1825	1825:039
Brown, Juliet C., by James Roy Micou	Suit Ref.	21 NOV 1832	1831:153
Brown, Mary to Jane Mills	Bond	10 MAY 1710	D&W13:324
Brown, Mary Hill, c/o Bennett to Mary Brown	Bond	21 DEC 1795	1761:216
Brown, Mereda [Meriday] to George Green	Bond	20 MAR 1753	1731:159
Brown, Pracilla Brooke, c/o Bennett to Mary Brown	Bond	21 DEC 1795	1761:216
Brown, Reuben, c/o William to William Brown	Bond	17 FEB 1868	1867:024
Brown, Richard Lewis, c/o Lewis to David W. Pitts	Bond	17 NOV 1828	1825:257
Brown, Stark, c/o William, by Stark Boulware	Account	16 OCT 1769	1761:077
Brown, Susan M., c/o Daniel to Elizabeth Brown	Bond	17 OCT 1825	1825:039
Brown, Susan A., c/o Daniel to Larkin Noel	Bond	20 MAY 1829	1825:280
Brown, Susan M.	Suit Ref.	21 NOV 1832	1831:153
Brown, Susan, c/o Jacob to Aaron Commodore	Bond	20 JUL 1868	1867:038
Brown, William to Samuel Stallard	Bond	10 MAR 1707/8	D&W13:073
Browne, Andrew Cochrane, c/o Bennett to Wm. Fleet	Bond	21 DEC 1795	1761:217
Browne, Andrew C., by William Fleet	Account	17 OCT 1797	1796:015
Browne, Andrew C., by William Fleet	Account	17 SEP 1798	1796:033
Browne, Andrew C., by William Fleet	Account	16 JUN 1800	1796:062
Browne, Andrew C., c/o Bennett to Charles Browne	Bond	17 OCT 1803	1796:140
Browne, Basil, by William Fleet	Account	17 SEP 1798	1796:034
Browne, Basil, by William Fleet	Account	16 JUN 1800	1796:064
Browne, Basil, c/o Bennett to Christopher Tompkins	Bond	20 OCT 1800	1796:078
Browne, Bennett, c/o Charles, Jr. to Ann Temple Browne	Bond	20 MAY 1811	1796:246
Browne, Charles, c/o Charles, Jr. to Ann Temple Browne	Bond	20 MAY 1811	1796:246
Browne, Charles A., dec., by Alexander Fleet	Account	19 MAR 1827	1825:164
Browne, Christopher T., c/o Charles, Jr. to Ann Temple Browne	Bond	20 MAY 1811	1796:246
Browne, Christopher, c/o Charles, to Kemp Gatewood	Bond	16 DEC 1822	WB19:344
Browne, Christopher T., by Kemp Gatewood	Account	17 OCT 1825	1825:033

Ward or Subject (and Parent, Guardian or Other)	Record Type	Date	Reference(s)
Browne, Christopher T., by Lawrence Muse	Account	19 SEP 1825	1825:032
Browne, Christopher T., from Kemp Gatewood	Receipt	15 JAN 1827	1825:127
Browne, Eliza L., c/o Charles, Jr. to Ann Temple Browne	Bond	20 MAY 1811	1796:246
Browne, Sally T., c/o Charles, Jr. to Ann Temple Browne	Bond	20 MAY 1811	1796:246
Browne, Sally, c/o Charles, to Kemp Gatewood	Bond	16 DEC 1822	WB19:344
Browne, Sally T., by Lawrence Muse	Account	19 SEP 1825	1825:032
Browne, Sally T., by Kemp Gatewood	Account	17 OCT 1825	1825:033
Browne, Sally T., by Kemp Gatewood	Account	18 AUG 1828	1825:242
Bunday, Thomas R., by Ryburn Bunday	Bond	17 DEC 1888	F
Burch, Nettie, c/o Sterling to Joshua W. Roane	Bond	22 NOV 1872	1867:185
Burhanan, Sarah [Bohanan], to Jonathan Dunn	Bond	16 JUL 1751	WB9:076
Burke, Betsey, c/o James, by John Jones	Account	21 FEB 1803	1796:131
Burke, Bettie W., by Thomas B. Garnett	Account	21 OCT 1861	1857:275
Burke, Betty W., c/o Thomas to Thomas B. Garnett	Bond	21 DEC 1857	1857:045
Burke, Elizabeth, c/o James to John Jones	Bond	21 DEC 1801	1796:111
Burke, James, c/o James to John Jones	Bond	21 DEC 1801	1796:111
Burke, James, c/o James, by John Jones	Account	21 FEB 1803	1796:131
Burke, James, c/o Graves to William Burke	Bond	16 OCT 1826	1825:120
Burke, James, by William Burke	Account	18 APR 1831	1831:015
Burke, James, at age 21, in Morengo Co. AL, fr. John Burke	Receipt	18 SEP 1837	1831:500, 501
Burke, James C.B., c/o James to Ann B. Burke	Bond	19 NOV 1849	1844:399
Burke, James C., c/o James, by Ann B. Burke	Account	17 MAY 1852	1851:100
Burke, James C.B., by Ann B. Burke	Account	17 JUL 1854	1851:247
Burke, James C.B., by Ann B. Burke	Account	19 JUL 1858	1857:093
Burke, James C.B., by Ann B. Burke	Account	21 JAN 1861	1857:237
Burke, James C.B., by Ann B. Burke	Account	18 APR 1864	1857:324
Burke, John William, c/o James to Ann B. Burke	Bond	19 NOV 1849	1844:399
Burke, John William, c/o James, by Ann B. Burke	Account	17 MAY 1852	1851:104
Burke, John W., by Ann B. Burke	Account	17 JUL 1854	1851:249
Burke, John William, by Ann B. Burke	Account	19 JUL 1858	1857:096
Burke, John William, by Ann B. Burke	Account	21 JAN 1861	1857:239
Burke, John William, by Ann B. Burke	Account	18 APR 1864	1857:322
Burke, Juliett, c/o Graves to William Burke	Bond	16 OCT 1826	1825:121
Burke, Lucinda, c/o Graves to William Burke	Bond	16 OCT 1826	1825:121
Burke, Mary, c/o Graves to William Burke	Bond	16 OCT 1826	1825:120
Burke, Mary, by William Burke	Account	18 APR 1831	1831:015
Burke, Mary Susan, c/o James to Edward Powers	Bond	20 AUG 1849	1844:386
Burke, Mary S., c/o James, by Edward Powers	Account	15 SEP 1851	1851:010
Burke, Mary Susan, by Edward Powers	Account	17 JAN 1853	1851:164
Burke, Mary Susan, c/o James to Thomas M. Burke	Bond	17 JAN 1853	1851:163
Burke, Nancy, c/o James to John Jones	Bond	21 DEC 1801	1796:111
Burke, Nancy, c/o James, by John Jones	Account	21 FEB 1803	1796:131
Burke, Richard, c/o Graves to William Burke	Bond	16 OCT 1826	1825:120
Burke, Richard G., by William Burke	Account	18 APR 1831	1831:015
Burke, Robert, c/o James to Edward Powers	Bond	20 AUG 1849	1844:386
Burke, Robert, by Edward Powers	Account	15 SEP 1851	1851:006
Burke, Robert, by Edward Powers	Account	15 NOV 1852	1851:150
Burke, Robert, from Edward Powers	Receipt	15 NOV 1852	1851:151
Burnett, Benjamin, c/o Joseph to Winifred Burnett	Bond	19 DEC 1825	1825:078
Burnett, Benjamin, by Winneyfred Burnett	Account	19 FEB 1827	1825:151
Burnett, Benjamin C., by Winnifred Burnett	Account	19 FEB 1828	1825:219

Ward or Subject (and Parent, Guardian or Other)	Record Type	Date	Reference(s)
Burnett, Benjamin C., c/o Joseph, by Winneyfred Burnett	Account	19 JAN 1829	1825:270
Burnett, Benjamin C., c/o Joseph, by Winneyfred Burnett	Account	18 APR 1831	1831:033
Burnett, Benjamin C., c/o Joseph, by Winneyfred Burnett	Account	20 FEB 1832	1831:091
Burnett, Benjamin C., c/o Joseph, by Winneyfred Burnett	Account	20 MAR 1833	1831:164
Burnett, Caty, c/o Richard to John Turner	Bond	15 DEC 1800	1796:083
Burnett, Gatewood, c/o James to Churchill Anderson	Bond	18 OCT 1819	1811:195
Burnett, James, c/o Joseph to Winifred Burnett	Bond	19 DEC 1825	1825:078
Burnett, James, by Winnyfred Burnett	Account	19 FEB 1827	1825:149
Burnett, James W., by Winneyfred Burnett	Account	19 FEB 1828	1825:218
Burnett, James W., c/o Joseph, by Winneyfred Burnett	Account	19 JAN 1829	1825:272
Burnett, James W., c/o Joseph, by Winneyfred Burnett	Account	18 APR 1831	1831:035
Burnett, James W., c/o Joseph, by Winneyfred Burnett	Account	20 FEB 1832	1831:090
Burnett, Lucretia to William Burnett	Bond	18 SEP 1753	1731:169
Burnett, Phebe to John Burnett	Bond	18 SEP 1753	1731:168
Burnett, Robert, c/o Joseph to Winifred Burnett	Bond	19 DEC 1825	1825:078
Burnett, Robert, by Winnyfred Burnett	Account	19 FEB 1827	1825:150
Burnett, Robert G., by Winneyfred Burnett	Account	19 FEB 1828	1825:220
Burnett, Robert, c/o Joseph, by Winneyfred Burnett	Account	19 JAN 1829	1825:273
Burnett, Robert G., c/o Joseph, by Winneyfred Burnett	Account	18 APR 1831	1831:035
Burnett, Robert G., c/o Joseph, by Winneyfred Burnett	Account	20 FEB 1832	1831:093
Burnett, Robert G., c/o Joseph, by Winneyfred Burnett	Account	20 MAR 1833	1831:165
Burnett, Robert, c/o Joseph to Wm. F. Burnett	Bond	16 OCT 1837	1831:503
Burnett, William, c/o Joseph to Winifred Burnett	Bond	19 DEC 1825	1825:078
Burnett, William, by Winneyfred Burnett	Account	19 FEB 1827	1825:147
Burnett, William, by Winney Burnett	Account	19 FEB 1828	1825:221
Burnett, Wm., c/o Joseph, by Winneyfred Burnett	Account	19 JAN 1829	1825:269
Burwell, Elizabeth, c/o James to Warner Lewis	Bond	18 DEC 1815	1811:109
Bush, Alice, c/o John to Robert Dobbins	Bond	15 JUL 1811	1796:251
Bush, Cordelia, c/o John to Jane Bush	Bond	15 JUL 1811	1796:251
Bush, Cordelia, by Jane Bush	Account	17 OCT 1825	1825:048
Bush, Cordelia, c/o John to Alexander S. Boughton	Bond	19 JAN 1829	1825:265
Bush, Fanny, c/o John to Jane Bush	Bond	15 JUL 1811	1796:251
Bush, Frances, from Jane Bush	Receipt	19 SEP 1825	1825:013
Bush, Jane, c/o John to Robert Dobbins	Bond	15 JUL 1811	1796:251
Bush, Robert, c/o John to Jane Bush	Bond	15 JUL 1811	1796:251
Bush, Robert, by Jane Bush	Account	17 OCT 1825	1825:050
Bush, Thomas, s/o Bibby to Stephen Neale	Bond	17 MAR 1752	1731:144
Bush, Thomas, c/o Bibby to Thomas Henry Brooke	Bond	19 DEC 1758	1731:237
Bush, Thomas, c/o Bibby to Stephen Neal	Bond	16 JUN 1760	1731:253
Bush, Thomas, by Henry Broocke	Account	18 AUG 1760	1731:258
Bush, Thomas, c/o Bibby, by Stephen Neale	Account	21 SEP 1761	1761:009
Bush, Thomas, c/o Bibby, by Stephen Neale	Account	16 AUG 1762	1761:012
Bush, William, c/o John to Jane Bush	Bond	15 JUL 1811	1796:251
Bush, William, from Jane Bush	Receipt	19 SEP 1825	1825:012
Butler, Catharine, c/o Thomas, by Augustine Moxley	Account	17 AUG 1772	1761:086
Butler, Catharine, c/o Reuben to Warner Lewis	Marriage Ref.	17 AUG 1835	1831:326
Butler, James, by Thomas Hawkins	Account	19 OCT 1789	1761:165
Butler, James, by Samuel Ayres	Account	21 JAN 1793	1761:191
Butler, John, c/o Thomas, by Augustine Moxley	Account	17 AUG 1772	1761:086
Butler, Thomas, c/o Thomas, by Augustine Moxley	Account	17 AUG 1772	1761:086
Butler, Thomas, orphans of, by Augustine Moxley	Account	17 AUG 1772	1761:086

Ward or Subject (and Parent, Guardian or Other)	Record Type	Date	Reference(s)
Butler, Thomas, orphans of, by Augustine Moxley	Account	15 AUG 1774	1761:117
Butler, Thomas, orphans of, by Augustine Moxley	Account	18 AUG 1777	1761:129
Butler, Thomas, orphans of, by Augustine Moxley	Account	20 SEP 1779	1761:138
Butler, Thomas, orphans of, by Augustine Moxley	Account	21 AUG 1780	1761:142
Butler, Thomas, by John Butler	Account	17 OCT 1785	1761:144
Butler, Thomas, by John Butler	Account	16 OCT 1786	1761:152
Butler, Thomas, orphans of, by Augustine Moxley	Account	18 JUN 1798	1796:030
Butler, William, c/o Thomas, by Augustine Moxley	Account	17 AUG 1772	1761:086
Byram, Frances to Jonathan Haile	Bond	17 FEB 1724/5	WB4:093
Byrom, Bryant to James Byrom	Bond	18 MAY 1725	WB4:103
Byrom, Mary to Thomas Davis	Bond	19 JAN 1724/5	WB4:089
Byrom, Peter to James Byrom	Bond	18 MAY 1725	WB4:103

C

Ward or Subject (and Parent, Guardian or Other)	Record Type	Date	Reference(s)
Callaun, M.W., under 14, c/o E.A. & W.A. to F.P. Callaun	Bond	17 MAY 1887	1867:585
Callis, Catharine F., c/o Richard N. to Sarah Callis	Bond	20 MAR 1820	1811:209
Callis, Hannah, Miss, by Benjamin H. Munday	Account	17 MAR 1828	1825:232
Callis, Sarah, c/o Richard N. to David Pitts	Bond	20 AUG 1827	1825:169
Callis, Sarah, Miss, by Benjamin H. Munday	Account	17 MAR 1828	1825:232
Callis, Susan, Miss, by Benjamin H. Munday	Account	17 MAR 1828	1825:232
Callis, Susannah, c/o Richard N. to David Pitts	Bond	20 AUG 1827	1825:169
Cammack, Frances Ann late Jones, by Sarah J. Dobyns	Account	16 NOV 1857	1857:037
Campbell, Annie B., under 14, c/o William to her father	Bond	19 JAN 1880	1867:417
Campbell, Daniel to Richard Jeffries	Bond	19 MAR 1750/1	WB8:418
Campbell, Hugh, c/o Hugh to Archibald Ritchie	Bond	15 FEB 1808	1796:197
Campbell, James, c/o Thacker to Hannah Campbell	Bond	15 DEC 1794	1761:206
Campbell, James L., under 14, c/o William to his father	Bond	19 JAN 1880	1867:417
Campbell, Jeanette R., under 14, c/o William to her father	Bond	19 JAN 1880	1867:417
Campbell, Mary Ann, c/o Hugh to Thomas Roane	Bond	16 JUN 1806	1796:177
Campbell, Mary, under 14, c/o William to her father	Bond	19 JAN 1880	1867:417
Campbell, Priscilla C., under 14, c/o William to her father	Bond	19 JAN 1880	1867:417
Campbell, Wade H., under 14, c/o William to his father	Bond	19 JAN 1880	1867:417
Campbell, William, under 14, c/o William to his father	Bond	19 JAN 1880	1867:417
Cannon, Juliet E., c/o Richard to Walter G. Covington	Bond	21 APR 1856	1851:341
Cannon, Juliet, by Walter G. Covington	Account	20 JUL 1857	1851:439
Cannon, Mary C., c/o Richard to Walter G. Covington	Bond	21 APR 1856	1851:341
Cannon, Mary, by Walter G. Covington	Account	20 JUL 1857	1851:439
Carlton, George F., over 14, c/o Benj. T. to James W. Evans	Bond	18 APR 1882	1867:488
Carlton, Leslie, c/o Benjamin F. to Thomas F. Taff	Bond	17 AUG 1868	1867:039
Cauthorn, Ada, c/o Thomas to Thomas H. Brizendine	Bond	17 JAN 1870	1867:117
Cauthorn, Adelaide, under 14, c/o Thomas to Roberta Cauthorn	Bond	15 OCT 1866	1857:415
Cauthorn, Alfred, c/o James to Ross A. Cauthorn	Bond	19 MAY 1834	1831:265
Cauthorn, Alfred H., by Arthur L. Barnes	Account	18 MAY 1835	1831:294
Cauthorn, Alfred, by Ross A. Cauthorn	Account	19 DEC 1836	1831:458
Cauthorn, Amey, c/o Richard to Catharine Cauthorn	Bond	18 JUL 1796	1761:226
Cauthorn, Ann Eliza, c/o Ethelbert to William A. Oliver	Bond	17 MAR 1856	1851:340
Cauthorn, Ann E., by William A. Oliver	Account	21 OCT 1861	1857:271
Cauthorn, Ann Elizabeth, c/o Ethelbert, by R.B. Boughton, Jr.	Bond	14 NOV 1864	CCW:035
Cauthorn, Benjamin, c/o Vincent G. to Vincent Cauthorn	Bond	17 AUG 1792	1761:178
Cauthorn, Benjamin, c/o Godfrey to John Miller	Bond	21 APR 1795	1761:209
Cauthorn, E.G., from George C. Nunn gdn. of Leah A. Oliver	Receipt	21 FEB 1848	1844:262

Ward or Subject (and Parent, Guardian or Other)	Record Type	Date	Reference(s)
Cauthorn, Elizabeth, co Vincent G. to John Trible	Bond	17 APR 1792	1761:177
Cauthorn, Fannie Bettie, c/o Ethelbert to William A. Oliver	Bond	17 MAR 1856	1851:340
Cauthorn, Frances, c/o James, by Carter Cauthorn	Account	16 NOV 1835	1831:340
Cauthorn, Frances, c/o James to William Oliver	Bond	21 SEP 1835	1831:334
Cauthorn, Frances, by Carter Cauthorn	Account	17 MAY 1836	1831:416
Cauthorn, Frances E., by William Oliver	Account	16 MAR 1841	1838:134
Cauthorn, Godfrey, c/o Richard to Catharine Cauthorn	Bond	18 JUL 1796	1761:226
Cauthorn, Henry S., c/o Gabriel, in Knox Co. IN, by Elihu Stout	Bond	23 NOV 1844	1844:083
Cauthorn, Iverson, c/o Reuben to John Cauthorn	Bond	21 AUG 1820	1811:233
Cauthorn, James, c/o William, by Thomas Cauthorn	Account	16 NOV 1772	1761:095
Cauthorn, James, c/o William, by Thomas Cauthorn	Account	15 NOV 1773	1761:110
Cauthorn, James, c/o James, by A.L. Barnes	Account	16 JUN 1834	1831:268
Cauthorn, Jane, by Henry Vass	Account	20 SEP 1762	1761:021
Cauthorn, Jean, by Henry Vass	Account	19 SEP 1763	1761:040
Cauthorn, Jean, by Henry Vass	Account	17 SEP 1764	1761:050
Cauthorn, John to George Coleman	Bond	21 MAR 1748/9	WB8:200
Cauthorn, John to Francis Smith	Bond	16 JAN 1754	1731:176
Cauthorn, John, c/o Vincent G. to Vincent Cauthorn	Bond	17 AUG 1792	1761:178
Cauthorn, Juliet, under 14, c/o Thomas to Roberta Cauthorn	Bond	15 OCT 1866	1857:415
Cauthorn, Keturah Ann, c/o Amos to her father	Bond	16 DEC 1816	1811:130
Cauthorn, Keturah A., by Amos Cauthorn	Account	17 OCT 1825	1825:053
Cauthorn, Laura Eugenia, c/o Richard S. to R. Temple Gwathmey	Bond	21 DEC 1863	1857:301
Cauthorn, Laura E., by R. Temple Gwathmey	Account	16 JUL 1866	1857:399
Cauthorn, Leroy, c/o Richard to Catharine Cauthorn	Bond	18 JUL 1796	1761:226
Cauthorn, Lorenzo D., c/o Rice to George T. Cauthorn	Bond	15 MAR 1852	1851:048
Cauthorn, Lucinda E., c/o Amos to Absalom W. Cauthorn	Bond	17 JAN 1851	1844:481
Cauthorn, Lucinda E., by Absalom W. Cauthorn	Account	20 DEC 1852	1851:160
Cauthorn, Lucinda E., by Absalom W. Cauthorn	Account	18 AUG 1856	1851:377
Cauthorn, Mary to George Coleman	Bond	18 APR 1749	WB8:228
Cauthorn, Mary to Francis Smith	Bond	16 JAN 1754	1731:176
Cauthorn, Mary E., c/o Thomas to John L. Boughton	Bond	21 MAY 1866	1857:388
Cauthorn, Ophelia, c/o Reuben to John Cauthorn	Bond	21 AUG 1820	1811:233
Cauthorn, Ophelia now Baird, by Leroy Cauthorn	Account	18 JUN 1832	1831:115
Cauthorn, Patty, c/o Richard to Catharine Cauthorn	Bond	18 JUL 1796	1761:226
Cauthorn, Polly, c/o Reuben to John Cauthorn	Bond	21 AUG 1820	1811:233
Cauthorn, R. Starke, by R. Temple Gwathmey	Account	16 JUL 1866	1857:400
Cauthorn, Richard Francis, c/o Amos to his father	Bond	16 DEC 1816	1811:130
Cauthorn, Richard F.Y., by Amos Cauthorn	Account	17 OCT 1825	1825:053
Cauthorn, Richard Starke, c/o Richard S. to R. Temple Gwathmey	Bond	21 DEC 1863	1857:301
Cauthorn, Richard S., c/o Richard S., to Montalbet A. Cauthorn	Bond	18 DEC 1865	1857:374
Cauthorn, Richd. S., age 16+, s/o Dr. Rich. S. to bro. M. Alonzo Cauthorn	Certificate	18 DEC 1865	1857:373
Cauthorn, Robert, under 14, c/o Thomas to Roberta Cauthorn	Bond	15 OCT 1866	1857:415
Cauthorn, Thomas, under 14, c/o Thomas to Roberta Cauthorn	Bond	15 OCT 1866	1857:415
Cauthorn, Vincent, c/o Vincent G. to Vincent Cauthorn	Bond	17 APR 1792	1761:178
Cauthorn, William A., c/o Richard S., to Montalbet A. Cauthorn	Bond	18 DEC 1865	1857:374
Cauthorn, William, by R. Temple Gwathmey	Account	16 JUL 1866	1857:397
Cauthorn, Wm. Adolphus, c/o Richard S. to R. Temple Gwathmey	Bond	21 DEC 1863	1857:301
Cauthorn, Wm. A., 2nd s/o Dr. Richd. S. to bro. M. Alonzo Cauthorn	Certificate	18 DEC 1865	1857:373
Chamberlain, Curtis, c/o Leonard to Thomas M. Henley	Bond	16 SEP 1811	1796:256
Chamberlain, Curtis, by Thomas M. Henley	Account	19 JAN 1818	1811:144
Chamberlain, John to Alexander Parker	Bond	15 FEB 1736/7	WB6:044

Ward or Subject (and Parent, Guardian or Other)	Record Type	Date	Reference(s)
Chamberlain, Laura, over 14, c/o Carter to Jesse Ruffin	Certificate	18 FEB 1867	1857:416
Chamberlain, Lucy, c/o Leonard to James Gatewood	Bond	20 OCT 1800	1796:080
Chamberlaine, Polly, c/o Leonard to John Jones	Bond	20 JUL 1812	1811:017
Chamberlane, Leonard, c/o Leonard to John Jones	Bond	17 JUN 1811	1796:250
Chamberlayne, Laura, freedwoman, above 14, to Jesse Ruffin	Bond	18 FEB 1867	1857:416
Chamberlayne, Leonard, c/o Leonard to John Chamberlayne	Bond	16 OCT 1815	1811:104
Chaney, John to Peter Brooke	Bond	19 NOV 1751	1731:142
Chaney, John, by Peter Brooke	Account	16 OCT 1753	1731:170
Chaney, John, orphans of, by William Cheaney	Account	17 AUG 1778	1761:136
Cheaney, Eliza, c/o John, by Henry Vass	Account	19 SEP 1774	1761:119
Cheaney, John, orphans of, by Ann Cheaney	Account	20 SEP 1779	1761:140
Cheaney, Mary, Miss, c/o John, by William Cheaney	Account	18 SEP 1786	1761:151
Chenault, John to Stephen Chenault	Bond	20 FEB 1738/9	WB6:155
Chenault, Stephen to Stephen Chenault	Bond	20 FEB 1738/9	WB6:156
Cheney, John, c/o Erasmus to Isaac Mitchell	Bond	21 FEB 1748/9	WB8:165
Cheney, Philip to John Webb	Bond	20 JUN 1749	WB8:253
Cheney, Phillip, by Francis Brizendine	Account	15 AUG 1763	1761:028
Cheyney, Eliza., c/o John, by Henry Vass	Account	19 OCT 1772	1761:089
Cheyney, Eliza., c/o John, by Henry Vass	Account	29 SEP 1773	1761:097
Cheyney, Elizabeth, c/o John, by Henry Vass	Account	21 SEP 1767	1761:065
Cheyney, Elizabeth, c/o John, by Henry Vass	Account	19 SEP 1768	1761:067
Cheyney, Elizabeth, c/o John, by Henry Vass	Account	16 OCT 1769	1761:076
Cheyney, Elizabeth, c/o John, by Henry Vass	Account	20 AUG 1770	1761:081
Cheyney, Elizabeth, c/o John, by Henry Vass	Account	19 AUG 1771	1761:085
Cheyney, John, by Isaac Mitchell	Account	17 JUN 1755	WB10:059
Cheyney, John, by Peter Brooke	Settlement	17 JUN 1755	1731:193
Clark, Angelina, c/o William to James Clark	Bond	18 APR 1749	WB8:213
Clark, Angelina, c/o William, by James Clark	Account	22 MAY 1751	1731:129
Clark, Angelina, c/o William, by James Clark	Account	22 NOV 1752	1731:155
Clark, James, c/o William to James Clark	Bond	18 APR 1749	WB8:213
Clark, James, Jr., c/o William, by James Clark	Account	22 MAY 1751	1731:128
Clark, James, Jr., c/o William, by James Clark	Account	22 NOV 1752	1731:155
Clark, James, fr. James Andrews, admr. of Thos. Andrews	Receipt	17 OCT 1825	1825:057
Clark, Robert to Wheeler Haile	Bond	22 APR 1806	1796:174
Clark, Susanna, c/o William to James Clark	Bond	18 APR 1749	WB8:213
Clark, Susannah, c/o William, by James Clark	Account	22 MAY 1751	1731:128
Clark, Susannah, c/o William, by James Clark	Account	22 NOV 1752	1731:155
Clarke, Betsey C., c/o James to Andrew Noel	Bond	16 NOV 1812	1811:027
Clarke, Betty, c/o John to Mary Ann Clarke	Bond	20 MAR 1854	1851:227
Clarke, Betty, by Mary A. Clarke	Account	18 FEB 1861	1857:252
Clarke, Emeline, c/o John to Mary Ann Clarke	Bond	20 MAR 1854	1851:227
Clarke, Emeline, by Mary A. Clarke	Account	18 FEB 1861	1857:253
Clarke, Euphema, by Robert B. Micou	Account	19 APR 1841	1838:138
Clarke, Feminini, c/o James E. to Robert B. Micou	Bond	17 FEB 1840	1838:071
Clarke, John, c/o B., by William Clark	Account	17 OCT 1785	1761:145
Clarke, John, H., idiotic, by brother James, and Richard Kay	Writing	15 JUN 1840	1838:086
Clarke, John, c/o John to Mary Ann Clarke	Bond	20 MAR 1854	1851:227
Clarke, Kitty, c/o Jessefern to Thomas Clarke	Bond	18 JAN 1836	1831:401
Clarke, Martha Ann, c/o John to Mary Ann Clarke	Bond	20 MAR 1854	1851:227
Clarke, Martha Ann, c/o John now wife of Thomas Hy. Cox	Receipt	16 MAY 1859	1857:146
Clarke, Martha Ann, by Mary A. Clarke	Account	16 MAY 1859	1857:145

Ward or Subject (and Parent, Guardian or Other)	Record Type	Date	Reference(s)
Clarke, Mary C., c/o Henry to Albert Gresham	Bond	18 APR 1859	1857:140
Clarke, Nancy alias Graves, c/o Thos. Graves	Bond	17 OCT 1796	1761:227
Clarke, Olivia, c/o John to Mary Ann Clarke	Bond	20 MAR 1854	1851:227
Clarke, Olivia, by Mary A. Clarke	Account	18 FEB 1861	1857:253
Clarke, Polly, c/o Thomas to Upshaw Davis	Bond	21 JAN 1828	1825:207
Clarke, Robert, c/o John to Mary Ann Clarke	Bond	20 MAR 1854	1851:227
Clarke, Ruffin, c/o John to Mary Ann Clarke	Bond	20 MAR 1854	1851:227
Clarke, Ruffin, by Mary A. Clarke	Account	18 FEB 1861	1857:251
Clarke, Sue C.E. to G.H. Dillard	Certificate	19 DEC 1864	1857:352
Clarke, Susan C.E. to Gabriel H. Dillard	Bond	19 DEC 1864	1857:353
Clarke, Thomas Henry, from Mrs. Mary Ann Clarke	Receipt	16 MAY 1859	1857:146
Clarke, William to John Webb	Bond	10 JUN 1707	D&W12:420
Clarkson, Lucy Bell, c/o Thomas G. to John H. Clarkson	Bond	17 SEP 1866	1857:413
Clarkson, Lucy Belle, by John H. Clarkson	Account	20 JUL 1868	1867:032
Clements, Mace, c/o Dr. Mace to Elizabeth Foster	Bond	20 NOV 1820	1811:238
Clements, William, c/o William to Ewen Clements	Bond	21 NOV 1810	1796:239
Cloudas, Ebbin Parsons, c/o Abner to Sarah Cloudas	Bond	15 DEC 1794	1761:205
Cloudas, Pitman, c/o John to John Clarke	Bond	15 JUL 1799	1796:048
Cloudas, Pitman, by John Clark	Account	15 SEP 1800	1796:068
Cloudas, Pitmon, c/o John, by John Clark	Account	21 SEP 1801	1796:099
Coates, Sarah Jane, c/o Thomas to James Durham, Jr.	Bond	15 SEP 1845	1844:058
Coates, Sarah Jane, by James Durham	Account	21 JUN 1847	1844:216
Coates, Sarah Jane, by James Durham	Account	21 MAY 1849	1844:361
Coates, Sarah Jane, by James Durham	Account	16 JUN 1851	1844:523
Coates, Sarah Jane, by James Durham	Account	16 AUG 1852	1851:124
Coates, Sarah J., by James Durham	Account	19 SEP 1853	1851:193
Coates, Sarah Jane, by James Durham	Account	20 NOV 1854	1851:273
Coates, Sarah J., by James Durham	Account	20 AUG 1855	1851:314
Coates, Sarah J., by James Durham	Account	18 AUG 1856	1851:373
Coates, Sarah Jane, by James Durham	Account	19 OCT 1857	1857:023
Coates, Sarah Jane now Muse, by James Durham	Account	18 JAN 1858	1857:053
Coghill, Betty Ann, c/o Smallwood, now Bayliss to S.P. Bayliss	Bond	16 JUL 1855	1851:309
Coghill, Thomas B., c/o Smallwood to Silas P. Bayliss	Bond	16 JUL 1855	1851:309
Cole, George, under 14, c/o James M. to Isaac A. Cole	Bond	17 MAR 1884	1867:539
Cole, George, c/o James M. to Edwin Forbes	Bond	18 FEB 1885	1867:561
Cole, Robert F., under 14, c/o James M. to Isaac A. Cole	Bond	17 MAR 1884	1867:539
Cole, Robert F., c/o James M. to Edwin Forbes	Bond	18 FEB 1885	1867:561
Cole, Thomas to James Webb	Bond	22 NOV 1752	1731:153
Coleman, Anna, c/o George to Dinah Coleman	Bond	17 FEB 1756	1731:197
Coleman, Caty L., by John Beazley	Account	21 AUG 1826	1825:119
Coleman, James, c/o Robt. Sp., by Robert Brooking	Account	21 OCT 1765	1761:060, 061
Coleman, Martha, c/o George to Dinah Coleman	Bond	17 FEB 1756	1731:197
Coleman, Mary W., c/o Whitehead to Ann Coleman	Bond	17 FEB 1812	1811:004
Coleman, Mary W. now Muse, d/o Anne Coleman	Report	17 OCT 1825	1825:040
Coleman, Mary, c/o Richard to Catharine Coleman	Bond	19 DEC 1831	1831:081
Coleman, Mary S., by Catharine Coleman	Account	18 NOV 1833	1831:216
Coleman, Mary S., by Catharine Coleman	Account	20 JUL 1835	1831:316
Coleman, Mary Susan, by Catharine Coleman	Account	20 MAR 1837	1831:472
Coleman, Mary Susan, by Catharine Coleman	Account	18 JUN 1838	1838:029
Coleman, Mary S., by Catharine Coleman	Account	19 OCT 1840	1838:108
Coleman, Mary Susan, by Catharine Coleman	Account	18 JUL 1842	1838:222

Ward or Subject (and Parent, Guardian or Other)	Record Type	Date	Reference(s)
Coleman, Mary Susan, by Catharine Coleman	Account	21 JUL 1845	1844:038
Coleman, Mary Susan now Montague, c/o Richard	Receipt	19 JUL 1847	1844:218
Coleman, Richard, by Mourning Johnston	Account	20 FEB 1832	1831:094
Coleman, Robert Spilsby to William Covington	Bond	18 AUG 1730	WB4:386
Coleman, Robert Spilsbee, by William Covington	Account	21 JUL 1731	1731:001
Coleman, Vincent, c/o George to Dinah Coleman	Bond	17 FEB 1756	1731:197
Coleman, Vincent, c/o George, by Ambrose Cox	Account	20 SEP 1762	1761:021
Collins, Catharine, c/o John to Thomas Pilcher	Bond	20 OCT 1828	1825:254
Collins, Catharine, c/o John H. to James Roy Micou	Bond	21 DEC 1874	1867:289
Collins, Catherine Ann, over 14, to William Hall	Certificate	15 JAN 1872	1867:177
Collins, Catherine, c/o John H. to William Hall	Bond	15 JAN 1872	1867:177
Collins, Eliz., d/o Thos., by George T.F. Lorimer & wife Va. [Collins]	Account	16 NOV 1835	1831:352
Collins, Elizabeth, c/o Thomas to Virginia Collins	Bond	16 JUL 1832	1831:125
Collins, Elizabeth, d/o Thos., now Smith, by Virginia Lorimer	Account	20 JUN 1842	1838:210
Collins, John H., c/o John to Madison H. Jones	Bond	21 NOV 1827	1825:188
Collins, John H., from Madison H. Jones	Receipt	21 JAN 1828	1825:217
Collins, Thomas, Jr. & wife Virginia Garland, fr. Jos. Janey	Report	19 SEP 1825	1825:028
Collins, Thomas, c/o Thomas to Virginia Collins	Bond	16 JUL 1832	1831:124
Collins, Thomas, by George T.F. Lorimer & wife Va. [Collins]	Account	16 NOV 1835	1831:356
Collins, Thomas, c/o Thomas, by Virginia Lorimer	Account	20 JUN 1842	WB24:709
Compton, Augustine, c/o Wm. to Theophilus Faver	Bond	17 JUN 1760	1731:254
Compton, William, dec., by Theophilus Faver	Account	16 JUN 1760	1731:255
Conner, Ann, c/o Martin, by Thomas Wiatt	Account	18 DEC 1753	1731:175
Conner, Anne to Thomas Wiatt	Bond	19 FEB 1750/1	WB8:407
Conner, Margaret to Thomas Wiatt	Bond	19 FEB 1750/1	WB8:407
Conner, Margaret, c/o Martin, by Thomas Wiatt	Account	18 DEC 1753	1731:173a
Conner, Mary to James Banks	Bond	19 FEB 1750/1	WB8:410
Conoley, Elizabeth, c/o Larkin to Catharine Conoley	Bond	21 NOV 1827	1825:189
Conoley, Emma Jane, c/o Silas to Thomas Boughan	Bond	18 OCT 1852	1851:130
Conoley, John Larkin, c/o Silas to Thomas Boughan	Bond	18 OCT 1852	1851:130
Cook, Ellen, c/o Pascal to Larkin Noel	Bond	19 DEC 1836	1831:457
Cook, Malinda, c/o Thomas to Warner Cook	Bond	20 SEP 1802	1796:128
Cook, Malinda, c/o Thomas to Mary Bristow	Bond	16 DEC 1816	1811:125
Cook, Mary C., c/o Pascal to Larkin Noel	Bond	19 DEC 1836	1831:457
Cook, Melinda, c/o Thomas to Lewis Dix	Bond	15 AUG 1814	1811:064
Cook, Thomas, c/o Thomas to Warner Cook	Bond	20 SEP 1802	1796:128
Cook, Warner, c/o Thomas to Warner Cook	Bond	20 SEP 1802	1796:128
Cook, Warner, c/o Thomas to Lewis Dix	Bond	21 JUN 1813	1811:042
Cook, Warner, c/o Thomas to Mary Bristow	Bond	16 DEC 1816	1811:125
Cook, William, c/o Thomas to Warner Cook	Bond	20 SEP 1802	1796:128
Corbin, Jane, c/o John, Gent. to Lettice Corbin	Bond	20 FEB 1759	1731:239
Corbin, Jane, by Lettice Corbin	Account	20 FEB 1769	WB12:355
Corthen, Mildred, by James Longest	Account	20 AUG 1770	1761:082
Corthen, Mildred, by James Longest	Account	19 AUG 1771	1761:085
Covington, Ann E., c/o Walter G. to Lucy E. Covington	Bond	18 APR 1859	1857:139
Covington, Ann E., by Lucy E. Covington	Account	20 AUG 1860	1857:216
Covington, Ann E., by Lucy E. Covington	Account	16 APR 1866	1857:382
Covington, Ann E., by Lucy E. Covington	Account	16 SEP 1867	1867:014
Covington, Ann E., by Lucy E. Covington	Account	19 AUG 1867	1867:001, 004
Covington, Benjamin T., c/o Walter G. to Lucy E. Covington	Bond	18 APR 1859	1857:139
Covington, Benjamin F., by Lucy E. Covington	Account	20 AUG 1860	1857:213

Ward or Subject (and Parent, Guardian or Other)	Record Type	Date	Reference(s)
Covington, Benjamin F., by Lucy E. Covington	Account	16 APR 1866	1857:381
Covington, Benjamin F., by Lucy E. Covington	Account	19 AUG 1867	1867:001, 006
Covington, Benjamin F., by Lucy E. Covington	Account	16 SEP 1867	1867:012
Covington, Benjamin F., by Lucy E. Covington	Account	16 MAR 1868	1867:026
Covington, Benjamin F., by Lucy E. Covington	Account	19 SEP 1870	1867:149
Covington, Bettie, c/o Thomas to John Wilson	Bond	19 MAY 1873	1867:213
Covington, Bettie, by John Wilson	Account	18 MAR 1878	1867:378
Covington, Bettie, by John Wilson	Account	20 SEP 1880	1867:443
Covington, Betty Campbell, c/o Thos. to Mildred Covington	Bond	16 MAR 1868	1867:029
Covington, Betty, above 14, c/o Thomas to John Wilson	Bond	21 MAY 1872	1867:183
Covington, Betty, by John Wilson	Account	19 APR 1875	1867:299
Covington, Campbell, c/o Thomas to John Wilson	Bond	21 MAY 1872	1867:183
Covington, Campbell, c/o Thomas to John Wilson	Bond	19 MAY 1873	1867:213
Covington, Campbell, by John Wilson	Account	19 APR 1875	1867:299
Covington, Campbell, by John Wilson	Account	18 MAR 1878	1867:378
Covington, Campbell, by John Wilson	Account	20 SEP 1880	1867:439
Covington, Edmond to Richard Covington	Bond	17 OCT 1738	WB6:148
Covington, Frances, c/o Thomas to John Wilson	Bond	21 MAY 1872	1867:183
Covington, Frances, c/o Thomas to John Wilson	Bond	19 MAY 1873	1867:213
Covington, Frances, by John Wilson	Account	19 APR 1875	1867:298
Covington, Frances, by John Wilson	Account	18 MAR 1878	1867:378
Covington, Frances, by John Wilson	Account	20 SEP 1880	1867:435
Covington, John, c/o Walter G. to Lucy E. Covington	Bond	18 APR 1859	1857:139
Covington, John Austin, by Lucy E. Covington	Account	20 AUG 1860	1857:219
Covington, John A., by Lucy E. Covington	Account	16 APR 1866	1857:381
Covington, John A., by Lucy E. Covington	Account	16 SEP 1867	1867:016
Covington, John A., by Lucy E. Covington	Account	19 AUG 1867	1867:001, 004
Covington, John A., by Lucy E. Covington	Account	16 MAR 1868	1867:025
Covington, Joseph B., c/o Richard to Thomas Bohannan	Bond	20 FEB 1815	1811:077
Covington, Julia, c/o John to Catherine Covington	Bond	19 JAN 1818	1811:141
Covington, Mary E., c/o Walter G. to Lucy E. Covington	Bond	18 APR 1859	1857:139
Covington, Mary E., by Lucy E. Covington	Account	20 AUG 1860	1857:215
Covington, Mary E., by Lucy E. Covington	Account	16 APR 1866	1857:381
Covington, Mary E., by Lucy E. Covington	Account	19 AUG 1867	1867:001, 006
Covington, Mary E.., by Lucy E. Covington	Account	16 SEP 1867	1867:013
Covington, Mary E., by Lucy E. Covington	Account	16 MAR 1868	1867:026
Covington, Mary E., by Lucy E. Covington	Account	19 SEP 1870	1867:149
Covington, Matilda Frances, c/o Thos. to Mildred Covington	Bond	16 MAR 1868	1867:029
Covington, R.R., by Reuben B. Boughton	Account	18 JUL 1864	1857:346
Covington, Richard, c/o Richard to Thomas Bohannan	Bond	20 FEB 1815	1811:077
Covington, Richard R., c/o Walter G. to Reuben B. Boughton, Jr.	Bond	16 AUG 1858	1857:104
Covington, Richard, by Reuben B. Boughton	Account	21 OCT 1861	1857:273
Covington, Richard, c/o Richard to Thomas Covington	Bond	19 JUL 1919	1811:190
Covington, Sophronia D., c/o Richard to William Howerton	Bond	21 JUN 1819	1811:189
Covington, Sophronia, by William Howerton	Account	19 SEP 1825	1825:022
Covington, Sophronia D., c/o Richard to Richard L. Covington	Bond	20 FEB 1832	1831:099
Covington, Sophronia D., by William Howerton	Account	17 APR 1833	1831:175
Covington, Thomas R., c/o Walter G. to Lucy E. Covington	Bond	18 APR 1859	1857:139
Covington, Thomas S., by Lucy E. Covington	Account	20 AUG 1860	1857:218
Covington, Thomas R., by Lucy E. Covington	Account	16 APR 1866	1857:381
Covington, Thomas R., by Lucy E. Covington	Account	16 SEP 1867	1867:011

Ward or Subject (and Parent, Guardian or Other)	Record Type	Date	Reference(s)
Covington, Thomas R., by Lucy E. Covington	Account	19 AUG 1867	1867:001, 002
Covington, Thomas, c/o Thos. to Mildred Covington	Bond	16 MAR 1868	1867:029
Covington, Thomas, c/o Thomas to John Wilson	Bond	21 MAY 1872	1867:183
Covington, Thomas, c/o Thomas to John Wilson	Bond	19 MAY 1873	1867:213
Covington, Thomas, by John Wilson	Account	19 APR 1875	1867:298
Covington, Thomas, by John Wilson	Account	18 MAR 1878	1867:378
Covington, Thomas, by John Wilson	Account	20 SEP 1880	1867:431
Covington, Walter G., c/o Richard to William Howerton	Bond	21 JUN 1819	1811:189
Covington, Walter G., by William Howerton	Account	19 SEP 1825	1825:021
Covington, Walter G., by William Howerton	Account	17 APR 1833	1831:175
Covington, Winfield S., c/o Walter G. to Lucy E. Covington	Bond	18 APR 1859	1857:139
Covington, Winfield S., by Lucy E. Covington	Account	20 AUG 1860	1857:217
Covington, Winfield S., by Lucy E. Covington	Account	16 APR 1866	1857:382
Covington, Winfield S., by Lucy E. Covington	Account	16 SEP 1867	1867:015
Covington, Winfield S., by Lucy E. Covington	Account	19 AUG 1867	1867:001, 004
Covington, Winfield S., by Lucy E. Covington	Account	16 MAR 1868	1867:025
Covington, Winfield S., by Lucy E. Covington	Account	19 SEP 1870	1867:148
Cox, Charles, c/o William to Henry Cox	Bond	21 JAN 1884	1867:535
Cox, Chester, under 14, c/o William to Henry Cox	Bond	20 FEB 1882	1867:483
Cox, Chester, by Henry Cox	Account	16 JAN 1888	1867:596
Cox, Elizabeth, c/o James, to her father	Bond	19 JUN 1815	1811:082
Cox, Hugh, c/o James, to his father	Bond	19 JUN 1815	1811:082
Cox, James T., c/o William to James Semple	Bond	15 DEC 1845	1844:086
Cox, Judson, c/o William to James Semple	Bond	15 DEC 1845	1844:086
Cox, Martha Ann late Clarke, from Mrs. Mary Ann Clarke	Receipt	16 MAY 1859	1857:146
Cox, Phebe, by James Wilson	Account	17 OCT 1785	1761:144
Cox, William, c/o William to James Semple	Bond	15 DEC 1845	1844:086
Cox, William, under 14, c/o William to Henry Cox	Bond	20 FEB 1882	1867:483
Cox, William, c/o William to Henry Cox	Bond	21 JAN 1884	1867:535
Cox, William, by Henry Cox	Account	16 JAN 1888	1867:596
Crewdson, Eliza, c/o Ellen to Thomas M. Henley	Bond	21 FEB 1814	1811:055
Crewdson, Eliza, by Thomas M. Henley	Account	19 JAN 1818	1811:143
Cross, Joseph, to William Rennolds	Bond	16 JUL 1751	WB9:078
Cross, Lucy, c/o Thomas to Polly Cross	Bond	18 APR 1831	1831:003
Crow, Betsey, c/o Thomas to Sarah Crow	Bond	22 MAR 1826	1825:094
Crow, Catharine, c/o Thomas to James Croxton, Jr.	Bond	17 MAR 1834	1831:245
Crow, Elizabeth, c/o Nathaniel S. to Joseph Mann, Jr.	Bond	16 MAR 1801	1796:087
Crow, Elizabeth now Broocke, by Sally Crow	Account	17 SEP 1832	1831:135
Crow, Elizabeth, c/o Nathaniel to Mary M. Crow	Bond	16 JUN 1834	1831:274
Crow, Eugene, c/o Alexander to Muscoe R. Dunn	Bond	18 OCT 1869	1867:108
Crow, Eugene, by Muscoe R. Dunn	Account	13 JAN 1871	1867:151
Crow, Evan, c/o Alexander to Muscoe R. Dunn	Bond	18 OCT 1869	1867:108
Crow, Fielding Saunders, c/o Nathaniel S. to John E. Crow	Bond	19 JAN 1801	1796:085
Crow, Frances Ann, c/o John to Fanny Crow	Bond	16 MAY 1842	1838:208
Crow, Henry, c/o William to Martha Crow	Bond	19 FEB 1821	1811:247
Crow, Inis, c/o William to Martha Crow	Bond	19 FEB 1821	1811:247
Crow, James H., c/o John to Fanny Crow	Bond	16 MAY 1842	1838:208
Crow, John, c/o William to Martha Crow	Bond	19 FEB 1821	1811:247
Crow, John, c/o Nathaniel to Mary M. Crow	Bond	16 JUN 1834	1831:274
Crow, John N., from Mary M. Crow	Receipt	20 DEC 1847	1844:248
Crow, Josiah B., over 14, c/o Josiah L. to James Roy Micou	Bond	20 JAN 1862	1857:279

Ward or Subject (and Parent, Guardian or Other)	Record Type	Date	Reference(s)
Crow, Kitty, c/o Thomas to Sarah Crow	Bond	22 MAR 1826	1825:094
Crow, Kitty, by Sally Crow	Account	17 SEP 1832	1831:137
Crow, Louisa, c/o John to Fanny Crow	Bond	16 MAY 1842	1838:208
Crow, Lucinda, c/o Nathaniel to Mary M. Crow	Bond	16 JUN 1834	1831:274
Crow, Lucinda C., from Mary M. Crow	Receipt	20 DEC 1847	1844:248
Crow, Malissa, c/o Thomas to Sarah Crow	Bond	22 MAR 1826	1825:094
Crow, Mary Jane, by H.H. Boughan	Account	19 MAR 1832	1831:101
Crow, Mary E., from Mary M. Crow	Receipt	20 DEC 1847	1844:248
Crow, Melissa, by Sally Crow	Account	17 SEP 1832	1831:133
Crow, Nancy, c/o William to Martha Crow	Bond	19 FEB 1821	1811:247
Crow, Nathaniel, c/o Nathaniel to Mary M. Crow	Bond	16 JUN 1834	1831:274
Crow, Polly E., c/o Nathaniel S. to John Crow	Bond	20 JUL 1807	1796:191
Crow, Sophronia, c/o Robert to Thomas Harper	Bond	16 MAR 1840	1838:074
Crow, St. Albion, c/o Nathaniel S. to John E. Crow	Bond	16 JUN 1806	1796:178
Crow, Thomas, c/o Nathaniel to Mary M. Crow	Bond	16 JUN 1834	1831:274
Crow, Winney, c/o Nathaniel Saunders Crow to Andrew Allen	Bond	20 OCT 1800	1796:079
Croxton, Ann, c/o Isaac to Catherine Croxton	Bond	16 JAN 1815	1811:073
Croxton, Ann E., by William S. Croxton	Account	17 JUL 1848	1844:286
Croxton, Ann E., by William S. Croxton	Report	20 MAR 1848	1844:262
Croxton, Ann E., c/o William S. to her father	Bond	17 JAN 1848	1844:250
Croxton, Anne, c/o Samuel, by Richard Jones	Account	19 SEP 1774	1761:121
Croxton, Carter, c/o John, by Richard Thomas Haile	Account	17 AUG 1778	1761:134
Croxton, Carter, c/o James to Barker Minter	Bond	21 FEB 1815	1811:078
Croxton, Carter, Jr., c/o James to Washington H. Purkins	Bond	19 OCT 1818	1811:163
Croxton, Carter, Jr., from Washington H. Purkins	Receipt	19 SEP 1825	1825:028
Croxton, Catharine, c/o John to Winter Bray	Bond	21 NOV 1810	1796:238
Croxton, Catherine, c/o Isaac to Catherine Croxton	Bond	16 JAN 1815	1811:073
Croxton, Cornelia Bert, c/o Carter to Frances Croxton	Bond	17 NOV 1845	1844:077
Croxton, Cornelia Burt, c/o Carter to John F. Faulconer	Bond	17 DEC 1849	1844:400
Croxton, Cornelia B., by John W. Faulconer	Account	16 JUN 1851	1844:527
Croxton, Cornelia Burt, by John W. Faulconer	Account	16 AUG 1852	1851:123
Croxton, Cornelia B., by John W. Faulconer	Account	15 MAY 1854	1851:231
Croxton, Cornelia Burt, by John W. Faulconer	Account	17 NOV 1856	1851:395
Croxton, Cornelia B., by John W. Faulconer	Account	20 APR 1857	1851:418
Croxton, Cornelia B., by John W. Faulconer	Account	19 APR 1858	1857:061
Croxton, Cornelia B., c/o Carter to Philip A. Sandy	Bond	16 MAY 1859	1857:140
Croxton, Cornelia B., by Philip A. Sandy	Account	19 MAR 1860	1857:199
Croxton, Cornelia B., by John W. Faulconer, dec. [Betty S.]	Account	19 MAR 1860	1857:197
Croxton, Cynthia Louisa, c/o Robert to Cynthia A. Croxton	Bond	16 NOV 1835	1831:350
Croxton, Eliz. Ann, c/o John, by Richard Thomas Haile	Account	17 AUG 1778	1761:134
Croxton, Eliza, c/o James to Barker Minter	Bond	21 FEB 1815	1811:078
Croxton, Eliza, Miss, by Moses Crow	Account	19 DEC 1827	1825:178
Croxton, Eliza., c/o Jas. to Moses Crow	Bond	15 FEB 1819	1811:175
Croxton, Elizabeth, by Cath. Shearwood	Account	15 MAY 1826	1825:099
Croxton, Fannie E., by John W. Faulconer	Account	16 JUN 1856	1851:355
Croxton, Fanny Ellen, c/o Carter to Frances Croxton	Bond	17 NOV 1845	1844:077
Croxton, Fanny Ellen, c/o Carter to John W. Faulconer	Bond	17 DEC 1849	1844:400
Croxton, Fanny Ellen, by John W. Faulconer	Account	16 JUN 1851	1844:527
Croxton, Fanny E., by John W. Faulconer	Account	16 AUG 1852	1851:126
Croxton, Fanny E., by John W. Faulconer	Account	15 MAY 1854	1851:229
Croxton, Fielding, c/o John to James Croxton, Jr.	Bond	16 DEC 1817	1811:137

Ward or Subject (and Parent, Guardian or Other)	Record Type	Date	Reference(s)
Croxton, Fielding and wife Juliett Dobbins, fr. Jas. Croxton	Receipt	19 SEP 1825	1825:010, 011
Croxton, Harriett, by Cath. Shearwood	Account	15 MAY 1826	1825:101
Croxton, Harriot, c/o Isaac to Catherine Croxton	Bond	16 JAN 1815	1811:073
Croxton, Joanna, c/o James to Barker Minter	Bond	21 FEB 1815	1811:078
Croxton, Joannah, c/o Samuel, by Richard Jones	Account	19 SEP 1774	1761:121
Croxton, John, orphans of, by Richard Thomas Haile	Account	17 AUG 1778	1761:134, 135
Croxton, John, orphans of, by Richard Thomas Haile	Account	20 SEP 1779	1761:139
Croxton, John T., c/o James to Leonard Henley	Bond	15 JUN 1857	1851:436
Croxton, John T., by Robt. Y. Henley, Admr. of Leonard, dec.	Account	19 JUL 1869	1867:086
Croxton, Louisa Carter, c/o Carter to Frances Croxton	Bond	17 NOV 1845	1844:077
Croxton, Louisa Carter, c/o Carter to John W. Faulconer	Bond	17 DEC 1849	1844:400
Croxton, Louisa C., by John W. Faulconer	Account	16 JUN 1851	1844:527
Croxton, Louisa C., by John W. Faulconer	Account	16 AUG 1852	1851:126
Croxton, Louisa C., by John W. Faulconer	Account	15 MAY 1854	1851:233
Croxton, Louisa C., by John W. Faulconer	Account	16 JUN 1856	1851:359
Croxton, Lucy A., c/o James to Leonard Henley	Bond	15 JUN 1857	1851:436
Croxton, Lucy Ann, by Robt. Y. Henley, Admr. of Leonard, dec.	Account	19 JUL 1869	1867:096
Croxton, Margaret Ann, c/o Richard to Frances G. Croxton	Bond	18 DEC 1848	1844:297
Croxton, Margaret A., by Frances G. Croxton	Account	16 MAY 1853	1851:180
Croxton, Mary Ann, c/o John, Jr. to Carter Croxton	Bond	20 NOV 1809	1796:221
Croxton, Mary E., c/o Robert to Cynthia A. Croxton	Bond	16 NOV 1835	1831:350
Croxton, Mary Ann, c/o Carter to Frances Croxton	Bond	17 NOV 1845	1844:077
Croxton, Mary C., by William S. Croxton	Account	20 MAY 1861	1857:263
Croxton, Maryan, c/o John, by Richard Thomas Haile	Account	17 AUG 1778	1761:134
Croxton, Molly, c/o John, by Richard Thomas Haile	Account	17 AUG 1778	1761:134
Croxton, Polly, c/o William S. to her father	Bond	17 JAN 1848	1844:250
Croxton, Polly, by William S. Croxton	Account	16 OCT 1854	1851:265
Croxton, Polly, by William S. Croxton	Account	16 JUN 1856	1851:351
Croxton, Polly, by William S. Croxton	Account	17 OCT 1859	1857:175
Croxton, Richard & wife Frances G. Ware, from Winter Bray	Receipt	21 NOV 1826	1825:125
Croxton, Richard, c/o Richard to Frances G. Croxton	Bond	18 DEC 1848	1844:297
Croxton, Richard, by Frances G. Croxton	Account	16 MAY 1853	1851:182
Croxton, Richard, by Frances G. Croxton	Account	20 JUL 1857	1851:443
Croxton, Susan late Taylor, by Frances Taylor	Account	17 MAY 1847	1844:212
Croxton, Susan F., c/o Richard to Frances G. Croxton	Bond	18 DEC 1848	1844:297
Croxton, Susan F. now Jeffries, by Frances G. Croxton	Account	16 MAY 1853	1851:178
Croxton, Susanna, c/o John to Winter Bray	Bond	21 NOV 1810	1796:238
Croxton, Thomas, c/o Richard to his father	Bond	20 FEB 1837	1831:462
Croxton, William S., c/o William S. to Peter Toombs	Bond	20 FEB 1860	1857:191
Croxton, William S., c/o William S., by Peter Toombs	Account	17 JUN 1861	1857:267
Croxton, William, c/o John to Richard H. Brizendine	Bond	15 JAN 1872	1867:178
Cunningham, John H., c/o Thornton to Milton Atwell	Bond	15 APR 1872	1867:180
Cunningham, Lawrence, c/o Thornton to Milton Atwell	Bond	15 APR 1872	1867:180
Cunningham, Martha A., c/o Thornton to Milton Atwell	Bond	15 APR 1872	1867:180
Curtis, Charles to James Gray	Bond	16 OCT 1750	WB8:372
Curtis, Frances Joanna, c/o Robert to Tunstall Banks	Bond	17 APR 1792	1761:178

D

Daingerfield, Hannah, c/o William, by John Beale	Account	19 OCT 1772	1761:091
Daingerfield, Leroy to William Daingerfield	Bond	22 FEB 1758	1731:219
Daingerfield, Leroy, by John Beale	Account	19 OCT 1772	1761:090

Ward or Subject (and Parent, Guardian or Other)	Record Type	Date	Reference(s)
Daingerfield, Lucy to William Daingerfield	Bond	22 FEB 1758	1731:219
Daingerfield, Martha to Edwin Daingerfield	Bond	15 FEB 1736/7	WB6:044
Daingerfield, Martha to William Daingerfield	Bond	22 FEB 1758	1731:219
Daingerfield, Molly to William Daingerfield	Bond	22 FEB 1758	1731:219
Davis, Becky, c/o William to Thomas Pickels	Bond	18 JUL 1791	1761:173
Davis, Catharine, wife of John Tune, by John Griffin	Certificate	19 SEP 1825	1825:025
Davis, Catherine, c/o Carter to Washington H. Purkins	Bond	18 JAN 1815	1811:075
Davis, Catherine, c/o Lindsay to Washington H. Purkins	Bond	18 JAN 1815	1811:076
Davis, Catherine A., over 14, to her father Richard	Bond	18 FEB 1878	1867:377
Davis, Charles W., c/o Richard, to his father	Bond	18 FEB 1878	1867:377
Davis, Clary, c/o Upshaw to Motta Ball	Bond	18 SEP 1820	1811:235
Davis, Conna, c/o George to Samuel Brooks	Bond	15 JUL 1811	1796:252
Davis, Conna, c/o George, by Richard Miller	Account	19 JUN 1815	1811:082
Davis, Constant, from Samuel Brooks	Receipt	19 SEP 1825	1825:027
Davis, Constine, c/o George to Richard Miller	Bond	22 APR 1806	1796:175
Davis, Edward, c/o Edward G. to William Noel	Bond	21 FEB 1814	1811:058
Davis, Eliza, c/o James to Lucy Davis	Bond	17 MAY 1813	1811:039
Davis, Eliza., c/o James to Gabriel Purkins	Bond	18 JAN 1815	1811:075
Davis, Elizabeth G., c/o Edward G. to Elizabeth G. Davis	Bond	21 FEB 1814	1811:057
Davis, Elizabeth, c/o Robinson to Nathaniel I.B. Whitlocke	Bond	22 MAR 1853	1851:174
Davis, Fannie E., c/o Richard, to her father	Bond	18 FEB 1878	1867:377
Davis, Fanny, c/o Philip to Agrippa Dogens	Bond	17 JAN 1803	1796:130
Davis, Fanny, c/o Philip to William Newbill	Bond	18 JUL 1803	1796:134
Davis, Fanny, c/o Carter to Washington H. Purkins	Bond	18 JAN 1815	1811:075
Davis, Francis Gouldman, c/o Edward G. to Eliza. G. Davis	Bond	21 FEB 1814	1811:056
Davis, George, c/o George to Thomas Harper	Bond	21 JUN 1852	1851:117
Davis, James, c/o Carter to Washington H. Purkins	Bond	18 JAN 1815	1811:075
Davis, James and Henry, from Washington H. Purkins	Receipt	19 SEP 1825	1825:028
Davis, James Franklin, c/o Richard, to his father	Bond	18 FEB 1878	1867:377
Davis, Kitty, by Washington H. Purkins	Account	17 DEC 1827	1825:211
Davis, McKinzie, by his brother Oswald Davis	Report	17 OCT 1825	1825:040
Davis, McKinzie, brother of Oswald, to Richard Croxton	Apprentice	17 OCT 1825	1825:040
Davis, Mildred Ellen, over 14, to her father Richard	Bond	18 FEB 1878	1867:377
Davis, Patsy, c/o Philip to Agrippa Dogens	Bond	17 JAN 1803	1796:130
Davis, Patsy, c/o Philip to William Newbill	Bond	18 JUL 1803	1796:134
Davis, Rebecca, c/o Thomas to John Davis	Bond	19 OCT 1756	1731:204
Davis, Robert B., c/o Richard, to his father	Bond	18 FEB 1878	1867:377
Davis, Sally, c/o Lindsay to Washington H. Purkins	Bond	18 JAN 1815	1811:076
Davis, Sarah, by Washington H. Purkins	Account	17 DEC 1827	1825:212
Davis, Walker, c/o James to Jno. Dunn	Bond	17 FEB 1812	1811:005
Davis, William Henry, c/o Carter to Washington H. Purkins	Bond	18 JAN 1815	1811:075
Davis, William A., c/o Tunstall to Richard J. Muse	Bond	18 AUG 1851	1844:544
Davis, Zachariah, c/o James to Jno. Dunn	Bond	17 FEB 1812	1811:005
Day, Henrietta, c/o Lucy to Benjamin H. Munday	Bond	16 AUG 1813	1811:043
Day, Nancy, c/o Lucy to Benjamin H. Munday	Bond	16 AUG 1813	1811:043
Dennett, Elizabeth, c/o Francis, to Samuel Doggins	Bond	15 JUL 1793	WB15:054
Dennett, Elizabeth, c/o Francis to Samuel Doggins	Bond	15 JUL 1793	1761:197
Dennett, Elizabeth, c/o Francis to Wm. Paridow	Bond	18 SEP 1798	1796:088
Dennett, Gregory, c/o Robert to Peter B. Davis	Bond	17 OCT 1814	1811:069
Dennett, Mary, c/o Francis to Charles Evans	Bond	21 JAN 1793	1761:190
Dennett, Mary Jane, by Henry H. Boughan	Account	17 DEC 1827	1825:197

Ward or Subject (and Parent, Guardian or Other)	Record Type	Date	Reference(s)
Dennett, Mary Jane, Miss, by Henry H. Boughan	Account	19 MAY 1829	1825:281
Dennett, Mary Jane, by H.H. Boughan	Account	18 APR 1831	1831:005
Dennett, Nancy, c/o Francis, to Samuel Doggins	Bond	15 JUL 1793	WB15:054
Dennett, Nancy, c/o Francis to Samuel Doggins	Bond	15 JUL 1793	1761:197
Dennett, Sally, c/o Robert to Peter B. Davis	Bond	17 OCT 1814	1811:069
Derieux, Amelia S., c/o Peter J. to John H. Wilson	Bond	17 FEB 1857	1851:399
Derieux, Susan C., c/o Peter J. to John H. Wilson	Bond	17 FEB 1857	1851:399
Dickenson, James, by John Saunders, Jr.	Account	17 MAR 1840	1838:076
Dickenson, James, c/o Wm., from John Saunders	Receipt	20 JUL 1840	1838:094
Dickenson, James, from William Bentley	Receipt	18 JAN 1841	1838:133
Dickenson, Peter to James Turner	Bond	21 FEB 1737/8	WB6:112
Dickerson, Anabel, under 14, c/o Frank to Richard Brooks	Bond	16 JUN 1884	1867:541
Dickinson, James, c/o William to John Saunders, Jr.	Bond	19 NOV 1832	1831:152
Dickinson, James, c/o William to John Saunders, Jr.	Bond	20 MAY 1833	1831:181
Dickinson, James, c/o William to William Bentley	Bond	17 DEC 1838	1838:038
Dickinson, James, by John Saunders, Jr., pur. land in K&Q Co.	Bond	16 AUG 1838	1838:209
Dickinson, Lucy Ann, c/o William to John Saunders, Jr.	Bond	19 NOV 1832	1831:152
Dickinson, Lucy Ann, c/o William to John Saunders, Jr.	Bond	20 MAY 1833	1831:181
Dillard, Robert H., dec., lands of	Bond	18 DEC 1848	1844:298
Dishman, John, c/o Samuel to Samuel Dishman	Bond	16 JUN 1794	1761:212
Dishman, Weedor, c/o Samuel to Samuel Dishman	Bond	16 JUN 1794	1761:212
Diskin, John to Robert Elliott	Bond	21 JUN 1715	D&W14:364
Dix, Catharine, c/o Walter to Benjamin Blake	Bond	18 NOV 1833	1831:219
Dix, Catharine, by Benjamin Blake	Account	15 APR 1850	1844:426
Dix, James, c/o Walter to Benjamin Blake	Bond	18 NOV 1833	1831:219
Dix, Lucy B., c/o Tandy to Graves Burke	Bond	21 MAR 1826	1825:093
Dix, Lucy B., c/o Tandy to Henry W. Latane	Bond	21 NOV 1826	1825:124
Dix, Lucy B., by Henry W. Latane	Account	15 JUL 1833	1831:186
Dix, Lucy B., c/o Tandy to Achilles Lumpkin	Bond	20 MAY 1833	1831:180
Dix, Lucy B., c/o Tandy, by Achilles Lumpkin	Account	21 SEP 1835	1831:332
Dix, Lucy B., c/o Tandy, by Achilles Lumpkin	Account	15 AUG 1836	1831:430
Dix, Lucy B., c/o Tandy, by Achilles Lumpkin	Account	19 JUN 1837	1831:482
Dix, Lucy B., c/o Tandy, by Achilles Lumpkin	Account	21 JAN 1839	1838:040
Dix, Lucy B. now Priddy, from Achilles Lumpkin	Receipt	19 JUN 1843	1838:269
Dix, Melissa, c/o James to Caty Dix	Bond	18 SEP 1815	1811:096
Dix, Tandy, c/o James to Lewis Dix	Bond	18 SEP 1815	1811:097
Dix, Walter, c/o James to Lewis Dix	Bond	18 SEP 1815	1811:098
Dix, Walter, c/o James to Thomas Dix	Bond	18 DEC 1815	1811:109
Dix, Walter, c/o Walter to Benjamin Blake	Bond	18 NOV 1833	1831:219
Dix, William, c/o Walter to Benjamin Blake	Bond	18 NOV 1833	1831:219
Dobbins, Juliett and husb. Fielding Croxton, fr. Jas. Croxton	Receipt	19 SEP 1825	1825:010, 011
Dobbins, Robert, c/o Robert to William Saddler	Bond	17 JUL 1820	1811:222
Dobyns, Annie B., c/o Thomas A. to Lucy E. Dobyns	Bond	17 APR 1871	1867:156
Dobyns, Frederick, c/o Thomas A. to Lucy E. Dobyns	Bond	17 APR 1871	1867:156
Dobyns, George H., c/o Thomas A. to Lucy E. Dobyns	Bond	17 APR 1871	1867:156
Dobyns, John H., c/o George H. to Judith E. Dobyns	Bond	19 OCT 1857	1857:034
Dobyns, John H., c/o George H. to Leroy W. Dobyns	Bond	15 NOV 1858	1857:106
Dobyns, John, by L.W. Dobyns	Account	19 MAR 1860	1857:195
Dobyns, John H., by Judith E. Dobyns	Account	19 MAR 1860	1857:193
Dobyns, John H., by L.W. Dobyns	Account	16 APR 1866	1857:385
Dobyns, John H., from L.W. Dobyns	Receipt	18 JUN 1866	1857:394

Ward or Subject (and Parent, Guardian or Other)	Record Type	Date	Reference(s)
Dobyns, Lucy R., c/o Thomas A. to Lucy E. Dobyns	Bond	17 APR 1871	1867:156
Dobyns, Maria E., c/o Thomas A. to Lucy E. Dobyns	Bond	17 APR 1871	1867:156
Dobyns, Sarah J., late Jones, gdn. of Frances Ann Jones	Account	15 APR 1850	1844:430
Dobyns, Thomas A., c/o Thomas A. to Lucy E. Dobyns	Bond	17 APR 1871	1867:156
Dogens, Elizabeth, c/o Agrippa, by Lucy Dogens	Account	17 OCT 1808	1796:204
Dogens, Elizabeth, c/o Agrippa, by Lucy Dogens	Account	18 DEC 1809	1796:222
Dogens, Elizabeth, c/o Agrippa, by Lucy Dogens	Account	15 OCT 1810	1796:238
Doggins, Betsey, c/o Agrippa to Lucy Doggins	Bond	19 DEC 1803	1796:143
Doggins, Betty, c/o Agrippa, by Lucy Doggins	Account	20 JAN 1806	1796:172
Doggins, Elizabeth, c/o Agrippa to Wm. Davis	Bond	21 OCT 1816	1811:124
Doggins, Elizabeth, c/o A., by William Davis	Settlement	21 AUG 1818	1811:161
Doggins, Elizabeth, c/o A., by Lucy Doggins	Settlement	21 AUG 1818	1811:160
Doggins, Jane, c/o Samuel to William Croxton, Sr.	Bond	19 JUN 1809	1796:216
Doggins, Nancy, c/o Samuel to William Croxton, Sr.	Bond	19 JUN 1809	1796:216
Doggins, Patsey, c/o Samuel to John Trible	Bond	21 DEC 1807	1796:194
Doggins, Priscilla, c/o Agrippa to John Crow	Bond	19 DEC 1803	1796:144
Doggins, Samuel, c/o Samuel to William Croxton, Sr.	Bond	19 JUN 1809	1796:216
Doggins, Samuel, c/o Samuel to James Croxton, Jr.	Bond	21 FEB 1815	1811:079
Doggins, Samuel, from James Croxton	Receipt	19 SEP 1825	1825:009
Doggins, William, c/o Agrippa, by Lucy Doggins	Account	20 JAN 1806	1796:172
Dogins, Elizabeth, c/o Agrippa, by Lucy Dogins	Account	15 JUN 1807	1796:190
Dogins, Wm., c/o Agrippa to Lucy Doggins	Bond	19 DEC 1803	1796:143
Douglas, William Bruce, c/o Robert F. to Richard T. Douglas	Bond	20 NOV 1865	1857:326
Duling, Augustine, c/o William, by Philip Duling	Account	19 MAR 1821	1811:252
Duling, Lucretia, c/o Wm. to Philip Duling	Bond	17 JAN 1814	1811:053
Duling, Lucretia, c/o William, by Philip Duling	Account	19 MAR 1821	1811:253
Duling, William, c/o William, by Philip Duling	Account	19 MAR 1821	1811:251
Duling, Wm. Augustine, c/o Wm. to Philip Duling	Bond	17 JAN 1814	1811:053
Dunn, Billington, c/o Thomas to Jane Dunn	Bond	17 DEC 1810	1796:240
Dunn, Billington, by Jane Dunn	Account	21 SEP 1812	1811:026
Dunn, Delila, c/o Robert L. to Thomas Covington	Bond	16 SEP 1811	1796:257
Dunn, Delila, c/o Wm. to Wm. Fisher	Bond	17 APR 1826	1825:098
Dunn, Delilah, c/o William, by William Fisher	Account	18 APR 1831	1831:021
Dunn, Dorinda M., c/o James to James A. Dunn	Bond	18 DEC 1843	1838:300
Dunn, Dorinda M., by James A. Dunn	Account	16 FEB 1846	1844:088
Dunn, Dorinda M., from James A. Dunn	Receipt	22 AUG 1848	1844:291
Dunn, Dorinda M., by James A. Dunn	Account	17 JUL 1848	1844:278
Dunn, Edmonia C., c/o Jackson to John Clarke	Bond	16 DEC 1833	1831:233
Dunn, Elizabeth, c/o Tolla to Thomas Harper	Bond	18 DEC 1820	1811:243
Dunn, Ellender Jane, c/o Jackson to Happy Dunn	Bond	19 OCT 1840	1838:107
Dunn, James Henry, c/o Henry to James Dunn	Bond	17 MAR 1834	1831:246
Dunn, James W., c/o James to James A. Dunn	Bond	16 JUL 1849	1844:384
Dunn, James W., by James A. Dunn	Account	18 MAR 1851	1844:505
Dunn, James W., by James A. Dunn	Account	17 MAY 1852	1851:056
Dunn, James W., by James A. Dunn	Account	16 MAY 1853	1851:175
Dunn, James W., by James A. Dunn	Account	17 JUL 1854	1851:240
Dunn, James W., by James A. Dunn	Account	18 JUN 1855	1851:309
Dunn, James W., by James A. Dunn	Account	16 JUN 1856	1851:353
Dunn, James W., by James A. Dunn	Account	20 JUL 1857	1851:453
Dunn, James William, by James A. Dunn	Account	20 DEC 1858	1857:107
Dunn, James W., by James A. Dunn	Account	19 SEP 1859	1857:155

Ward or Subject (and Parent, Guardian or Other)	Record Type	Date	Reference(s)
Dunn, James W., by James A. Dunn	Account	17 SEP 1860	1857:225
Dunn, James W., by James A. Dunn	Account	16 JUL 1866	1857:406
Dunn, James M., under 14, c/o Muscoe R. to Iverson L. Dunn	Bond	15 NOV 1886	1867:583
Dunn, Jonathan to William Gray	Bond	19 FEB 1733	WB5:174
Dunn, Josephine, c/o Alexander Crow to Muscoe R. Dunn	Bond	18 OCT 1869	1867:108
Dunn, Maggie H., c/o Tazwell to Winter M. Dunn	Bond	15 MAR 1869	1867:082
Dunn, Maggie H., over 14, c/o Tazwell to Winter M. Dunn	Certificate	15 MAR 1869	1867:081
Dunn, Margaret D., c/o Richard to Warner Shackelford	Bond	18 DEC 1820	1811:243a
Dunn, Margaret H., c/o Tazewell to Peter T. Campbell	Bond	18 SEP 1871	1867:170
Dunn, Maria, c/o Thomas to Jane Dunn	Bond	17 DEC 1810	1796:240
Dunn, Maria, by Jane Dunn	Account	21 SEP 1812	1811:025
Dunn, Mary E., d/o John to G.G. Roy	Certificate	21 NOV 1859	1857:186
Dunn, Mary E., c/o John to Gustavus G. Roy	Bond	21 NOV 1859	1857:186
Dunn, Mildred, c/o Patsey Dunn to Edmund Dunn	Bond	21 SEP 1835	1831:330
Dunn, Molly, c/o Dickinson to Jesse Griggs	Bond	20 FEB 1809	1796:209
Dunn, Nannie D., under 14, c/o Muscoe R. to Iverson L. Dunn	Bond	15 NOV 1886	1867:583
Dunn, Robert, c/o Thomas to Jane Dunn	Bond	17 DEC 1810	1796:240
Dunn, Roberta, c/o Henry to James Dunn	Bond	17 MAR 1834	1831:246
Dunn, Roberta, c/o Henry to James H. Dunn	Bond	17 APR 1843	1838:247
Dunn, Roberta P., by James Dunn	Account	17 MAR 1845	1844:026
Dunn, Sarah, c/o Wm. to Wm. Fisher	Bond	17 APR 1826	1825:098
Dunn, Sarah, c/o William, by William Fisher	Account	18 APR 1831	1831:021, 027
Dunn, Sthreshly, c/o Wm. to Wm. Fisher	Bond	17 APR 1826	1825:098
Dunn, Sthreshly, c/o William, by William Fisher	Account	18 APR 1831	1831:021, 029
Dunn, Sthreshly, by William Fisher	Account	17 DEC 1832	1831:157
Dunn, Susan Baylie, c/o Jackson to Happy Dunn	Bond	19 OCT 1840	1838:107
Dunn, Thomas, c/o Thomas to Jane Dunn	Bond	17 DEC 1810	1796:240
Dunn, Thomas, by Jane Dunn	Account	21 SEP 1812	1811:024
Dunn, Virginia A., c/o John to Gustavus G. Roy	Bond	21 NOV 1859	1857:186
Dunn, Virginia A., d/o John to G.G. Roy	Certificate	21 NOV 1859	1857:186
Dunn, Virginia A., c/o John P. to Richard M. McKan	Bond	15 SEP 1862	1857:295
Dunn, William, orphans of, by William Fisher	Account	18 APR 1831	1831:021
Dunn, William J., by James A. Dunn	Account	20 JAN 1862	1857:285
Durham, Ann, c/o James to Catharine Durham	Bond	19 OCT 1801	1796:103
Durham, Anna, c/o James to George Durham	Bond	19 OCT 1801	1796:108
Durham, Catharine, c/o James to Catharine Durham	Bond	19 OCT 1801	1796:103
Durham, Fanny, c/o James to Catharine Durham	Bond	21 JAN 1811	1796:241
Durham, Frances now Taylor, c/o Catharine & James	Receipt	19 SEP 1825	1825:019
Durham, George, c/o James to James Durham	Bond	19 MAR 1827	1825:161
Durham, Jacob, c/o James to Catharine Durham	Bond	19 OCT 1801	1796:103
Durham, Jacob, c/o Catharine & James, from Catharine	Receipt	19 SEP 1825	1825:019
Durham, Joseph, c/o James to Catharine Durham	Bond	19 OCT 1801	1796:103
Durham, Joseph, c/o Catharine & James, from Catharine	Receipt	19 SEP 1825	1825:019
Durham, Olivia, c/o Joseph to her father	Bond	16 NOV 1840	1838:126
Durham, Polly, c/o James to Catharine Durham	Bond	19 OCT 1801	1796:103
Durham, Polly, c/o Catharine & James, from Catharine	Receipt	19 SEP 1825	1825:019
Durham, Samuel, c/o James to James Durham	Bond	19 MAR 1827	1825:161
Durham, Susanna, c/o James to George Durham	Bond	19 OCT 1801	1796:108
Durham, Susanna, c/o James to John Minter	Bond	16 JUN 1806	1796:176
Dyer, Andrew to Francis Meriwether	Bond	10 DEC 1709	D&W13:262
Dyer, Elizabeth to John Gatewood	Bond	10 OCT 1709	D&W13:256

Ward or Subject (and Parent, Guardian or Other)	Record Type	Date	Reference(s)
Dyke, Catharine, by Larkin Hundley	Account	18 MAY 1835	1831:298
Dyke, Catharine, by Larkin Hundley	Account	17 MAY 1836	1831:420
Dyke, Catharine, by Larkin Hundley	Account	19 JUN 1837	1831:479
Dyke, Catharine, by Larkin Hundley	Account	21 MAY 1838	1838:026
Dyke, Catharine, by Larkin Hundley	Account	15 APR 1839	1838:054
Dyke, Catharine	Receipt	02 NOV 1839	1838:090
Dyke, Catharine, by Larkin Hundley	Account	20 JUL 1840	1838:090
Dyke, Catharine	Receipt	15 JUN 1840	1838:092
Dyke, Charlotte C., c/o William to Larkin Hundley	Bond	19 SEP 1831	1831:069
Dyke, Charlotte Catharine, by Larkin Hundley	Account	16 DEC 1833	1831:220
Dyke, Charlotte Catharine, c/o William to Elijah Hundley	Bond	16 SEP 1839	1838:059
Dyke, Eliza Pace, c/o William to Miskel Dyke	Bond	17 OCT 1831	1831:070
Dyke, Eliza P., by Miskel H. Dyke	Account	21 JAN 1833	1831:160
Dyke, Eliza P., by Miskel H. Dyke	Account	16 JUN 1834	1831:271
Dyke, Eliza P., by Miskel H. Dyke	Account	15 AUG 1836	1831:432
Dyke, Fanny, c/o Jackson to Wm. H. Faulconer	Bond	17 JUN 1799	1796:044
Dyke, Fanny, c/o Jack to her father	Bond	16 DEC 1816	1811:129
Dyke, Fanny, by Jack Dyke	Account	21 NOV 1825	1825:065
Dyke, Jackson, c/o Jack to his father	Bond	16 DEC 1816	1811:129
Dyke, Jackson	Receipt	21 NOV 1825	1825:066
Dyke, Jackson, by Jack Dyke	Account	21 NOV 1825	1825:065
Dyke, John, c/o William to his father	Bond	15 MAR 1819	1811:186
Dyke, John, by William Dyke	Account	17 OCT 1825	1825:049
Dyke, John & wife Ann C. Roy, from Larkin Hundley	Receipt	16 APR 1832	1831:111
Dyke, John, c/o Jackson to Catharine L. Dyke	Bond	21 JUN 1852	1851:117
Dyke, Lewis, c/o Jackson to Catharine L. Dyke	Bond	21 JUN 1852	1851:117
Dyke, Lucy Walker, c/o William to Miskel Dyke	Bond	17 OCT 1831	1831:070
Dyke, Maria, c/o Jackson to Catharine L. Dyke	Bond	21 JUN 1852	1851:117
Dyke, Mary Ann, c/o William to Miskel Dyke	Bond	17 OCT 1831	1831:070
Dyke, Mary A., by Miskel H. Dyke	Account	21 JAN 1833	1831:161
Dyke, Mary Ann, by Miskel H. Dyke	Account	16 JUN 1834	1831:270
Dyke, Mary A., c/o Vincent to Elzer Fogg	Bond	15 NOV 1852	1851:153
Dyke, Mary A. now Taylor, by Elzer Fogg	Account	19 MAR 1855	1851:286
Dyke, Nancy, d/o Jackson to Philip Dunn	Bond	20 FEB 1792	1761:176
Dyke, Peggy Ellen, c/o Jackson to Catharine L. Dyke	Bond	21 JUN 1852	1851:117
Dyke, Polly, c/o Jackson to Micajah Munday	Bond	19 OCT 1801	1796:107
Dyke, Polly, an infant, by Micajah Munday	Account	19 SEP 1803	1796:135
Dyke, Polly, c/o Jack to her father	Bond	16 DEC 1816	1811:129
Dyke, Polly, by Jack Dyke	Account	21 NOV 1825	1825:065
Dyke, Robert, c/o Jack to his father	Bond	16 DEC 1816	1811:129
Dyke, Robert, by Jack Dyke	Account	21 NOV 1825	1825:065
Dyke, Susan E., c/o William to Larkin Hundley	Bond	19 SEP 1831	1831:069
Dyke, Susan, by Larkin Hundley	Account	16 DEC 1833	1831:224
Dyke, Susan, by Larkin Hundley	Account	18 MAY 1835	1831:298
Dyke, Susan E., by Larkin Hundley	Account	17 MAY 1836	1831:418
Dyke, Susan E,, by Larkin Hundley	Account	19 JUN 1837	1831:480
Dyke, Susan E., by Larkin Hundley	Account	21 MAY 1838	1838:027
Dyke, Susan E., by Larkin Hundley	Account	15 APR 1839	1838:054
Dyke, Susan E., by Larkin Hundley	Account	20 JUL 1840	1838:088
Dyke, Susan E., by Larkin Hundley	Account	17 MAY 1841	1838:139
Dyke, Susan E., by Larkin Hundley	Account	20 JUN 1842	1838:220

Ward or Subject (and Parent, Guardian or Other)	Record Type	Date	Reference(s)
Dyke, Susan E., by Larkin Hundley	Account	17 NOV 1845	1844:072
Dyke, Susan E., by Larkin Hundley	Account	17 JUL 1848	1844:289
Dyke, William A., c/o William to Larkin Hundley	Bond	19 SEP 1831	1831:069
Dyke, William, by Larkin Hundley	Account	16 DEC 1833	1831:222
Dyke, William, by Larkin Hundley	Account	18 MAY 1835	1831:296
Dyke, William, by Larkin Hundley	Account	17 MAY 1836	1831:418
Dyke, William, by Larkin Hundley	Account	19 JUN 1837	1831:480
Dyke, William, by Larkin Hundley	Account	21 MAY 1838	1838:027
Dyke, William, by Larkin Hundley	Account	15 APR 1839	1838:056
Dyke, William, by Larkin Hundley	Account	20 JUL 1840	1838:088
Dyke, William, by Larkin Hundley	Account	17 MAY 1841	1838:139
Dyke, William A., by Larkin Hundley	Account	20 JUN 1842	1838:218
Dyke, William A., by Larkin Hundley	Account	20 OCT 1845	WB25:442
Dyke, William A., by Larkin Hundley	Account	20 OCT 1845	1844:060

E

Edmonds, Meredith M., from Leroy Cauthorn	Receipt	18 JUN 1832	1831:115
Edmondson, Betty, c/o Robert, by J. Edmondson	Account	19 AUG 1766	1761:062
Edmondson, Clack, c/o William to William L. Montague	Bond	15 OCT 1804	1796:158
Edmondson, Clack R., c/o William to James G. Row	Bond	16 JAN 1809	1796:208
Edmondson, Clack R., by James G. Row	Account	20 JUL 1818	1811:153
Edmondson, John, c/o William to John Croxton, Jr.	Bond	15 JUL 1805	1796:165
Edmondson, Judith, c/o Thomas to Edmund Pendleton	Bond	18 FEB 1760	1731:251
Edmondson, Patsey M., by James Montague	Account	20 OCT 1806	1796:188
Edmondson, Patsy, c/o William to James Montague	Bond	15 OCT 1804	1796:158
Edmondson, Polly, c/o William to James Montague	Bond	15 OCT 1804	1796:158
Edmondson, Robert to Philip Stockdell	Bond	21 MAY 1734	WB5:257
Edmondson, Samuel to Robert Edmondson	Bond	15 MAY 1739	WB6:180
Edmondson, Samuel, by Robert Edmondson	Account	20 OCT 1741	1731:045
Edmondson, Suckey to Gabriel Jones	Bond	21 MAR 1743/4	WB7:107
Edmondson, Sukey, by Gabriel Jones	Account	18 SEP 1744	1731:077
Edmondson, Sukey, h/o John, by Gabriel Jones	Account	17 JUL 1744	1731:063, 068
Edmondson, Sukey, Miss, by Gabriel Jones	Account	20 NOV 1745	1731:090
Edmondson, Wenifred to George Stubblefield	Bond	21 MAY 1734	WB5:256
Edwards, Judith, c/o Edmund to Achilles Ball	Bond	20 DEC 1819	1811:204
Edwards, Mary C. late Owen, w/o Robert D., by Wm. A. Wright	Account	19 MAR 1849	1844:330
Elliott, Fanny, c/o Caleb to Frederick Fogg	Bond	15 APR 1793	1761:192
Elliott, Morton, c/o Caleb to Frederick Fogg	Bond	15 APR 1793	1761:192
Elliott, Streshly, c/o Caleb to Frederick Fogg	Bond	15 APR 1793	1761:192
Eubank, Anna R., c/o Thomas P. to James M. Brown	Bond	20 NOV 1865	1857:327
Eubank, Anna R., by James M. Brown	Account	15 JUL 1867	1857:434
Eubank, Camma A., c/o Richard S. to Thomas J. Talbott	Bond	18 SEP 1865	1857:325
Eubank, Charles, c/o Richard S. to Thomas J. Talbott	Bond	18 SEP 1865	1857:325
Eubank, Estell, c/o Richard S. to Thomas J. Talbott	Bond	18 SEP 1865	1857:325
Eubank, Honoria, c/o Richard S. to Thomas J. Talbott	Bond	18 SEP 1865	1857:325
Eubank, Isabella J., by Richard S. Eubank	Account	21 JUN 1852	1851:118
Eubank, Judith, c/o William to Richard S. Eubank	Bond	19 AUG 1850	1844:467
Eubank, Judith E., by Richard S. Eubank	Account	21 JUN 1852	1851:120
Eubank, Judith E., by Richard S. Eubank	Account	19 SEP 1853	1851:204
Eubank, Judith E., by Richard S. Eubank	Account	15 JAN 1855	1851:279
Eubank, Judith E., by R.S. Eubank	Account	17 NOV 1856	1851:387, 389

Ward or Subject (and Parent, Guardian or Other)	Record Type	Date	Reference(s)
Eubank, Judith E., by R.S. Eubank	Account	19 OCT 1857	1857:025
Eubank, Judith E., by R.S. Eubank	Account	20 DEC 1858	1857:117
Eubank, Juliet Isabella, c/o William to Richard S. Eubank	Bond	19 AUG 1850	1844:467
Eubank, Juliet J., by Richard S. Eubank	Account	19 SEP 1853	1851:196
Eubank, Juliet J., by Richard S. Eubank	Account	15 JAN 1855	1851:281
Eubank, Philip E., c/o William to Thomas P. Eubank	Bond	18 NOV 1850	1844:479
Eubank, Philip C., by Thomas P. Eubank	Account	16 JAN 1854	1851:226
Eubank, Philip C., by Thomas P. Eubank	Account	19 MAR 1855	1851:289
Eubank, Philip C., by Thomas P. Eubank	Account	18 AUG 1856	1851:367
Eubank, Philip C., now 21, from Thomas P. Eubank	Receipt	19 DEC 1859	1857:191
Eubank, Richard W., c/o Richard S. to Thomas J. Talbott	Bond	18 SEP 1865	1857:325
Eubank, Thomas, c/o Thomas P. to James M. Brown	Bond	20 NOV 1865	1857:327
Eubank, Thomas T., by James M. Brown	Account	15 JUL 1867	1857:433
Eubank, William T., c/o Thomas P. to James M. Brown	Bond	20 NOV 1865	1857:327
Eubank, William T., by James M. Brown	Account	15 JUL 1867	1857:433
Evans, Charles, c/o Charles, by Clack Row	Account	19 OCT 1772	1761:095
Evans, Charles, c/o Charles, by Clack Row	Account	20 SEP 1773	1761:097
Evans, Charles, c/o Charles, by Clack Row	Account	19 SEP 1774	1761:120
Evans, Charles R., c/o James B., to John S. McCauley	Bond	15 SEP 1880	CCW:114
Evans, James, c/o Thomas to Wm. Upshaw Davis	Bond	15 MAY 1750	WB8:332
Evans, James to Thomas Waring, Jr.	Bond	20 FEB 1750/1	WB8:414
Evans, James to John Seayres	Bond	17 JUL 1750	WB8:340
Evans, Joseph, to Thomas Waring, Jr.	Bond	20 AUG 1751	WB9:085
Evans, Thomas, to Thomas Waring, Jr.	Bond	20 AUG 1751	WB9:085
Evans, William to Thomas Waring, Jr.	Bond	20 FEB 1750/1	WB8:414
Evans, William T., c/o James B. to his father	Bond	17 SEP 1855	1851:327
Evat, Agatha to Thomas Evat	Bond	18 AUG 1740	WB6:268
Evat, Agatha, by Thomas Evat	Account	15 DEC 1741	1731:044
Evat, John to Thomas Evat	Bond	18 AUG 1740	WB6:268
Evat, John, by Thomas Evat	Account	15 DEC 1741	1731:044
Evatt, Ann to John Pettit	Bond	18 MAR 1728	WB4:285a
Eyles, John to Thomas Cox	Bond	10 MAY 1711	D&W13:412

F

Farmer, Anne, c/o Ralph	Account	21 JUN 1763	WB12:062
Farmer, Hannah, c/o Ralph	Account	21 JUN 1763	WB12:063
Farmer, Mary, c/o Ralph	Account	21 JUN 1763	WB12:062
Farmer, Thomas, c/o Ralph	Account	21 JUN 1763	WB12:061
Faulconer, Bettie P., c/o John W. to Bettie S. Faulconer	Bond	19 SEP 1859	1857:154
Faulconer, Bettie P., h/o John W., by John S. Trible	Account	18 JAN 1864	1857:306, 308
Faulconer, Bettie P., by John S. Trible	Account	20 JAN 1873	1867:198
Faulconer, Elizabeth S. late Waring, by Robt. P. Waring	Account	19 OCT 1846	1844:176
Faulconer, Fannie, h/o John W., by John S. Trible	Account	18 JAN 1864	1857:306
Faulconer, Fanny Ida., c/o John W. to Bettie S. Faulconer	Bond	19 SEP 1859	1857:154
Faulconer, Harriet alias Noel to Wm. H. Faulconer	Bond	17 OCT 1808	1796:203
Faulconer, Ida F. [Fannie I.], by John S. Trible	Account	18 JAN 1864	1857:310
Faulconer, Ida, by John S. Trible	Account	21 DEC 1874	1867:292
Faulconer, John W., c/o John W. to Bettie S. Faulconer	Bond	19 SEP 1859	1857:154
Faulconer, John W., h/o John W., by John S. Trible	Account	18 JAN 1864	1857:306, 312
Faulconer, John W., by John S. Trible	Account	20 JAN 1873	1867:202
Faulkner, Anabella to John Haile	Bond	17 JUN 1740	WB6:254

Ward or Subject (and Parent, Guardian or Other)	Record Type	Date	Reference(s)
Faulkner, Arabella, c/o Edward, by James Fargeson	Account	20 OCT 1730	WB4:399
Fauntleroy, M.G., h/o Wm. J.L. Latane	Writing	17 OCT 1825	1825:041
Faver, Elizabeth, c/o Theophilus to William Faver	Bond	16 JUL 1792	WB14:323
Faver, Elizabeth, c/o Thomas to James Sale	Bond	21 DEC 1801	1796:110
Faver, Fanny, c/o Theophilus, by Joseph Sale	Account	15 SEP 1800	1796:075
Faver, Florella J. to H.W. Daingerfield	P. of Atty.	21 MAY 1872	1867:183
Faver, James, c/o Theophilus to William Faver	Bond	16 JUL 1792	WB14:323
Faver, James, c/o Theophilus to Edmund Noel	Bond	15 OCT 1792	1761:185
Faver, Richard, by Thomas Faver	Account	17 OCT 1785	1761:143
Faver, Susanna, c/o Thomas to Lewis Sale	Bond	17 NOV 1794	1761:209
Faver, Theophilus, c/o Theophilus to William Faver	Bond	16 JUL 1792	WB14:323
Faver, Theophilus, c/o Theophilus to Edmund Noel	Bond	15 OCT 1792	1761:185
Favor, Caleb, c/o Theophilus, dec. to Theophilus Favor	Bond	21 APR 1760	1731:252
Favor, Thomas, c/o Theophilus to Theophilus Favor	Bond	21 APR 1760	1731:252
Fer, Julia E., c/o Gustavus A. to Lewis Allen	Bond	21 AUG 1837	1831:498
Ferguson, Bettie, c/o Absolom to Robert Waller	Bond	19 OCT 1885	1867:568
Ferrill, Jane, of unknown parent to Joseph H. Fidler	Bond	16 MAR 1840	1838:073
Ferris, Elizabeth M. to Thomas Pitts	Bond	12 JAN 1829	1825:265
Fisher, Alfred, c/o Lewis to Alfred H. Garnett	Bond	18 DEC 1843	1838:298
Fisher, B.L., from Josiah W. Fisher	Receipt	18 JAN 1836	1831:398
Fisher, Benjamin, c/o Benjamin to William Fisher	Bond	18 JAN 1819	1811:169
Fisher, Benjamin, by Richard Motley	Account	15 SEP 1828	1825:252
Fisher, Benjamin, c/o Benjamin to Josiah W. Fisher	Bond	20 FEB 1832	1831:100
Fisher, Eliza Ellen, c/o John W. to William A. Baynham	Bond	17 SEP 1860	1857:220
Fisher, Eliza Ellen, over 14, c/o John W. to Dr. Wm. A. Baynham	Certificate	17 SEP 1860	1857:220
Fisher, Ella Ann, c/o William to Washington H. Purkins	Bond	17 NOV 1840	1838:129
Fisher, Ella Ann, c/o William to Washington H. Purkins	Bond	16 FEB 1846	1844:092
Fisher, Ella Ann, c/o William to Washington H. Purkins	Bond	20 JUL 1846	1844:151
Fisher, Ella A., c/o William to John W. Fisher	Bond	16 FEB 1852	1851:043
Fisher, Ellar Ann, by Washington H. Purkins	Account	20 APR 1846	1844:127
Fisher, Emma O., c/o John W., to Martha S. Fisher	Bond	14 NOV 1860	CCW:019
Fisher, Harriett D., c/o Lewis to John W. Fisher	Bond	18 DEC 1843	1838:297
Fisher, Henry, c/o Benjamin to William Fisher	Bond	18 JAN 1819	1811:169
Fisher, Isaac, c/o James to Reuben Cauthorn	Bond	20 FEB 1815	1811:077
Fisher, J.W., from Richard Motley	Receipt	21 JUL 1828	1825:240
Fisher, Jane, c/o William to Wm. Clark	Bond	21 OCT 1816	1811:121
Fisher, John, c/o Benjamin to William Fisher	Bond	18 JAN 1819	1811:169
Fisher, John, c/o Benjamin to Josiah Waller Fisher	Bond	16 JUL 1827	1825:168
Fisher, John, by Benjamin H. Munday, Jr.	Account	21 JAN 1828	1825:214
Fisher, John, c/o William to Washington H. Purkins	Bond	15 JAN 1838	1838:004
Fisher, John W., c/o William to Washington H. Purkins	Bond	17 NOV 1840	1838:129
Fisher, John W., c/o William to Washington H. Purkins	Bond	20 JUL 1846	1844:151
Fisher, John W., Master, by Washington H. Purkins	Account	20 APR 1846	1844:101
Fisher, John W., c/o William to Washington H. Purkins	Bond	16 FEB 1846	1844:092
Fisher, John W., c/o John W. to William W. Dishman	Bond	21 JAN 1861	1857:236
Fisher, John W., c/o John W. to his uncle Wm. W. Dishman	Certificate	21 JAN 1861	1857:235
Fisher, Joseph W., c/o John W., to Martha S. Fisher	Bond	14 NOV 1860	CCW:019
Fisher, Kitty, c/o Nancy to Lewis Fisher	Bond	21 DEC 1818	1811:167
Fisher, Lucy, c/o Richard to Thomas Turner	Bond	16 DEC 1816	1811:127
Fisher, Lucy, c/o Nancy to Francis Trigger	Bond	20 DEC 1819	1811:204
Fisher, Martha, c/o Lewis to Alfred H. Garnett	Bond	18 DEC 1843	1838:298

Ward or Subject (and Parent, Guardian or Other)	Record Type	Date	Reference(s)
Fisher, Mary Ellen, c/o William to Washington H. Purkins	Bond	15 JAN 1838	1838:004
Fisher, Mary S., c/o Lewis to John W. Fisher	Bond	18 DEC 1843	1838:297
Fisher, Muscoe R., c/o John W., to Martha S. Fisher	Bond	14 NOV 1860	CCW:019
Fisher, Rebecca G., over 14, c/o John W. to Dr. Wm. A. Baynham	Certificate	17 SEP 1860	1857:220
Fisher, Rebecca G., c/o John W. to William A. Baynham	Bond	17 SEP 1860	1857:220
Fisher, Rebecca G., by William A. Baynham	Account	16 APR 1866	1857:386
Fisher, Rebecca G., by William A. Baynham	Account	20 OCT 1873	1867:221
Fisher, Robert, c/o Lewis to Alfred H. Garnett	Bond	18 DEC 1843	1838:298
Fisher, Samuel G., c/o John W. to William W. Dishman	Bond	21 JAN 1861	1857:236
Fisher, Selina P., c/o John W., to Martha S. Fisher	Bond	14 NOV 1860	CCW:019
Fisher, Thomas, c/o William to Washington H. Purkins	Bond	15 JAN 1838	1838:004
Fisher, Thomas E., c/o William to Washington H. Purkins	Bond	17 NOV 1840	1838:129
Fisher, Thomas E., c/o William to Washington H. Purkins	Bond	16 FEB 1846	1844:092
Fisher, Thomas E., by Washington H. Purkins	Account	20 APR 1846	1844:110
Fisher, Thomas E., c/o William to Washington H. Purkins	Bond	20 JUL 1846	1844:151
Fisher, William, by Richard Cauthorn	Account	15 SEP 1777	1761:132
Fisher, William, c/o William to Washington H. Purkins	Bond	15 JAN 1838	1838:004
Fisher, William, c/o William to Washington H. Purkins	Bond	17 NOV 1840	1838:129
Fisher, William, by Washington H. Purkins	Account	20 APR 1846	1844:118
Fisher, William, c/o William to Washington H. Purkins	Bond	16 FEB 1846	1844:092
Fisher, William, c/o William to John W. Fisher	Bond	15 NOV 1852	1851:152
Fisher, William Obed, c/o John W., to Martha S. Fisher	Bond	14 NOV 1860	CCW:019
Fletcher, Carter, c/o John to Barker Minter	Bond	15 SEP 1800	1796:070
Fletcher, Carter, by Barker Minter	Account	16 SEP 1805	1796:167
Fletcher, Carter, c/o John, by Barker Minter	Account	19 SEP 1808	1796:202
Fletcher, Carter, c/o John, by Barker Minter	Settlement	21 JUL 1818	1811:156
Fletcher, Fanny, c/o John to Barker Minter	Bond	15 SEP 1800	1796:070
Fletcher, Fanny, by Barker Minter	Account	16 SEP 1805	1796:168
Fletcher, Fanny, c/o John, by Barker Minter	Settlement	21 JUL 1818	1811:158
Fletcher, Jno., c/o John, by Barker Minter	Account	19 SEP 1808	1796:202
Fletcher, John Young, c/o John to Barker Minter	Bond	15 SEP 1800	1796:070
Fletcher, John Bush, by Barker Minter	Account	16 SEP 1805	1796:168
Fletcher, John Bush, c/o John, by Barker Minter	Settlement	21 JUL 1818	1811:159
Fletcher, Leroy A. to Rachael Fletcher	Bond	20 FEB 1882	1867:484
Fletcher, Lucy A., under 14, c/o Booker to Rachel Fletcher	Bond	20 NOV 1876	1867:358
Fletcher, Mary E., under 14, c/o Booker to Rachel Fletcher	Bond	20 NOV 1876	1867:358
Fletcher, Mary E. to Rachael Fletcher	Bond	20 FEB 1882	1867:484
Fletcher, Nathan, c/o John to Barker Minter	Bond	15 SEP 1800	1796:070
Fletcher, Nathan, by Barker Minter	Account	16 SEP 1805	1796:168
Fletcher, Nathan, c/o John, by Barker Minter	Account	19 SEP 1808	1796:202
Fletcher, Nathan, by Barker Minter	Settlement	16 JUN 1817	1811:132
Fletcher, Sally, c/o John to James Davis	Bond	15 SEP 1800	1796:071
Fletcher, Thomas, c/o John to James Davis	Bond	15 SEP 1800	1796:071
Fletcher, Thomas, by James Davis	Account	15 JUL 1805	1796:164
Florilla, Floriel, natural child of Phillip Henshaw to Sally Gatewood	Bond	19 FEB 1821	1811:246
Fogg, Celestine, by Elzer Fogg	Account	17 MAR 1873	1867:211
Fogg, Celestine, above 14, c/o Wilcey to Joseph Scott	Bond	17 MAR 1874	1867:229
Fogg, Celestine, by Joseph Scott	Account	26 JUN 1875	1867:322
Fogg, Celestine, by Elzer Fogg	Account	26 JUN 1875	1867:318
Fogg, Celestine, by Joseph Scott	Account	19 FEB 1877	1867:362
Fogg, Elizabeth, c/o James, by John Garnett, Jr.	Account	18 AUG 1752	1731:147

Ward or Subject (and Parent, Guardian or Other)	Record Type	Date	Reference(s)
Fogg, Elizabeth, c/o James, by John Garnett, Jr.	Account	21 AUG 1753	1731:167
Fogg, Elizabeth, by John Garnett, Jr.	Account	20 AUG 1754	1731:180
Fogg, Elizabeth, c/o James to John Garnett	Bond	21 JAN 1755	1731:190
Fogg, Elizabeth, c/o Thomas to James Green	Bond	17 AUG 1795	1761:223
Fogg, Hillyard, c/o Major to John Beazley	Bond	19 FEB 1821	1811:249
Fogg, John & Elizabeth, c/o James, by Nathaniel Fogg	Account	17 OCT 1752	1731:152
Fogg, John, c/o James, by John Garnett, Jr.	Account	18 AUG 1752	1731:147
Fogg, John, c/o James, by Nathaniel Fogg	Account	17 OCT 1752	1731:152
Fogg, John to John Garnett	Bond	20 NOV 1753	1731:173
Fogg, John, c/o James, by John Garnett, Jr.	Account	21 AUG 1753	1731:166
Fogg, John, by John Garnett, Jr.	Account	20 AUG 1754	1731:180
Fogg, Mourning, c/o Thomas to John Beazley	Bond	20 DEC 1802	1796:122
Fogg, Polly Colstone Cavanaugh, c/o Thomas to Peggy Fogg	Bond	18 APR 1796	1761:224
Fogg, Tena, c/o Wilcey to Elzer Fogg	Bond	18 MAY 1868	1867:030
Foreacre, Loulie W., under 14, c/o Wm. to Geo. P. Crispin	Bond	20 FEB 1882	1867:485
Foreacres, Henrietta D., above 14, c/o George to Robt. P. Brooks	Bond	18 JUN 1877	1867:368
Foreacres, Loulie H, c/o Wm. L., to Robert C. Brizendine	Bond	15 SEP 1882	CCW:125
Fortune, Rebecca, c/o Susan to Dandridge Bush	Bond	19 DEC 1831	1831:084
Foster, Anne to John Tayloe	Bond	21 JUL 1724	WB4:067
Fowler, John to Theophilus Faver	Bond	20 NOV 1744	WB7:225
Fowler, John to Robert Harbin	Bond	18 MAR 1745/6	WB7:428
Fowler, John, by Robert Harbin	Account	19 APR 1748	1731:116
Fowler, Susa: to Theophilus Faver	Bond	18 DEC 1744	WB7:231
Fowler, Susanna, by Robert Harbin	Account	19 APR 1748	1731:117
Fowler, Susannah to Robert Harbin	Bond	18 MAR 1745/6	WB7:428
Frank, Mildred Harvie, c/o William H. to her father	Bond	16 SEP 1844	1838:358
Frank, Mildred H., by Maria J.G. Frank	Account	18 FEB 1861	1857:255
Franklin, Lewis Henry, c/o Richard W. to Henry Clarke	Bond	15 JAN 1855	1851:285
Franklin, Lewis H., c/o Richard W. to his father	Bond	16 AUG 1858	1857:103
Franklin, Lewis H., by Henry Clarke	Account	19 JUL 1858	1857:101
Franklin, Lewis H., c/o Richard W. to his father	Bond	21 JAN 1861	1857:250
Franklin, Richard W., c/o John to William A. Wright	Bond	19 APR 1847	1844:208
Franklin, Richard W., c/o Richard W. to Henry Clarke	Bond	15 JAN 1855	1851:285
Franklin, Richard W., by Henry Clarke	Account	19 JUL 1858	1857:101
Franklin, Richard W., c/o Richard W. to his father	Bond	16 AUG 1858	1857:103
Franklin, Richard W., c/o Richard W. to his father	Bond	21 JAN 1861	1857:250

G

Gains, John, orphan of to Mark Thomas	Marriage Ref.	16 MAY 1738	WB6:125
Galloway, Estave, c/o George to James Jones	Bond	15 OCT 1792	1761:184
Games, Carter, c/o Thomas to William Games	Bond	20 MAY 1811	1796:247
Games, Carter, by William Games	Report	21 FEB 1826	1825:086
Games, John, c/o Thomas to William Games	Bond	20 MAY 1811	1796:247
Games, John, by William Games	Report	21 FEB 1826	1825:086
Games, William to John Games	Bond	19 MAY 1730	WB4:353
Garland, Virginia, c/o William B. to Joseph Janey	Bond	17 MAY 1819	1811:187
Garland, Virginia now Collins, from Joseph Janey	Report	19 SEP 1825	1825:028
Garnett, Alexander, c/o Robert S. to Robert S. Garnett	Bond	18 OCT 1841	1838:154
Garnett, Alfred, c/o James T. to Sarah A. Garnett	Bond	18 APR 1859	1857:139
Garnett, Ann, c/o Augustine to Theodorick Noel	Bond	16 SEP 1811	1796:253
Garnett, Augustine, c/o Augustine to Theodorick Noel	Bond	16 SEP 1811	1796:253

Ward or Subject (and Parent, Guardian or Other)	Record Type	Date	Reference(s)
Garnett, Austin, c/o Austin to Joseph Jones Monroe	Bond	22 APR 1800	1796:057
Garnett, Austin, c/o Austin to Robert Hill	Bond	15 NOV 1813	1811:048
Garnett, Austin, c/o Austin, by Theodk. Noel	Account	21 JUN 1814	1811:062
Garnett, Austin, c/o Austin, by Joseph Jones Monroe	Settlement	17 MAR 1818	1811:147
Garnett, Caroline, c/o William F.G. to William C. Garnett	Bond	21 OCT 1878	1867:385
Garnett, Caroline, by William C. Garnett	Account	22 NOV 1881	1867:462
Garnett, Caroline, above 14, c/o Wm. F.G. to C.F. Goss	Bond	18 SEP 1882	1867:499
Garnett, Caroline to Charles F. Goss	Certificate	18 SEP 1882	1867:499
Garnett, Caroline, by Charles F. Goss	Account	15 SEP 1884	1867:542
Garnett, Edith G., over 14, c/o Wm. F.G. to Wm. C. Garnett	Bond	21 OCT 1878	1867:385
Garnett, Edith G., under 14, to W.C. Garnett	Certificate	21 OCT 1878	1867:387
Garnett, Edith G., by William C. Garnett	Account	20 SEP 1880	1867:429
Garnett, Edith G., by William C. Garnett	Account	22 NOV 1881	1867:458
Garnett, Edith G. now Goss, by William C. Garnett	Account	20 NOV 1882	1867:540
Garnett, Elizabeth, c/o Thomas to Richard Noell	Bond	20 JUN 1758	1731:227
Garnett, Elizabeth, c/o Augustine to Henry Garnett	Bond	15 DEC 1794	1761:205
Garnett, James M., c/o M.R. to Robert M.T. Hunter	Bond	18 APR 1864	1857:313
Garnett, Jno. M., c/o Muscoe to James M. Garnett	Bond	18 APR 1803	1796:131
Garnett, Jno. M., c/o Muscoe to brother James M. Garnett	Account	21 NOV 1814	1811:070
Garnett, John F.W., c/o Robert S. to Robert S. Garnett	Bond	18 OCT 1841	1838:154
Garnett, Leonard, c/o James T. to Sarah A. Garnett	Bond	18 APR 1859	1857:139
Garnett, Milly, c/o William to Muscoe Garnett	Bond	19 NOV 1759	1731:246
Garnett, Muscoe, c/o Muscoe to James M. Garnett	Bond	18 APR 1803	1796:131
Garnett, Muscoe, dec., by John T. Brooke & Cary Selden	Executors	12 FEB 1803	1796:133
Garnett, Muscoe, c/o Muscoe to brother James M. Garnett	Account	21 NOV 1814	1811:070
Garnett, Nancy, c/o Austin to Joseph Jones Monroe	Bond	22 APR 1800	1796:057
Garnett, Nancy M., c/o Austin to Robert Hill	Bond	15 NOV 1813	1811:048
Garnett, Nancy M., c/o Austin, by Theodk. Noel	Account	21 JUN 1814	1811:062
Garnett, Nancy, c/o Austin, by Joseph Jones Monroe	Settlement	17 MAR 1818	1811:147
Garnett, Richard P., c/o James T. to Sarah A. Garnett	Bond	18 APR 1859	1857:139
Garnett, Robert S., c/o William W., by William Wright	Account	19 FEB 1844	1838:305
Garnett, Robt. S., c/o Muscoe to James M. Garnett	Bond	18 APR 1803	1796:131
Garnett, Robt. S., c/o Muscoe to brother James M. Garnett	Account	21 NOV 1814	1811:070
Garnett, Rosa D., c/o William F.G. to William C. Garnett	Bond	21 OCT 1878	1867:385
Garnett, Rosa D., by William C. Garnett	Account	20 SEP 1880	1867:428
Garnett, Rosa D., by William C. Garnett	Account	22 NOV 1881	1867:460
Garnett, Sarah, c/o William to Muscoe Garnett	Bond	19 NOV 1759	1731:246
Garnett, Thomas, c/o Thomas to Richard Noell	Bond	20 JUN 1758	1731:227
Garnett, Wm., c/o Muscoe to James M. Garnett	Bond	18 APR 1803	1796:131
Garnett, Wm., c/o Muscoe to brother James M. Garnett	Account	21 NOV 1814	1811:070
Garrett, Elizabeth Jane, c/o John G. to Thomas Durham, Jr.	Bond	17 MAR 1856	1851:338
Garrett, Elizabeth, by Thomas M. Durham	Account	18 JAN 1864	1857:302
Garrett, Richard H., c/o William to Clara Garrett	Bond	21 NOV 1825	1825:068
Garrett, Richard H., from Mrs. Clara Garrett	Receipt	21 JUL 1828	1825:238
Garrett, Robert S., c/o William W. to William Wright	Bond	17 DEC 1832	1831:155
Garrett, Silas S., c/o William to Clara Garrett	Bond	21 NOV 1825	1825:068
Garrett, William Ryburn, c/o John G. to Thomas Durham, Jr.	Bond	17 MAR 1856	1851:338
Garrett, William, by Thomas M. Durham	Account	18 JAN 1864	1857:302
Gatewood, Amey, d/o James, by James Gatewood	Account	16 AUG 1748	1731:121
Gatewood, Amy to James Gatewood	Bond	20 NOV 1745	WB7:402
Gatewood, Amy, c/o William to Hannah Gatewood	Bond	18 JAN 1758	1731:216

Ward or Subject (and Parent, Guardian or Other)	Record Type	Date	Reference(s)
Gatewood, Ann to James Gatewood	Bond	20 NOV 1745	WB7:402
Gatewood, Ann, d/o James, by James Gatewood	Account	16 AUG 1748	1731:123
Gatewood, Ann, by William Gatewood	Account	18 OCT 1773	1761:106
Gatewood, Ann, by William Gatewood	Account	17 JUL 1775	1761:123
Gatewood, Ann L., c/o Lewis, by George Richards	Account	15 OCT 1787	1761:157
Gatewood, Ann, c/o Lewis, by George Richards	Account	16 JUN 1788	1761:158
Gatewood, Ann L., c/o Lewis, by Thomas & Ann Sears	Account	17 OCT 1796	1761:228
Gatewood, Ann L., c./o Lewis, by Thomas & Ann Sears	Account	15 JUN 1801	1796:091
Gatewood, Ann R., from Laneus C. Gatewood	Receipt	17 JUL 1826	1825:117
Gatewood, Anthony, c/o William to Hannah Gatewood	Bond	18 JAN 1758	1731:216
Gatewood, Benjamin to James Gatewood	Bond	20 NOV 1745	WB7:402
Gatewood, Benjamin, s/o James, by James Gatewood	Account	16 AUG 1748	1731:120
Gatewood, Bennett, c/o Joseph to Reuben Garnett	Bond	15 DEC 1794	1761:207
Gatewood, Caleb, c/o William to Hannah Gatewood	Bond	18 JAN 1758	1731:216
Gatewood, Cordelia, c/o Thomas to Thomas M. Henley	Bond	19 JAN 1829	1825:266
Gatewood, Edmond, c/o Joseph to Reuben Garnett	Bond	16 DEC 1793	1761:210
Gatewood, Edmund, c/o Joseph to Robert Park	Bond	20 JAN 1794	1761:199a crossed
Gatewood, Elizabeth to John Hunt	Bond	18 MAR 1745/6	WB7:424
Gatewood, Elizabeth, by William Gatewood	Account	18 OCT 1773	1761:101
Gatewood, Ellen A., c/o Traverse to Ann Gatewood	Bond	16 NOV 1835	1831:343
Gatewood, Ellen Ann Eliz., c/o Traverse to Orville Jeffries	Bond	19 MAY 1845	1844:032
Gatewood, Elton A., by Orville Jeffries	Account	16 OCT 1848	1844:291
Gatewood, Elton A., by Orville Jeffries	Account	21 FEB 1848	1844:258
Gatewood, Henry, c/o Thomas to Thomas M. Henley	Bond	17 APR 1826	1825:098
Gatewood, Henry S., by Thomas M. Henley	Account	18 MAY 1835	1831:291
Gatewood, James to James Gatewood	Bond	20 NOV 1745	WB7:402
Gatewood, James, Jr., s/o James, by James Gatewood	Account	16 AUG 1748	1731:119
Gatewood, James, c/o William to William Gatewood	Bond	18 JAN 1758	1731:217
Gatewood, John, c/o Joseph to Reuben Garnett	Bond	16 DEC 1793	1761:210
Gatewood, John, c/o Joseph to Robert Park	Bond	20 JAN 1794	1761:199a crossed
Gatewood, John H., by John Clarkson	Account	19 JUN 1826	1825:112
Gatewood, John H., by John Clarkson	Account	15 DEC 1828	1825:263
Gatewood, John H., from John Clarkson	Receipt	16 MAR 1835	1831:286
Gatewood, John F., c/o Traverse to Ann Gatewood	Bond	16 NOV 1835	1831:343
Gatewood, John F., c/o Travis to Richard F. Gatewood	Bond	15 DEC 1845	1844:087
Gatewood, John T., by Richard F. Gatewood	Account	17 JAN 1848	1844:252
Gatewood, John F., by R.F. Gatewood	Account	18 MAR 1850	1844:417
Gatewood, Joseph, c/o Joseph to Reuben Garnett	Bond	16 DEC 1793	1761:210
Gatewood, Joseph, c/o Joseph to Robert Park	Bond	20 JAN 1794	1761:199a crossed
Gatewood, Julia Rebecca, c/o Traverse to Orville Jeffries	Bond	19 MAY 1845	1844:032
Gatewood, Juliet R., by Orville Jeffries	Account	21 FEB 1848	1844:260
Gatewood, Juliet R., by Orville Jeffries	Account	16 OCT 1848	1844:293
Gatewood, Juliet R., by Orville Jeffries	Account	20 JAN 1851	1844:499
Gatewood, Juliet R., by Orville Jeffries	Account	19 SEP 1853	1851:198
Gatewood, Juliett R., c/o Traverse to Ann Gatewood	Bond	16 NOV 1835	1831:343
Gatewood, Katharine, c/o Richard to Richard Tyler	Bond	21 JUL 1760	1731:256
Gatewood, Leonard, c/o Joseph to Reuben Garnett	Bond	16 DEC 1793	1761:210
Gatewood, Leonard, c/o Joseph to Robert Park	Bond	20 JAN 1794	1761:199a crossed
Gatewood, Lucy, c/o William to Hannah Gatewood	Bond	18 JAN 1758	1731:216
Gatewood, Lucy, c/o Caleb to John Burke	Bond	21 SEP 1801	1796:098
Gatewood, Mary M., c/o Traverse to Ann Gatewood	Bond	16 NOV 1835	1831:343

Ward or Subject (and Parent, Guardian or Other)	Record Type	Date	Reference(s)
Gatewood, Mary Elton, by Benjamin Blake	Account	18 MAR 1850	1844:419
Gatewood, Matilda Barker, c/o Richd. to Agnes West Gatewood	Bond	19 JUN 1797	1796:007
Gatewood, Matilda B., c/o Richd., by Agnes W. Gatewood	Account	21 JUN 1802	1796:118
Gatewood, Nancy Lewis, c/o Lewis, by Geo. Richards	Account	19 JUN 1786	1761:150
Gatewood, Nancy Lewis, c/o Lewis, by T. & A. Seayres	Bond	15 SEP 1794	1761:204
Gatewood, Patty, c/o William to Hannah Gatewood	Bond	18 JAN 1758	1731:216
Gatewood, Philip, c/o Lewis, by George Richards	Account	19 JUN 1786	1761:150
Gatewood, Philip, c/o Lewis, by George Richards	Account	15 OCT 1787	1761:157
Gatewood, Philip, c/o Lewis, by George Richards	Account	16 JUN 1788	1761:158
Gatewood, Philip, c/o Lewis by Thos. & Ann Seayres	Bond	15 SEP 1794	1761:203
Gatewood, Philip, c/o Lewis, by Thomas & Ann Sears	Account	17 OCT 1796	1761:228
Gatewood, Richard F., c/o Traverse to Ann Gatewood	Bond	16 NOV 1835	1831:343
Gatewood, Robert W., c/o Robert to Joseph J. Gouldman	Bond	16 MAR 1857	1851:416
Gatewood, Ryburn M., c/o Traverse to Ann Gatewood	Bond	16 NOV 1835	1831:343
Gatewood, Sarah to Joseph Burnett	Bond	15 OCT 1745	WB7:379
Gatewood, Susan, c/o Philip P. to Lineus C. Gatewood	Bond	17 JUN 1839	1838:058
Gatewood, Susan P., c/o Philip P. to Thomas N. Clarke	Bond	19 SEP 1842	1838:229
Gatewood, Susan P., by L.C. Gatewood	Account	20 FEB 1843	1838:242
Gatewood, Thomas, c/o William to William Gatewood	Bond	18 JAN 1758	1731:217
Gatewood, Thomas, from Philip P. Gatewood	Receipt	15 MAY 1826	1825:104
Gatewood, Thomas O., c/o Traverse to Ann Gatewood	Bond	16 NOV 1835	1831:343
Gatewood, William, by Richard Allen	Account	18 JUL 1791	1761:172
Gibson, Fleming, c/o John to William Deshazo	Bond	21 FEB 1815	1811:078
Gibson, Horace, c/o John to William Deshazo	Bond	21 FEB 1815	1811:078
Gibson, John H., c/o John to Thomas Pilcher	Bond	16 OCT 1820	1811:237
Gibson, John H., from Thomas Pilcher	Receipt	21 NOV 1826	1825:124
Gibson, John H., by Thomas Pilcher	Account	21 NOV 1826	1825:123
Goar, John to Timothy Driscoll	Bond	10 APR 1710	D&W13:308
Goode, John, c/o James to Larkin Hundley	Bond	18 JAN 1841	1838:132
Goode, Richard, c/o Elizabeth to John Conoley	Bond	19 FEB 1827	1825:152
Goode, Thomas, c/o Edward, by Thomas Goode	Account	15 OCT 1751	1731:137
Gordon, Alexander, c/o Alexander to Susanna Gordon	Bond	20 MAR 1815	1811:080
Gordon, Alexander, by Susanna Gordon	Account	21 FEB 1826	1825:080
Gordon, Alexander, from his mother Susanna Gordon	Receipt	19 MAY 1828	1825:236
Gordon, Alfred Beale, c/o Vincent to Elizabeth Gordon	Bond	21 OCT 1816	1811:123
Gordon, Alfred B., young negro of, named Allen, in March	Death	17 APR 1826	1825:095
Gordon, Alfred B., by Philip Montague	Account	17 APR 1826	1825:096
Gordon, Alfred B., by Philip Montague	Account	19 MAR 1827	1825:156
Gordon, Arthur, c/o Thomas to Lucy C. Gordon	Bond	16 JUN 1828	1825:236
Gordon, Arthur Gabriel, c/o Thomas to Thomas Marlow	Bond	21 MAR 1833	1831:169
Gordon, Arthur G., by Thomas Marlow	Account	18 MAY 1835	1831:306
Gordon, Arthur G., by Thomas Marlow	Account	18 SEP 1837	1831:496
Gordon, Fanny, under 14, c/o Vincent to Leroy R. Taylor	Bond	20 AUG 1866	1857:409
Gordon, Horace, c/o Thomas to Lucy C. Gordon	Bond	16 JUN 1828	1825:236
Gordon, Horace, c/o Thomas to John P. Shackelford	Bond	18 MAY 1835	1831:292
Gordon, Horace, by John P. Shackelford	Account	15 DEC 1845	1844:078
Gordon, Horace, by John P. Shackelford	Account	15 DEC 1845	1844:080
Gordon, Isham, c/o Alexander to Susanna Gordon	Bond	20 MAR 1815	1811:080
Gordon, Isham, from Mrs. Susannah Gordon	Receipt	19 SEP 1825	1825:013
Gordon, John, c/o Alexander to Purkins Armstrong	Bond	21 FEB 1815	1811:079
Gordon, John, from Purkins Armstrong	Receipt	17 OCT 1825	1825:058

Ward or Subject (and Parent, Guardian or Other)	Record Type	Date	Reference(s)
Gordon, Lucy, c/o Alexander to Susanna Gordon	Bond	20 MAR 1815	1811:080
Gordon, Mary, c/o Alexr. to Purkins Armstrong	Bond	21 DEC 1813	1811:052
Gordon, Matilda Roy, c/o Vincent to Elizabeth Gordon	Bond	21 OCT 1816	1811:123
Gordon, Peggy, Mrs., by William Dunn	Account	18 OCT 1779	1761:141
Gordon, Peggy, c/o William, by Thomas Gordon	Account	18 OCT 1784	WB13:447
Gordon, Rebecca, c/o Gabriel to Gregory Dennett	Bond	20 SEP 1819	1811:193
Gordon, Robert, c/o Vincent to Philip Montague	Bond	21 NOV 1825	1825:067
Gordon, Robert, by Thomas Boughan	Account	21 FEB 1826	1825:081
Gordon, Robert W.S., by Philip Montague	Negroes	21 FEB 1826	1825:084
Gordon, Robert, by Philip Montague	Account	19 MAR 1827	1825:157
Gordon, Robert W.S., by Philip Montague	Account	17 MAR 1828	1825:228
Gordon, Robert S., by Philip Montague	Account	16 FEB 1829	1825:275
Gordon, Robert W.S., by Philip Montague	Account	18 APR 1831	1831:031
Gordon, Robt. Wm. Smith, c/o Vincent to Elizabeth Gordon	Bond	21 OCT 1816	1811:123
Gordon, Thomas C.	Receipt	19 NOV 1828	1825:260
Gordon, Vincent G., c/o George to his father	Bond	19 FEB 1838	1838:020
Gordon, Vincent, c/o George to William B.B. Seward	Bond	18 MAY 1840	1838:080
Gordon, Vincent, c/o George to Muscoe Garnett	Bond	17 JUL 1843	1838:293
Gordon, Vincent, by Muscoe Garnett	Account	18 DEC 1848	1844:314
Gordon, Vincent, by Muscoe Garnett	Account	21 APR 1851	1844:513
Gordon, Vincent, by Muscoe Garnett	Account	16 MAR 1857	1851:413
Goss, Edith G. late Garnett, by William C. Garnett	Account	20 NOV 1882	1867:540
Gouddy, Phebe, c/o Sarah to John Weyman	Bond	15 OCT 1792	1761:186
Goudy, Louisa, over 14, c/o Edmund Goudy to Elzer Fogg	Bond	17 MAR 1856	1851:339
Goudy, Louisa, by Elzer Fogg	Account	19 JUL 1858	1857:099
Goudy, Phebe, c/o Sally to Theodrick Noel	Bond	21 DEC 1795	1761:219
Goudy, Thomas, c/o Sally to Theodrick Noel	Bond	21 DEC 1795	1761:219
Goudy, Thomas, by Theodorick Noel	Account	17 SEP 1798	1796:032
Goudy, Thomas, s/o Sally to Nicholas Faulconer	Bond	16 JUN 1800	1796:061
Goudy, Thomas, by Theodk. Noel	Account	15 SEP 1800	1796:069
Goudy, Thomas, by Nicholas Faulconer	Account	15 FEB 1802	1796:115
Goulden, John M., c/o Dr. J.M. to Eliza J. Wright	Bond	21 DEC 1887	1867:594
Gouldman, Albert Payne, c/o Jesse to Happy Gouldman	Bond	21 MAY 1838	1838:025
Gouldman, Alma, above 14, c/o Joseph J. to H.H. Robinson	Bond	21 DEC 1874	1867:288
Gouldman, Betsey, c/o Thomas to Phoebe Gouldman	Bond	21 OCT 1816	1811:121
Gouldman, Catharine P., c/o Thomas, by Phebe Gouldman	Account	17 OCT 1825	1825:043
Gouldman, Catharine P., from mother Phebe Gouldman	Receipt	17 OCT 1825	1825:045
Gouldman, Caty, c/o Thomas to Phoebe Gouldman	Bond	21 OCT 1816	1811:121
Gouldman, Dallas, over 14, c/o Fendal to Lucy B. Gouldman	Bond	19 MAR 1860	1857:201
Gouldman, Francis & Thomas, by Thomas Waring	Account	19 SEP 1721	WB3:276
Gouldman, Francis & Thomas, by Thomas Waring	Account	21 AUG 1722	WB3:312
Gouldman, Henry B., c/o Jesse to Happy Gouldman	Bond	21 MAY 1838	1838:025
Gouldman, John, c/o Thomas to Phoebe Gouldman	Bond	21 OCT 1816	1811:121
Gouldman, Joseph Jesse, c/o Jesse to Happy Gouldman	Bond	21 MAY 1838	1838:025
Gouldman, Margarett, by McKenzie Gouldman	Account	18 APR 1842	1838:184
Gouldman, Nancy, c/o Thomas to Phoebe Gouldman	Bond	21 OCT 1816	1811:121
Gouldman, Nancy, c/o Thomas, by Phebe Gouldman	Account	17 OCT 1825	1825:043
Gouldman, Nancy, from Phebe Gouldman	Receipt	17 OCT 1825	1825:045
Gouldman, Phoebe, c/o Thomas to Phoebe Gouldman	Bond	21 OCT 1816	1811:121
Gouldman, Polly, c/o Thomas to Phoebe Gouldman	Bond	21 OCT 1816	1811:121
Gouldman, Polly, c/o Thomas, by Phebe Gouldman	Account	17 OCT 1825	1825:042

Ward or Subject (and Parent, Guardian or Other)	Record Type	Date	Reference(s)
Gouldman, Polly, from Phebe Gouldman	Receipt	17 OCT 1825	1825:046
Gouldman, Richard, c/o Thomas to Phoebe Gouldman	Bond	21 OCT 1816	1811:121
Gouldman, Richard, c/o Thomas, by Phebe Gouldman	Account	17 OCT 1825	1825:044
Gouldman, Richard, from Phebe Gouldman	Receipt	17 OCT 1825	1825:046
Gouldman, Robert, c/o Thomas to Phoebe Gouldman	Bond	21 OCT 1816	1811:121
Gouldman, Robert, c/o Thomas, by Phebe Gouldman	Account	17 OCT 1825	1825:042
Gouldman, Robert, from mother Phebe Gouldman	Receipt	17 OCT 1825	1825:045
Gouldman, Roland R.R., c/o Joseph J., to Henry H. Robinson	Bond	21 DEC 1874	1867:288
Gouldman, Sally, c/o Thomas to Phoebe Gouldman	Bond	21 OCT 1816	1811:121
Gouldman, Susan, c/o Thomas to Phoebe Gouldman	Bond	21 OCT 1816	1811:121
Gouldman, Virginia A., c/o Jesse to Happy Gouldman	Bond	21 MAY 1838	1838:025
Gowdy, Thomas, c/o Sally to Theodk. Noel	Bond	16 SEP 1799	1796:047
Gowdy, Thomas, by Theodk. Noel	Account	16 SEP 1799	1796:048
Gowdy, Thomas H., from, Nicholas Faulconer	Receipt	16 JUN 1806	1796:176
Grafton, Sally, c/o Jno. to William Shelton, Junr.	Bond	15 FEB 1802	1796:114
Graham, John to John Meggs	Bond	19 DEC 1732	WB5:116
Graham, John to John Powel Rein	Bond	19 SEP 1732	WB5:101
Graves, Nancy, c/o Thomas to Thomas Coleman	Bond	17 OCT 1796	1761:227
Gray, Ann, c/o William to Philip Gray	Bond	20 DEC 1802	1796:121
Gray, Birkett, from Barbee Spindle	Receipt	19 SEP 1825	1825:016
Gray, Burkett, c/o Philip to Barbee Spindle	Bond	21 JUL 1806	1796:183
Gray, Catharine W., c/o Thomas B.W. to Robert Weir	Bond	17 MAR 1829	1825:278
Gray, Elizabeth Wormley, c/o William to Philip Gray	Bond	20 DEC 1802	1796:121
Gray, Elizabeth late Hawkins, by John Miller	Account	23 MAY 1810	1796:234
Gray, George, c/o William to Susan W. Gray	Bond	16 MAR 1846	1844:097
Gray, Jane, c/o William to Susan W. Gray	Bond	16 MAR 1846	1844:097
Gray, Lucy, c/o William to Thomas B.W. Gray	Bond	21 JAN 1811	1796:242
Gray, Lucy, c/o William to Susan W. Gray	Bond	16 MAR 1846	1844:097
Gray, Maria, c/o William to Philip Gray	Bond	20 DEC 1802	1796:121
Gray, Martha, c/o Philip to Barbee Spindle	Bond	21 JUL 1806	1796:181
Gray, Mary Ann, c/o William to Philip Gray	Bond	20 DEC 1802	1796:121
Gray, Mary, c/o Philip to Barbee Spindle	Bond	21 JUL 1806	1796:181
Gray, Mary, c/o William to Susan W. Gray	Bond	16 MAR 1846	1844:097
Gray, Mary Susan, c/o Lemuel to James Buniff	Bond	17 FEB 1879	1867:404
Gray, Mary Susan, age 17, to James Buniff	Certificate	17 FEB 1879	1867:404
Gray, Obed, c/o Obed to Joseph Taylor	Bond	18 DEC 1815	1811:111
Gray, Obed, from Joseph Taylor	Receipt	19 SEP 1825	1825:025
Gray, Philip, c/o William to Susan W. Gray	Bond	16 MAR 1846	1844:097
Gray, William Mark, c/o William to Philip Gray	Bond	20 DEC 1802	1796:121
Gray, William, c/o Philip to Mordecai Spindle	Bond	15 SEP 1806	1796:185
Gray, William, dec. of Petersburg, dec., by Philip Gray	Account	16 APR 1810	1796:227
Gray, William, from Mordecai Spindle	Receipt	19 SEP 1825	1825:015
Gray, William, dec., three tracts: *Hawkins, Thomas', Fishers'*	Bond	17 AUG 1846	1844:173
Green, George to Robert Harrison	Bond	21 AUG 1716	D&W14:636
Green, George, c/o Richard to Thomas L. Oneale	Bond	20 APR 1818	1811:151
Green, George, from Thomas L. Oneale	Receipt	19 SEP 1825	1825:024
Green, Lucy, c/o James to Danl. Gouldman	Bond	20 JAN 1817	1811:131
Green, Mary E., c/o Richard to Spencer Harrison	Bond	15 JUN 1812	1811:011
Green, Thomas P., c/o Richard to Spencer Harrison	Bond	15 JUN 1812	1811:011
Greenfield Estate, The, by Frances Brockenbrough	Account	18 APR 1864	1857:328
Greenhill, Angelinah to John Allen	Bond	19 NOV 1751	1731:140

Ward or Subject (and Parent, Guardian or Other)	Record Type	Date	Reference(s)
Greenhill, Elizabeth to John Allen	Bond	19 NOV 1751	1731:140
Greenhill, Joseph to John Allen	Bond	19 NOV 1751	1731:140
Greenwood, Benjamin, from Amos Cauthorn	Receipt	17 OCT 1825	1825:041
Greenwood, Eliza, c/o James to Richard H. Street	Bond	17 NOV 1828	1825:255
Greenwood, Isaac, c/o Isaac to Martha Crow	Bond	18 AUG 1828	1825:240
Greenwood, Isaac, by William Crow	Account	15 JUN 1829	1825:297
Greenwood, Mary Ellen, c/o Thomas to Benjamin Blake	Bond	16 MAR 1846	1844:098
Greenwood, Mary E., c/o Thomas to Richard F.T. Cauthorn	Bond	18 JUN 1849	1844:382
Greenwood, Mary Elton, by Richard F.T. Cauthorn	Account	16 DEC 1850	1844:485
Greenwood, Mary Ellen, by Richard F.T. Cauthorn	Account	17 NOV 1851	1851:025
Greenwood, Nancy W., c/o Thomas to Benjamin Blake	Bond	16 MAR 1846	1844:098
Greenwood, Susan Eliz., c/o James H. to Alfred C. Greenwood	Bond	15 DEC 1856	1851:398
Gregory, John to William Bourne	Bond	12 DEC 1712	D&W14:093
Gregory, Sarah to William Bourne	Bond	12 DEC 1712	D&W14:093
Gresham, Evelyn Dew, c/o Dr. Henry to Laura M. Gresham	Bond	17 SEP 1883	1867:525
Gresham, Genevieve, c/o Dr. Henry to Laura M. Gresham	Bond	17 SEP 1883	1867:525
Gresham, Laura Howard, c/o Dr. Henry to Laura M. Gresham	Bond	17 SEP 1883	1867:525
Gresham, Thomas to Simon Minor	Bond	21 MAR 1731/2	WB5:075
Griffin, Elizabeth to John Holder	Bond	18 APR 1744	WB7:143
Griffing, Betty, Miss, by John Holder	Account	17 SEP 1745	1731:087
Griffing, Betty, Miss, h/o Mary Griffing, by John Holder	Account	21 OCT 1746	1731:099
Griffing, Betty Miss, by John Holder	Account	15 SEP 1747	1731:108
Griffing, Betty, by John Holder	Account	15 NOV 1748	1731:126
Griffing, James to William Roane	Bond	17 NOV 1742	WB6:408
Griffing, James, by William Roane, Gent.	Account	18 SEP 1744	1731:074
Griffing, James, by William Roane, Gent.	Account	20 NOV 1745	1731:088
Griffing, James, by William Roane, Gent.	Account	21 OCT 1746	1731:102
Griffing, James, by William Roane, Gent.	Account	16 MAR 1747/8	1731:114
Griffing, James, orphan of James	Account	19 JUL 1768	WB12:302
Griffing, James, by Griffing Boughan	Account	16 MAY 1774	1761:112
Griffing, Margaret to John Upshaw	Bond	22 MAR 1748/9	WB8:209
Griffith, John R., c/o Richard to William Watts	Bond	19 JUN 1837	1831:476
Griffith, Joseph R., c/o Richard to William Watts	Bond	20 NOV 1837	1831:504
Griggs, Anderson, c/o Philip to James Croxton, Jr.	Bond	17 JUN 1816	1811:117
Griggs, Anderson, from James Croxton, Jr.	Receipt	19 SEP 1825	1825:010
Griggs, Dolly, c/o Philip to James Croxton, Jr.	Bond	17 JUN 1816	1811:117
Griggs, Dorothy, from James Croxton, Jr.	Receipt	19 SEP 1825	1825:010
Griggs, Fanny, c/o Philip to James Croxton, Jr.	Bond	17 JUN 1816	1811:117
Griggs, Fanny, from James Croxton, Jr.	Receipt	19 SEP 1825	1825:009
Griggs, Lucy, c/o Jesse to Thomas Harper	Bond	17 SEP 1827	1825:176
Griggs, Wesley, from James Croxton	Receipt	19 SEP 1825	1825:009
Griggs, Westley, c/o Philip to James Croxton, Jr.	Bond	17 JUN 1816	1811:117
Grigsby, Larkin, c/o Polly to Lewis Fisher	Bond	21 DEC 1818	1811:167
Guess, Austin, above 14, c/o Howard to Robert Harmon	Bond	16 FEB 1874	1867:228
Guess, James O., c/o Howard to Lucy A. Greenwood	Bond	18 OCT 1869	1867:106
Guess, Oscar, by Robert Harmon	Account	16 SEP 1878	1867:391
Guess, Robert H., c/o Howard to Lucy A. Greenwood	Bond	18 OCT 1869	1867:106
Guess, Robert, above 14, c/o Howard to Robert Harmon	Bond	16 FEB 1874	1867:228
Guess, Robert, by Robert Harmon	Account	16 SEP 1878	1867:391

Ward or Subject (and Parent, Guardian or Other)	Record Type	Date	Reference(s)
H			
Haile, Benjamin B., by Robert G. Haile	Account	19 MAY 1834	1831:258
Haile, Benjamin B., by Robert G. Haile	Account	19 JUN 1837	1831:486
Haile, Benjamin B., from Robert G. Haile	Receipt	20 JAN 1840	1838:068
Haile, Benjamin B., by Robert G. Haile	Account	20 JAN 1840	1838:066
Haile, Bettie B., under 14, c/o Robert G., Jr. to John D. Hutchinson	Bond	19 OCT 1863	1857:301
Haile, Bettie B., by John D. Hutchinson	Account	17 JUN 1867	1857:430
Haile, Bettie B., by John D. Hutchinson	Account	19 AUG 1882	1867:497
Haile, Bettie B., by John D. Hutchinson	Account	15 SEP 1884	1867:553
Haile, Bettie B., from John D. Hutchinson	Receipt	15 SEP 1884	1867:554
Haile, Betty B., by John D. Hutchinson	Account	21 AUG 1871	1867:160-171
Haile, Catharine E., c/o John to Robert G. Haile	Bond	19 OCT 1829	1825:312
Haile, Emily A., c/o Robert G. to her father	Bond	16 FEB 1818	1811:145
Haile, Emily A., c/o Robert G., by her father, 29 acres land	Account	19 SEP 1825	1825:026
Haile, Emily A. now Whitlocke, by Robert G. Haile	Account	15 FEB 1836	1831:404
Haile, Emma, under 14, c/o Robert G., Jr. to John D. Hutchinson	Bond	19 OCT 1863	1857:301
Haile, John to Peter Harwood	Bond	10 APR 1708	D&W13:098
Haile, Lucy E., by John D. Hutchinson	Account	17 JUN 1867	1857:430
Haile, Lucy E., by John D. Hutchinson	Account	21 AUG 1871	1867:160-171
Haile, Lucy E., by John D. Hutchinson	Account	18 AUG 1873	1867:214
Haile, Lucy E., by John D. Hutchinson	Account	20 DEC 1875	1867:329-345
Haile, Lucy E., c/o John D. Hutchinson	Account	19 FEB 1877	1867:365
Haile, Lucy E., by John D. Hutchinson	Account	20 JAN 1879	1867:399
Haile, Lucy E., by John D. Hutchinson	Account	16 JUN 1879	1867:407
Haile, Lucy E., by John D. Hutchinson	Account	15 SEP 1884	1867:545, 548, 556
Haile, Lucy Emma, from John D. Hutchinson	Receipt	15 SEP 1884	1867:551
Haile, Mary C., c/o Robert G. to her father	Bond	16 FEB 1818	1811:145
Haile, Mary C., c/o Robert G., by her father, 20 acres land	Account	19 SEP 1825	1825:026
Haile, Mary C. now Barnes, by father Robert G. Haile	Account	16 FEB 1829	1825:277
Haile, Robert A., by Robert G. Haile	Account	19 MAY 1834	1831:254
Haile, Robert A., by Robert G. Haile	Account	17 JUL 1837	1831:490
Haile, Robert A., by Robert G. Haile	Account	18 MAR 1839	1838:048
Haile, Robert G., Jr., for M.S. Burke, from T.M. Burke	Receipt	15 DEC 1856	1851:397
Haile, Susan, under 14, c/o Robert G., Jr. to John D. Hutchinson	Bond	19 OCT 1863	1857:301
Haile, Susan B., by John D. Hutchinson	Account	17 JUN 1867	1857:430
Haile, Susan B., by John D. Hutchinson	Account	21 AUG 1871	1867:160-171
Haile, Susan B. and Betty B., by John D. Hutchinson	Account	18 AUG 1873	1867:215
Haile, Susan B. and Bettie B., by John D. Hutchinson	Account	20 DEC 1875	1867:330-345
Haile, Susan B. and Bettie B., by John D. Hutchinson	Account	19 FEB 1877	1867:366
Haile, Susan B. & Bettie B., by John D. Hutchinson	Account	16 JUN 1879	1867:408
Haile, Susan B. & Bettie B., by John D. Hutchinson	Account	20 JAN 1879	1867:402
Haile, Susan & Bettie, by John D. Hutchinson	Account	21 JUN 1881	1867:449
Haile, Susan B., from John D. Hutchinson	Receipt	15 SEP 1884	1867:550
Haile, Susan B. and Bettie, by John D. Hutchinson	Account	15 SEP 1884	1867:546, 549, 557
Halbert, James, Jr. & wife Nancy Rennolds, from Andrew Rennolds	Receipt	19 SEP 1825	1825:018
Hardy, Agnes, c/o Conna to Susanna Gordon	Bond	17 JUN 1816	1811:116
Hardy, Agnes, legatee of Robert Gordon, by Susanna Gordon	Account	16 SEP 1817	1811:133
Hardy, Laura G., legatee of Robert Gordon, by Susanna Gordon	Account	16 SEP 1817	1811:133
Hardy, Lorinda, c/o Conna to Susanna Gordon	Bond	17 JUN 1816	1811:116
Harford, Henry A., c/o Henry to William J. Duff	Bond	15 FEB 1875	1867:294
Harford, Leland, c/o Henry to William J. Duff	Bond	15 FEB 1875	1867:294

Ward or Subject (and Parent, Guardian or Other)	Record Type	Date	Reference(s)
Harford, Myrtle H., c/o Henry to William J. Duff	Bond	15 FEB 1875	1867:294
Harford, Willie Ann, c/o Henry to William J. Duff	Bond	15 FEB 1875	1867:294
Harper, Ann Eliza, c/o Thomas to Francis G.W. Smith	Bond	17 JAN 1842	1838:170
Harper, Ann Eliza, c/o Thomas to Joseph T. Tompkins	Bond	20 MAY 1844	1838:319
Harper, Ann E., by Francis G.W. Smith	Account	17 JUN 1844	1838:354
Harper, Ann E., by Jos. T. Tompkins	Account	15 DEC 1845	1844:081
Harper, Ann E., by Jos. T. Tompkins	Account	16 APR 1849	1844:353
Harper, Ann Eliza, by Joseph T. Tompkins	Account	16 JUN 1851	1844:537
Harper, Ann Eliza, by Joseph T. Tompkins	Account	20 DEC 1852	1851:154
Harper, Ann E., by Joseph T. Tompkins	Account	16 JUN 1856	1851:345
Harper, Henry, c/o Thomas to William S. Croxton	Bond	17 JAN 1842	1838:169
Harper, Henry, by William S. Croxton	Account	15 MAY 1843	1838:250
Harper, Henry, by William S. Croxton	Account	21 JUL 1845	1844:044
Harper, Henry, by William S. Croxton	Account	19 FEB 1849	1844:328
Harper, James, c/o George to Thomas Harper	Bond	17 AUG 1835	1831:327
Harper, Laurence, by Wm. S. Croxton	Account	21 JUL 1845	1844:040
Harper, Laurence, from Capt. Wm. S. Croxton	Receipt	21 JUL 1845	1844:043
Harper, Lawrence, c/o Thomas to William S. Croxton	Bond	17 JAN 1842	1838:169
Harper, Lawrence, by William S. Croxton	Account	15 MAY 1843	1838:250
Harper, Richard Thos., over 14, c/o James H. to Wm. J. Clarkson	Bond	18 NOV 1861	1857:277
Harper, Susan, over 14, c/o James H. to Wm. J. Clarkson	Bond	18 NOV 1861	1857:277
Harrison, Sally late McCarty, by John Games	Report	19 SEP 1825	1825:020
Hart, Thomas, s/o William to William Hart	Bond	18 FEB 1799	1796:042
Hartz, Lewis, under 14, to George W. Johnson	Bond	15 MAR 1886	1867:570
Harvey, Mary, d/o John to John Harvey	Bond	20 JUN 1758	1731:226
Harwarr, Harwarr [sic] to Daniel Hornby	Bond	16 JUL 1728	WB4:268
Harwood, John Wm. Edmondson, c/o Wm. to Warner Harwood	Bond	20 OCT 1806	1796:186
Harwood, John Wm. Edmondson, c/o Wm. to James Montague	Bond	16 APR 1810	1796:228
Hawes, Betsey, c/o Samuel to William Hawes	Bond	17 JUL 1797	1796:008
Hawes, Burtin, c/o Samuel to William Hawes	Bond	17 APR 1797	1796:005
Hawes, Eliza., c/o Saml. to Thomas Gouldman	Bond	17 APR 1797	1796:004
Hawes, Elizabeth, c/o Samuel to Francis Gouldman, Jr.	Bond	16 JUN 1800	1796:058
Hawes, Elizabeth by William Hawes	Account	20 JUN 1808	1796:200
Hawes, Isaac, c/o John to William Hawes	Bond	16 JUL 1792	1761:182
Hawes, Spencer, c/o Samuel to William Hawes	Bond	17 JUL 1797	1796:008
Hawes, Spencer, c/o Saml. to Thomas Gouldman	Bond	17 APR 1797	1796:004
Hawes, Susanna, c/o Samuel to William Hawes	Bond	17 JUL 1797	1796:008
Hawes, Susanna, c/o Saml. to Thomas Gouldman	Bond	17 APR 1797	1796:004
Hawkins, Betty Mosely, c/o Thos. to John Rennolds	Bond	15 APR 1793	1761:193
Hawkins, Catharine, c/o Thomas to Thomas Pitts, Jr.	Bond	15 OCT 1798	1796:035
Hawkins, Catharine, by Thomas Pitts, Jr.	Inventory	18 FEB 1799	1796:056
Hawkins, Catharine, by Thomas Pitts, Jr.	Account	15 SEP 1800	1796:072
Hawkins, Caty Rennolds, c/o Thos. to John Rennolds	Bond	15 APR 1793	1761:193
Hawkins, Caty, by John Rennolds	Account	16 OCT 1797	1796:017
Hawkins, Elizabeth Mosely, c/o Thomas to John Miller	Bond	18 APR 1797	1796:006
Hawkins, Elizabeth, by John Rennolds	Account	16 OCT 1797	1796:017
Hawkins, Elizabeth now Gray, by John Miller	Account	23 MAY 1810	1796:234
Hawkins, Fanny, by Thomas Boulware	Account	18 DEC 1797	1796:020
Hawkins, John, c/o John to John Hord	Bond	18 JUL 1791	1761:172
Hawkins, Lucy to William Hawkins	Bond	17 MAY 1748	WB8:056
Hawkins, Mary to Joseph Rennolds	Bond	17 JAN 1726/7	WB4:198

Ward or Subject (and Parent, Guardian or Other)	Record Type	Date	Reference(s)
Hawkins, Mary, by Harry Beverley	Account	21 AUG 1728	WB4:270a
Hawkins, Mary, by Joseph Reynolds	Account	21 JUL 1731	1731:001
Hawkins, Mary to William Hawkins	Bond	17 MAY 1748	WB8:056
Hawkins, William, by Harry Beverley	Account	21 AUG 1728	WB4:271
Hawkins, William Mosely, c/o Thos. to John Rennolds	Bond	15 APR 1793	1761:193
Hawkins, William, by John Rennolds	Account	16 OCT 1797	1796:017
Hawkins, William, c/o Thomas to John Hawkins	Bond	15 OCT 1798	1796:037
Hawkins, Young to Ann Hawkins	Bond	21 JUL 1741	WB6:326
Hawkins, Young, by Ann Hawkins	Account	16 AUG 1743	1731:055
Haws, Burtin, c/o Samuel to Spencer Haws	Bond	20 JAN 1800	1796:052
Hayes, Rosa alias Webb, c/o John alias Webb to James Wright	Bond	21 SEP 1840	1838:106
Hayne, Elizabeth to Thomas Waring	Bond	20 SEP 1737	WB6:090
Haynes, John to Philemon Byrd	Bond	15 FEB 1736/7	WB6:045
Hazlewood, Ann to Robert Beverley	Bond	10 MAR 1707/8	D&W13:067
Henley, Ambrose, c/o Ambrose to Elizabeth Henley	Bond	18 DEC 1815	1811:106
Henley, Ann H., c/o Ambrose to Elizabeth Henley	Bond	18 DEC 1815	1811:106
Henley, Catherine, c/o Ambrose to Elizabeth Henley	Bond	18 DEC 1815	1811:106
Henley, John Thomas, c/o Ambrose to Elizabeth Henley	Bond	18 DEC 1815	1811:106
Henley, Mary R., c/o Ambrose to Elizabeth Henley	Bond	18 DEC 1815	1811:106
Henley, Ransom, c/o Ambrose to Elizabeth Henley	Bond	18 DEC 1815	1811:106
Henley, Sarah M., c/o Ambrose to Elizabeth Henley	Bond	18 DEC 1815	1811:106
Henley, Susan D., c/o Ambrose to Elizabeth Henley	Bond	18 DEC 1815	1811:106
Henley, Thomas M., from Edward Wright	Receipt	21 NOV 1831	1831:079
Henshall, Frances N. to Harrison Southworth	P. of Atty.	22 DEC 1887	1867:595
Henshaw, Charles Lee, c/o John to Thos. Pitts, Jr.	Bond	15 DEC 1794	1761:207
Hill, Anna, age 20, c/o Samuel to Samuel Robinson	Certificate	17 APR 1882	1867:486
Hill, Anna, over 14, c/o Samuel to Samuel Robinson	Bond	17 APR 1882	1867:487
Hill, Catharine, c/o William to John Beazley	Bond	16 OCT 1820	1811:236
Hill, Elizabeth, c/o Leonard to Richard Tunstall	Bond	16 MAY 1758	1731:224
Hill, Elizabeth, c/o Leonard	Account	15 MAY 1759	WB11:168
Hill, Elizabeth, c/o Humphrey, Sr. to Humphrey Hill	Bond	17 MAR 1828	1825:230
Hill, Katherine to Leonard Hill	Bond	16 FEB 1730/1	WB5:014
Hill, Leonard, by James Campbell	Account	18 SEP 1769	1761:069
Hill, Mary, c/o Leonard to Richard Tunstall	Bond	16 MAY 1758	1731:224
Hill, Mary, c/o Leonard	Account	15 MAY 1759	WB11:168
Hill, Polly, c/o Lewis to Benoni Broach	Bond	19 DEC 1825	1825:069
Hill, Susanna, c/o Wm. to Robt. Hill	Bond	16 FEB 1818	1811:146
Hinshaw, John to Samuel Hinshaw	Bond	17 MAR 1723/4	WB4:050
Hodges, Mary Eleanor, c/o Philip T. to her father	Bond	15 JAN 1838	1838:002
Hoomes, George L., c/o John W. to Augustine M. Braxton	Bond	16 NOV 1835	1831:346
Hoomes, George Landon, c/o John W. to Augustine Braxton	Bond	16 MAR 1840	1838:127
Hoomes, George L., c/o John W. to Thomas Haynes	Bond	21 DEC 1840	1838:131
Hoomes, George L., by Thomas Haynes	Account	17 MAY 1852	1851:058
Hoomes, John A., c/o John W. to Augustine M. Braxton	Bond	16 NOV 1835	1831:346
Hoomes, John Armistead, c/o John W. to Augustine Braxton	Bond	16 MAR 1840	1838:127
Hoomes, John A., c/o John W. to Thomas Haynes	Bond	21 DEC 1840	1838:131
Hoomes, Martha C., c/o John W. to Augustine M. Braxton	Bond	16 NOV 1835	1831:346
Hoomes, Martha Caroline, d/o John W. to Augustine Braxton	Bond	16 MAR 1840	1838:127
Hoomes, Martha W. [sic], c/o John W. to Thomas Haynes	Bond	21 DEC 1840	1838:131
Hoskins, Addie, c/o Richard L. to Robt. H. Waring	Bond	21 APR 1879	1867:406
Hoskins, Catherine Y. [Montague], by James Montague	Account	17 JUL 1820	1811:225

Ward or Subject (and Parent, Guardian or Other)	Record Type	Date	Reference(s)
Hoskins, Gabriella T., c/o R.C., by R.H. Waring	Account	17 OCT 1887	1867:588
Hoskins, James T., c/o George to Nathaniel I. Whitlocke	Bond	21 JUL 1851	1844:543
Hoskins, James T., c/o George to John T. Hoskins	Bond	18 JUL 1853	1851:185
Hoskins, James T., by John T. Hoskins	Account	20 JUL 1857	1851:442
Hoskins, Louisa W., c/o George to Nathaniel I. Whitlocke	Bond	21 JUL 1851	1844:543
Hoskins, Maggie Lawson, c/o Richard L. to Robt. H. Waring	Bond	21 APR 1879	1867:406
Hoskins, Maggie L., c/o R.C., by R.H. Waring	Account	17 OCT 1887	1867:588
Hoskins, Mary Gabriella, c/o Richard L. to Robt. H. Waring	Bond	21 APR 1879	1867:406
Hoskins, William R., c/o George to Nathaniel I. Whitlocke	Bond	21 JUL 1851	1844:543
House, Ella T., c/o Selah T. to her father	Bond	20 FEB 1871	1867:153
Houston, Jane, c/o Alexander to Robert Wright	Bond	17 AUG 1835	1831:326
Houston, Jane, c/o Alexander to William Wright	Bond	20 FEB 1837	1831:463
Houston, Jane, by Robert Wright	Account	15 NOV 1841	1838:158
Houston, Jane, by William Wright	Account	15 DEC 1841	1838:155
Houston, Mary, c/o Alexander to William Wright	Bond	20 FEB 1837	1831:463
Houston, Mary, by William Wright	Account	15 NOV 1841	1838:165
Houston, Mary, by Robert Wright	Account	15 NOV 1841	1838:164
Houston, Polly, c/o Alexander to Robert Wright	Bond	17 AUG 1835	1831:326
Houston, Sarah, c/o Alexander to Robert Wright	Bond	17 AUG 1835	1831:326
Houston, Thomas, c/o Alexander to Robert Wright	Bond	17 AUG 1835	1831:326
Houston, Thomas, c/o Alexander to William Wright	Bond	20 FEB 1837	1831:463
Houston, Thomas, by William Wright	Account	15 NOV 1841	1838:161
Houston, Thomas, by Robert Wright	Account	15 NOV 1841	1838:159
Howerton, Benjamin F., c/o William to Ann W. Howerton	Bond	19 MAY 1834	1831:267
Howerton, Benjamin F., infant, by Ann W. Howerton	Account	21 SEP 1840	1838:098
Howerton, Eleanor A., c/o William to Ann W. Howerton	Bond	19 MAY 1834	1831:267
Howerton, Elizabeth W., c/o Ambrose to Charles Howerton	Bond	19 OCT 1801	1796:104
Howerton, Harry c/o Ambrose to John St. John	Bond	15 FEB 1802	1796:116
Howerton, John, c/o Jno. to Lewis Booker	Bond	17 JAN 1814	1811:054
Howerton, John, c/o John to John St. John	Bond	19 JUN 1815	1811:083
Howerton, John, from John St. John	Receipt	19 SEP 1825	1825:014
Howerton, Martha Jane Coleman Lumpkin, c/o Jno. to William Howerton	Bond	17 JAN 1814	1811:053
Howerton, Martha J.C.L., c/o John to John Howerton	Bond	15 FEB 1819	1811:177
Howerton, Martha J.C.L., c/o John, by William Howerton	Account	15 FEB 1819	1811:182
Howerton, Martha J.C.L., c/o John to Richard Howerton	Bond	19 FEB 1827	1825:155
Howerton, Mary Ann, c/o Jno. to William Howerton	Bond	17 JAN 1814	1811:053
Howerton, Mary Ann, c/o John to Henry C. Howerton	Bond	16 NOV 1818	1811:164
Howerton, Mary Ann, c/o John, by Henry Howerton	Account	19 DEC 1825	1825:076
Howerton, Maryann, c/o John, by William Howerton	Account	15 FEB 1819	1811:184
Howerton, Patsey G., c/o Ambrose to Catharine Howerton	Bond	15 FEB 1802	1796:117
Howerton, Rachel, c/o Ambrose to Catharine Howerton	Bond	15 FEB 1802	1796:117
Howerton, Richard, c/o Jno. to William Howerton	Bond	17 JAN 1814	1811:053
Howerton, Richard, c/o John to Henry C. Howerton	Bond	16 NOV 1818	1811:164
Howerton, Richard, c/o John, by William Howerton	Account	15 FEB 1819	1811:179
Howerton, Richard, c/o John, by Henry Howerton	Account	19 DEC 1825	1825:076
Howerton, Robert G., c/o Ambrose to Catharine Howerton	Bond	15 FEB 1802	1796:117
Howerton, Robert G., c/o Ambrose to Robert G. Haile	Bond	17 SEP 1810	1796:233
Howerton, Robert G., by Robert G. Haile	Account	16 DEC 1817	1811:138
Howerton, Temple, c/o Jno. to Lewis Booker	Bond	17 JAN 1814	1811:054
Howerton, William, from John Howerton	Receipt	21 FEB 1820	1811:209
Howerton, William, from Henry C. Howerton	Receipt	21 FEB 1820	1811:208

Ward or Subject (and Parent, Guardian or Other)	Record Type	Date	Reference(s)
Howlett, Elizabeth, by Lewis Booker	Account	15 OCT 1798	1796:038
Hucklescott, Mary to Erasmus Allen	Bond	12 APR 1711	D&W13:402
Hundley, Alwin, over 14, c/o Thomas J. to Jack M. Hundley	Bond	21 FEB 1876	1867:348
Hundley, Alwyn, by Jack M. Hundley	Account	16 JUL 1877	1867:370
Hundley, Alwyn, by Jack M. Hundley	Account	20 JAN 1879	1867:396
Hundley, Alwyn, by Jack M. Hundley	Account	20 SEP 1880	1867:425
Hundley, Andrew, c/o Thomas to Elizabeth Hundley	Bond	17 JUL 1815	1811:085
Hundley, Andrew, by Elizabeth Hundley	Account	21 NOV 1820	1811:239
Hundley, Andrew, c/o Thomas to George M. Hundley	Bond	15 JAN 1821	1811:243a
Hundley, Andrew, from George M. Hundley	Receipt	19 SEP 1825	1825:012
Hundley, Austin, c/o Thomas to Elizabeth Hundley	Bond	17 JUL 1815	1811:085
Hundley, Edwin, c/o Thomas to Elizabeth Hundley	Bond	17 JUL 1815	1811:085
Hundley, Edwin, by Elizabeth Hundley	Account	21 NOV 1820	1811:240
Hundley, Edwin, c/o Thomas to Thomas Hundley	Bond	21 AUG 1820	1811:233
Hundley, Edwin, *Montagues*, from Thomas Hundley, Jr.	Receipt	19 SEP 1825	1825:013
Hundley, Edwin F., c/o Edwin to Virginia F. Hundley	Bond	21 FEB 1842	1838:180
Hundley, Edwin F., by Virginia F. Dunn	Account	17 JUN 1844	1838:352
Hundley, Edwin F., c/o Edwin, by Virginia F. Dunn	Account	20 JUL 1846	1844:168
Hundley, Edwin F., by Virginia F. Dunn	Account	18 DEC 1848	1844:310
Hundley, Edwin F., c/o Edwin to Thomas J. Hundley	Bond	18 JUN 1849	1844:381
Hundley, Edwin F., by Virginia F. Dunn, dec.	Account	21 JAN 1850	1844:402
Hundley, Edwin F., by Virginia F. Dunn	Account	18 MAR 1850	1844:415
Hundley, Edwin F., by Thomas J. Hundley	Account	16 JUN 1851	1844:533
Hundley, Edwin F., by Thomas J. Hundley	Account	21 JUN 1852	1851:114
Hundley, Edwin F., by Thomas J. Hundley	Account	19 SEP 1853	1851:206
Hundley, Edwin F., s/o Edwin to Christopher Newbill	Bond	18 SEP 1854	1851:263
Hundley, Edwin F., by Thomas J. Hundley	Account	21 AUG 1854	1851:261
Hundley, Edwin F., by Thomas J. Hundley	Account	16 APR 1855	1851:291
Hundley, Edwin F., by Christopher Newbill	Account	17 NOV 1856	1851:393
Hundley, Edwin F., by Christopher Newbill	Account	21 DEC 1857	1857:047
Hundley, Edwin F., by Christopher Newbill	Account	21 FEB 1859	1857:131
Hundley, Elijah, from Larkin Hundley, gdn. to Cath. Dyke	Receipt	02 NOV 1839	1838:090
Hundley, Elizabeth, c/o Thomas to Elizabeth Hundley	Bond	17 JUL 1815	1811:085
Hundley, Elizabeth to Lewis B. [sic] Birch	Certificate	16 DEC 1872	1867:187
Hundley, Elizabeth, c/o James B. to Lewis P. Birch	Bond	16 DEC 1872	1867:186
Hundley, Georgeana, by Lucy E. Covington	Account	19 APR 1875	1867:302
Hundley, Georgeanna, by Lucy E. Covington	Account	19 AUG 1867	1867:001, 002
Hundley, Georgeanna, by Lucy E. Covington	Account	16 MAR 1868	1867:028
Hundley, Georgeanna, by Lucy E. Covington	Account	19 SEP 1870	1867:124
Hundley, Georgeanna, by Lucy E. Covington	Account	20 MAR 1872	1867:179
Hundley, Georgianna, under 14, c/o George K. to Lucy E. Covington	Bond	19 MAR 1866	1857:379
Hundley, Gertrude L., c/o Thomas J. to Jack M. Hundley	Bond	21 FEB 1876	1867:348
Hundley, Gertrude L., by Jack M. Hundley	Account	16 JUL 1877	1867:371
Hundley, Gertrude L., by Jack M. Hundley	Account	20 JAN 1879	1867:397
Hundley, Gertrude L., by Jack Hundley	Account	20 SEP 1880	1867:423
Hundley, Gertrude L., by J.M. Hundley	Account	15 OCT 1883	1867:529
Hundley, Gertrude L., by Jack M. Hundley	Account	17 SEP 1883	1867:523
Hundley, Gertrude L., by J.M. Hundley	Account	20 APR 1885	1867:564
Hundley, Gertrude L., by Jack M. Hundley	Account	23 AUG 1886	1867:576
Hundley, Janet C., c/o Arthur J. to her father	Bond	21 FEB 1848	1844:256
Hundley, Laura, by James Dyke	Account	15 AUG 1836	1831:434

Ward or Subject (and Parent, Guardian or Other)	Record Type	Date	Reference(s)
Hundley, Louisa, c/o Daniel to James Dyke	Bond	16 DEC 1833	1831:240
Hundley, Mary Ann, c/o Edwin to Virginia F. Hundley	Bond	21 FEB 1842	1838:180
Hundley, Mary A., by Virginia F. Dunn	Account	17 JUN 1844	1838:350
Hundley, Mary A., c/o Edwin, by Virginia F. Dunn	Account	20 JUL 1846	1844:168
Hundley, Mary A., by Virginia F. Dunn	Account	18 DEC 1848	1844:312
Hundley, Mary A., c/o Edwin to John A. Jesse	Bond	16 JUL 1849	1844:383
Hundley, Mary A., by Virginia F. Dunn, dec.	Account	21 JAN 1850	1844:403
Hundley, Mary A., by John A. Jesse	Account	16 DEC 1850	1844:488
Hundley, Mary A., by Virginia F. Dunn	Account	18 MAR 1850	1844:415
Hundley, Mary A., by John A. Jesse	Account	15 SEP 1851	1851:002
Hundley, Mary A., by John A. Jesse	Account	15 MAR 1852	1851:050
Hundley, Nancy, c/o Thomas to Elizabeth Hundley	Bond	17 JUL 1815	1811:085
Hundley, Nancy, c/o Thomas to Charles G. Layton	Bond	21 AUG 1820	1811:232
Hundley, Nancy, by Elizabeth Hundley	Account	21 NOV 1820	1811:241
Hundley, Thomas & wife Frances Philips	Report	15 MAY 1826	1825:106
Hunley, Ambrose, infants of, to Elizabeth Hunley	Bond	25 OCT 1817	WB19:260
Hunley, Ambrose, by Elizabeth Hunley	Account	17 JUL 1826	1825:114
Hunley, Ann, c/o John to George P. Young	Bond	18 DEC 1809	1796:224
Hunley, Catharine C., by Elizabeth Hunley	Account	17 JUL 1826	1825:114
Hunley, Francis, c/o John to Benjamin Pace	Bond	20 JAN 1800	1796:052
Hunley, John H., by Elizabeth Hunley	Account	17 JUL 1826	1825:115
Hunley, Lucy, c/o John to George P. Young	Bond	18 DEC 1809	1796:224
Hunley, Richard Thomas, by Elizabeth Hunley	Account	17 JUL 1826	1825:115
Hunley, Sarah M., by Elizabeth Hunley	Account	17 JUL 1826	1825:116
Hunt, Eliza to Forest Upshaw	Bond	19 SEP 1749	WB8:277
Hunt, John to William Sthreshley	Bond	21 FEB 1748/9	WB8:183
Hunt, John, by Suca Sthreshley	Account	15 OCT 1751	1731:139
Hunt, Rachel to Forrest Upshaw	Bond	18 AUG 1752	1731:146
Hunt, Rachel, by Forest Upshaw	Account	21 SEP 1756	1731:200
Hunt, Rachel, recorded by John Lee, clerk	Account	20 SEP 1757	1731:212
Hunt, Rachel, c/o John to Archibald Ritchie	Bond	21 FEB 1759	1731:239
Hunt, Rachel, Miss, by Archibald Ritchie	Account	17 SEP 1759	1731:245
Hunt, Rachel, Miss, by Archibald Ritchie	Account	18 AUG 1760	1731:260
Hunt, Rachell, by Forest Upshaw	Account	17 OCT 1758	1731:236
Hunter, Edgar Malcom, c/o Muscoe G. to Grace Fenton Hunter	Bond	21 DEC 1818	1811:165
Hunter, Grace Fenton, c/o Muscoe G. to Grace Fenton Hunter	Bond	21 DEC 1818	1811:165
Hunter, Grace Fenton, Jr., by Grace Fenton Hunter	Account	19 SEP 1825	1825:001
Hunter, Grace Fenton, Jr., by Grace Fenton Hunter	Account	15 JUN 1829	1825:293
Hunter, M.G., from, to James Hunter	Receipt	18 JUN 1804	1796:155
Hunter, M.T., from, to James Hunter	Receipt	18 JUN 1804	1796:155
Hunter, Martha Taliaferro, c/o Wm. to James Hunter	Bond	21 SEP 1795	1761:213
Hunter, Muscoe Garnett, c/o Wm. to James Hunter	Bond	21 SEP 1795	1761:213
Hunter, Taliaferro, c/o Wm. to James Hunter	Bond	21 SEP 1795	1761:213
Hunter, Taliaferro, from, to James Hunter	Receipt	18 JUN 1804	1796:155
Hunter, William G., c/o James to David W. Pitts	Bond	21 JAN 1828	1825:206

I

Ingram, Alice, under 14, c/o William to Mary Ingram	Bond	18 JUN 1866	1857:389
Ingram, Ann Eliza, under 14, c/o William to Mary Ingram	Bond	18 JUN 1866	1857:389
Ingram, Samuel to Nicholas Faulkner	Bond	19 NOV 1751	1731:141

Ward or Subject (and Parent, Guardian or Other)	Record Type	Date	Reference(s)
J			
Jameson, David to Thomas Jameson	Bond	18 DEC 1739	WB6:217
Jameson, David, by Thomas Jameson	Account	15 SEP 1741	1731:043
Jameson, David, by Thomas Jameson	Account	20 SEP 1743	1731:058
Jameson, Isabella, h/o Thomas to Alfred Boyd	Bond	14 JUN 1841	1838:182
Jameson, James to Thomas Jameson	Bond	18 DEC 1739	WB6:218
Jameson, James, by Thomas Jameson	Account	15 SEP 1741	1731:043
Jameson, Marion, h/o Thomas to Alfred Boyd	Bond	14 JUN 1841	1838:182
Jameson, Martha, d/o James to James Jameson	Bond	20 JUN 1758	1731:225
Jameson, Mildred, h/o Thomas to Alfred Boyd	Bond	14 JUN 1841	1838:182
Jameson, Thomas, heirs of, in Trigg Co. KY	Bond	21 MAR 1842	1838:182
Jameson, William, h/o Thomas to Alfred Boyd	Bond	14 JUN 1841	1838:182
Jamison, Elizabeth, dec., by Reuben M. Garnett, Exor.	Estate Ref.	17 JAN 1842	1838:175
Jamison, James M., c/o John D., Todd Co. KY, to A.G. Slaughter	Bond	09 AUG 1842	1838:172
Jamison, Robert C., c/o John D., Todd Co. KY, to A.G. Slaughter	Bond	09 AUG 1842	1838:172
Janey, Mary Adelaide, c/o Claudius to John Janey	Bond	19 MAR 1827	1825:159
Jeffries, Alfred, c/o Robert to John Belfield	Bond	21 JUN 1813	1811:040
Jeffries, Ann, c/o Richard to Lewis Booker	Bond	17 OCT 1796	1761:228
Jeffries, Ann, by Lewis Booker	Account	17 SEP 1798	1796:032
Jeffries, Catharine, by John Jones	Account	19 SEP 1825	1825:005
Jeffries, Catharine, from John Jones	Receipt	18 JUN 1827	1825:167
Jeffries, Catharine, c/o William to Thomas Jeffries	Bond	21 JAN 1828	1825:205
Jeffries, Catharine, by Thomas Jeffries	Account	16 NOV 1835	1831:338
Jeffries, Caty, c/o John to John Jones	Bond	17 JUL 1820	1811:221
Jeffries, Edward, by John Jones	Account	19 SEP 1825	1825:003
Jeffries, Edwin, from John Jones	Receipt	21 JAN 1828	1825:213
Jeffries, Ewen, c/o John to John Jones	Bond	19 JUN 1820	1811:213
Jeffries, Fidelia, c/o Robert to John Belfield	Bond	21 JUN 1813	1811:040
Jeffries, Isaac Alfred, c/o Robert, by John Belfield	Account	19 JUN 1820	1811:216
Jeffries, Louisa, c/o Brooking to Willis Brooks	Bond	15 JAN 1838	1838:005
Jeffries, Martha, c/o William to Thomas Jeffries	Bond	21 JAN 1828	1825:205
Jeffries, Martha, from Thomas Jeffries	Receipt	24 MAY 1832	1831:112
Jeffries, Matilda, c/o Robert to John Belfield	Bond	21 JUN 1813	1811:040
Jeffries, Matilda, c/o Robert, by John Belfield	Account	19 JUN 1820	1811:214
Jeffries, Moses, c/o John to John Jones	Bond	19 JUN 1820	1811:213
Jeffries, Richard, c/o Richard to Lewis Booker	Bond	17 OCT 1796	1761:228
Jeffries, Richard, by Lewis Booker	Account	17 SEP 1798	1796:032
Jeffries, Richard Orlander, c/o Robert to John Belfield	Bond	21 JUN 1813	1811:040
Jeffries, Richard O., c/o Robert, by John Belfield	Account	19 JUN 1820	1811:217
Jeffries, Robert, orphans of, by John Belfield	Account	19 JUN 1820	1811:219
Jeffries, Sarah, c/o William to Thomas Jeffries	Bond	21 JAN 1828	1825:205
Jeffries, Sarah now Tate, from Thomas Jeffries	Receipt	24 MAY 1832	1831:112
Jeffries, Susan, c/o William to Thomas Jeffries	Bond	21 JAN 1828	1825:205
Jeffries, Susan F. late Croxton, by Frances S. Croxton	Account	16 MAY 1853	1851:178
Jesse, Jno. A., c/o Thomas, Jr. to Edwin Hundley	Bond	21 SEP 1835	1831:331
Jesse, John A., by Aneas Montague	Account	17 APR 1833	1831:173
Jesse, John A., by Aeneas Montague	Account	15 AUG 1836	1831:436
Jesse, Thomas P., c/o John A. to his father	Bond	17 MAR 1856	1851:339
Jesse, Thomas P., from John A. Jesse	Receipt	21 OCT 1861	1857:271
Jesse, William, by Aeneas Montague	Account	16 JUL 1832	1831:123
Johnson, Edmonia, c/o John to John Johnson	Bond	19 DEC 1836	1831:460

Ward or Subject (and Parent, Guardian or Other)	Record Type	Date	Reference(s)
Johnson, Katherine to Francis Taliaferro	Bond	10 MAY 1707	D&W12:411
Johnson, Martha M., c/o Samuel to Ross A. Cauthorn	Bond	17 APR 1843	1838:246
Johnson, Sarah, c/o unknown to Isaac Johnson	Bond	13 JAN 1871	1867:152
Johnson, Susan, c/o Samuel, Jr. to Edmund Dunn	Bond	17 AUG 1840	1838:095
Johnson, William, c/o Richard to Henry Johnson	Bond	17 AUG 1829	1825:309
Johnston, Ann, c/o Samuel, by Richard Fidler	Account	18 OCT 1773	1761:101
Johnston, John Williamson, c/o Patsey to Foushee G. Tebbs	Bond	19 DEC 1825	1825:079
Johnston, Polly, c/o Richard to Lewis Dunn	Bond	16 JAN 1832	1831:086
Jones, Anne, c/o William to William Jones	Bond	16 MAY 1758	1731:222
Jones, Aubrey H., by Alice J. Jones	Account	19 OCT 1857	1857:011
Jones, Benjamin F., c/o Benjamin F. to Alice J. Jones	Bond	15 AUG 1853	1851:184
Jones, Benjamin F., over 14, c/o Benjamin F., to James Roy Micou	Bond	19 MAY 1856	1851:343
Jones, Benjamin F., c/o Benjamin F. to James Roy Micou	Certificate	19 MAY 1856	1851:343
Jones, Benjamin F., by Alice J. Jones	Account	20 APR 1857	1851:425
Jones, Benjamin F., by James Roy Micou	Account	19 OCT 1857	1857:005
Jones, Benjamin F., by James Roy Micou	Account	19 JUL 1858	1857:081
Jones, Benjamin F., by Alice J. Jones	Account	19 JUL 1858	1857:069
Jones, Benjamin F., by James Roy Micou	Account	19 SEP 1859	1857:163
Jones, Benjamin F., by James Roy Micou	Account	20 AUG 1860	1857:205
Jones, Benjamin F., by James Roy Micou	Account	17 DEC 1860	1857:233
Jones, Betsey, c/o Thomas to Walter Jones	Bond	19 OCT 1801	1796:102
Jones, Betty, c/o James to Cornelius Sale	Bond	16 JUN 1760	1731:253
Jones, Dorothea Jane, c/o Thomas to John Jones (B)	Bond	16 JUN 1834	1831:275
Jones, Dorothea, c/o Benjamin to Richard D. Dunn	Bond	16 MAR 1835	1831:287
Jones, Dorothea, by John Jones	Account	21 NOV 1837	1831:505
Jones, Edward, c/o James to William Fisher	Bond	15 OCT 1804	1796:157
Jones, Edward, by Wm. Fisher	Account	15 JUL 1805	1796:164
Jones, Eliza., by Cornelius Sale	Account	15 AUG 1763	1761:029
Jones, Elizabeth, c/o James, by Cornelius Sale	Account	21 SEP 1761	1761:008
Jones, Elizabeth, c/o James to William Jones	Bond	15 APR 1799	1796:043
Jones, Elizabeth, c/o Richard to Richard Jones	Bond	19 DEC 1808	1796:204
Jones, Elizabeth, c/o Joseph to Ann Jones	Bond	19 MAR 1827	1825:160
Jones, Elizabeth, by Ann Jones	Account	21 JUL 1828	1825:239
Jones, Elizabeth now Brooks, from Nancy Jones	Receipt	16 MAR 1835	1831:290
Jones, Ellen Harvie, c/o John to William B. Matthews	Bond	17 JAN 1820	1811:206
Jones, Ellen H., c/o Capt. John, by Reuben M. Garnett	Account	21 NOV 1825	1825:062
Jones, Ellen H., by Reuben M. Garnett	Account	15 JAN 1827	1825:146
Jones, Ellen H., by Reuben M. Garnett	Account	17 DEC 1827	1825:203
Jones, Ellen H., c/o John, by Reuben M. Garnett	Account	19 JAN 1829	1825:267
Jones, Ellen Harvie, by Reuben M. Garnett	Account	18 APR 1831	1831:001
Jones, Ellen Harvie, by Reuben M. Garnett	Account	18 JUN 1832	1831:113
Jones, Ellen H., by Reuben M. Garnett	Account	15 JUL 1833	1831:184
Jones, Ellen, c/o Thomas to John Jones (B)	Bond	16 JUN 1834	1831:275
Jones, Ellen H., by Reuben M. Garnett	Account	19 MAY 1834	1831:252
Jones, Ellen H., by Reuben M. Garnett	Account	21 SEP 1835	1831:314
Jones, Ellen, by John Jones	Account	21 NOV 1837	1831:505
Jones, Ellen, c/o Thomas M. to Jefferson Minor	Bond	15 JAN 1838	1838:003
Jones, Frances Ann, c/o James W., by Sarah J. Jones	Account	20 MAY 1844	1838:326
Jones, Frances Ann, c/o James W., by Sarah J. Jones	Account	21 MAY 1849	1844:370
Jones, Frances Ann, c/o James W., by Sarah J. Dobyns	Account	15 APR 1850	1844:430
Jones, Frances Ann, c/o James W., by Sarah J. Dobyns	Account	17 MAY 1852	1851:094

Ward or Subject (and Parent, Guardian or Other)	Record Type	Date	Reference(s)
Jones, Frances Ann now Cammack, by Sarah J. Dobyns	Account	16 NOV 1857	1857:037
Jones, James, c/o John to Ann Jones	Bond	15 JUN 1818	1811:151
Jones, James W., from Mrs. Ann Jones	Receipt	19 SEP 1825	1825:006
Jones, Jane, c/o Thomas to Walter Jones	Bond	19 OCT 1801	1796:102
Jones, John, c/o John to William B. Matthews	Bond	17 JAN 1820	1811:206
Jones, John T., c/o John to his father	Bond	15 DEC 1828	1825:261
Jones, Keturah W., c/o John to George Wright	Bond	18 OCT 1819	1811:196
Jones, Laura M., by Alice J. Jones	Account	20 APR 1857	1851:421
Jones, Laura M., by Alice J. Jones	Account	19 JUL 1858	1857:077
Jones, Lewis Lunsford, c/o Armstead to Coleman Jones	Bond	21 DEC 1801	1796:113
Jones, Lewis Lunsford, c/o Armstead to Elizabeth Jones	Bond	18 OCT 1802	1796:119
Jones, Lucy, c/o James to Benjamin Haile Munday	Bond	19 SEP 1803	1796:135
Jones, Lucy C., c/o James W., by Sarah J. Jones	Account	20 MAY 1844	1838:324
Jones, Lucy Catharine, c/o James W., by Sarah J. Jones	Account	21 MAY 1849	1844:364
Jones, Lucy Catharine, c/o James W., by Sarah J. Dobyns	Account	15 APR 1850	1844:430
Jones, Lucy Catharine, c/o James W., by Sarah J. Dobyns	Account	17 MAY 1852	1851:098
Jones, Lucy Catharine, c/o James W. to Albert G. O'Neale	Bond	19 NOV 1855	1851:328
Jones, Lucy C., by Sarah J. Dobyns	Account	16 NOV 1857	1857:035
Jones, Maria, c/o Armstead to Coleman Jones	Bond	21 DEC 1801	1796:113
Jones, Maria, c/o Armstead to Elizabeth Jones	Bond	18 OCT 1802	1796:119
Jones, Martha M.M., c/o John to William B. Matthews	Bond	17 JAN 1820	1811:206
Jones, Martha M.M., c/o John, by Reuben M. Garnett	Account	21 NOV 1825	1825:058
Jones, Martha, c/o Joseph to Ann Jones	Bond	19 MAR 1827	1825:160
Jones, Martha M.M., by Reuben M. Garnett	Account	15 JAN 1827	1825:144
Jones, Martha M.M., Miss, by Reuben M. Garnett	Account	17 DEC 1827	1825:200
Jones, Martha, by Ann Jones	Account	21 JUL 1828	1825:239
Jones, Martha M.M., by Reuben M. Garnett	Account	19 NOV 1828	1825:258
Jones, Mary, c/o Philip to her father	Bond	20 MAY 1757	WB7:532
Jones, Mary, c/o John to George Wright	Bond	18 OCT 1819	1811:196
Jones, Mary Ann, c/o Thomas to John Jones (B)	Bond	16 JUN 1834	1831:275
Jones, Mary Ann, by John Jones	Account	21 NOV 1837	1831:505
Jones, Mary Ann, c/o Thomas M. to Benjamin F. Jones	Bond	15 JAN 1838	1838:001
Jones, Mary Lindsay, c/o James W., by Sarah J. Jones	Account	20 MAY 1844	1838:326
Jones, Mary Ann now Wright, from B.F. Jones	Receipt	15 SEP 1845	1844:059
Jones, Mary Lindsay, c/o James W., by Sarah J. Jones	Account	21 MAY 1849	1844:366
Jones, Mary Lindsay, c/o James W., by Sarah J. Dobyns	Account	15 APR 1850	1844:432
Jones, Mary Lindsay, c/o James W., by Sarah J. Dobyns	Account	17 MAY 1852	1851:096
Jones, Mary Lindsay, c/o James W. to Albert G. O'Neale	Bond	19 NOV 1855	1851:328
Jones, Mary L., by Sarah J. Dobyns late Jones	Account	16 NOV 1857	1857:041
Jones, Olander S., c/o John to his father	Bond	15 DEC 1828	1825:261
Jones, Patsy now Smither, from Nancy Jones	Receipt	16 MAR 1835	1831:291
Jones, Patty, c/o Philip to her father	Bond	20 MAY 1757	WB7:532
Jones, Peggy, c/o Richard to Lewis Booker	Bond	18 JAN 1813	1811:038
Jones, Priscilla, c/o Philip to her father	Bond	20 MAY 1757	WB7:532
Jones, Robert to James Garnett	Bond	16 DEC 1740	WB6:279
Jones, Sally, c/o Thomas to Walter Jones	Bond	19 OCT 1801	1796:102
Jones, Sally, c/o Richard to Lewis Booker	Bond	18 JAN 1813	1811:038
Jones, Sarah to George Stubblefield	Bond	21 SEP 1736	WB6:036
Jones, Sarah to John Rowzee	Bond	28 OCT 1737	WB6:092
Jones, Sarah Ann, c/o John to George Wright	Bond	18 OCT 1819	1811:196
Jones, Suca, Mrs., by Samuel Hipkins	Account	20 OCT 1741	1731:044

Ward or Subject (and Parent, Guardian or Other)	Record Type	Date	Reference(s)
Jones, Suca, Mrs., by Samuel Hipkins	Account	21 SEP 1742	1731:048
Jones, Susan, c/o Thomas to John Jones (B)	Bond	16 JUN 1834	1831:275
Jones, Susan, c/o Thomas M. to Arthur Temple	Bond	18 DEC 1837	1831:508
Jones, Susan, by John Jones	Account	21 NOV 1837	1831:505
Jones, Susanah, by John Dailey	Account	17 FEB 1772	1761:086
Jones, Susanah, c/o Francis, by Erasmus Jones	Account	19 OCT 1772	1761:092
Jones, Susanna to Samuel Hipkings	Bond	16 SEP 1740	WB6:270
Jones, Susanna, by Erasmus Jones	Account	15 AUG 1774	1761:116
Jones, Susannah, c/o William to John Clements, Gent.	Bond	15 AUG 1758	1731:228
Jones, Susannah	Account	18 SEP 1769	1761:072
Jones, Susannah, by Erasmus Jones	Account	18 OCT 1773	1761:099
Jones, Susannah, by Erasmus Jones	Account	18 SEP 1775	1761:126
Jones, Thomas, c/o Thomas to Walter Jones	Bond	19 OCT 1801	1796:102
Jones, Thomas Monroe, c/o Benjamin F. to Alice J. Jones	Bond	15 AUG 1853	1851:184
Jones, Thomas M., under 14, c/o Benjamin F., to James Roy Micou	Bond	19 MAY 1856	1851:343
Jones, Thomas M., by James Roy Micou	Account	19 OCT 1857	1857:017
Jones, Thomas M., by Alice J. Jones	Account	20 APR 1857	1851:431
Jones, Thomas M., by James Roy Micou	Account	19 JUL 1858	1857:087
Jones, Thomas M., by Alice J. Jones	Account	19 JUL 1858	1857:075
Jones, Thomas M., by James Roy Micou	Account	19 SEP 1859	1857:167
Jones, Thomas M., by James Roy Micou	Account	20 AUG 1860	1857:209
Jones, Thomas M., from James Roy Micou	Receipt	18 APR 1864	1857:343
Jones, Thomas M., by James Roy Micou	Account	18 APR 1864	1857:336
Jones, Virginia F., c/o John to his father	Bond	15 DEC 1828	1825:261
Jones, Walter S., c/o Benjamin F. to James Roy Micou	Certificate	19 MAY 1856	1851:343
Jones, Walter S., over 14, c/o Benjamin F., to James Roy Micou	Bond	19 MAY 1856	1851:343
Jones, Walter S., by Alice J. Jones	Account	20 APR 1857	1851:425
Jones, Walter S., by James Roy Micou	Account	19 OCT 1857	1857:001
Jones, Walter S., by James Roy Micou	Account	19 JUL 1858	1857:063
Jones, Walter S., by Alice J. Jones	Account	19 JUL 1858	1857:073
Jones, William, by Elizabeth Jones	Account	19 JUN 1786	1761:148
Jones, William, by William Montague	Account	18 OCT 1786	1761:153
Jordan, Susanna, c/o Isaac to John Howerton	Bond	16 JUN 1794	1761:212
Jourdan, Thomas, c/o Isaac to Thomas Jourdan	Bond	16 DEC 1793	1761:199

K

Kay, Elizabeth, c/o Christopher to her father	Bond	17 DEC 1804	1796:160
Kay, James, re: his sister Sally before her marriage	Report	19 SEP 1825	1825:008
Kay, Lucy, c/o Christopher to her father	Bond	17 DEC 1804	1796:160
Kay, Lucy, from Christopher Kay	Receipt	21 NOV 1825	1825:069
Kay, Richard, c/o Richard to James Kay	Bond	15 APR 1811	1796:245
Kay, Richard, from James Kay	Receipt	19 SEP 1825	1825:008
Kay, Richard, from Christopher Kay	Receipt	21 NOV 1825	1825:069
Kay, Sally, c/o Christopher to her father	Bond	17 DEC 1804	1796:160
Kay, Sally, c/o Richard to James Kay	Bond	15 APR 1811	1796:245
Kay, Sarah, from Christopher Kay	Receipt	21 NOV 1825	1825:069
Kay, Thomas, c/o Christopher to his father	Bond	17 DEC 1804	1796:160
Kay, Thomas, from Christopher Kay	Receipt	21 NOV 1825	1825:069
Keese, Sally, c/o George to Taylor Noel	Bond	21 DEC 1795	1761:219
Keese, Susan Lee late Micou, by John Micou, Jr.	Account	17 JUL 1843	1838:270
Keezee, Sally, c/o George to Theoderick Noel	Bond	18 DEC 1797	1796:026
Keezee, Sally, by Theoderick Noel	Account	20 OCT 1800	1796:093
Kemp, Sarah, c/o William to Robert S. Anderson	Bond	20 JUL 1829	1825:301

Ward or Subject (and Parent, Guardian or Other)	Record Type	Date	Reference(s)
Kendall, Samuel, c/o Jesse to John Beazley	Bond	20 DEC 1819	1811:205
Kerr, Thomas, over 14, to Morton B. Evans	Bond	19 JUL 1886	1867:574
Key, Betsey, c/o Christopher to Christopher Key	Bond	18 JUN 1798	1796:028
Key, Lucy, c/o Christopher to Christopher Key	Bond	18 JUN 1798	1796:028
Key, Polly, c/o Christopher to Christopher Key	Bond	18 JUN 1798	1796:028
Key, Sally, c/o Christopher to Christopher Key	Bond	18 JUN 1798	1796:028
Key, Solomon, c/o Christopher to Christopher Key	Bond	18 JUN 1798	1796:028
Key, Thomas, c/o Christopher to Christopher Key	Bond	18 JUN 1798	1796:028
Kidd, Benjamin, by Henry Kidd	Account	18 AUG 1777	1761:128
Kidd, Isaac, by Henry Kidd	Account	18 AUG 1777	1761:131
Kidd, Isaac, by Henry Kidd	Account	16 AUG 1779	1761:138
Kidd, Isaac, by Philip Kidd	Account	17 SEP 1787	1761:154
Kidd, Pitman, c/o Isaac, by Henry Kidd	Account	18 AUG 1777	1761:130

L

Ward or Subject (and Parent, Guardian or Other)	Record Type	Date	Reference(s)
Lafon, Elizabeth to John Rennolds	Bond	16 OCT 1750	WB8:373
Lafon, Elizabeth, by John Rennolds	Account	15 AUG 1758	1731:229
Lafon, Elizabeth, by John Rennolds	Account	20 AUG 1759	1731:244
Lafon, Elizabeth, by John Rennolds	Account	18 AUG 1760	1731:257
Lafon, Elizabeth, by John Rennolds	Account	16 AUG 1762	1761:013
Lafon, Hannah to John Rennolds	Bond	16 OCT 1750	WB8:373
Lafon, Mary to John Rennolds	Bond	16 OCT 1750	WB8:373
Lafon, Mary, by John Rennolds	Account	15 AUG 1758	1731:229
Lafon, Mary, by John Rennolds	Account	20 AUG 1759	1731:244
Lafon, Mary, by John Rennolds	Account	18 AUG 1760	1731:257
Lafon, Mary, by Jno. Rennolds	Account	21 SEP 1761	1761:008
Lafon, Mary, by Jno. Rennolds	Account	16 AUG 1762	1761:013
Lafon, Richard to John Rennolds	Bond	16 OCT 1750	WB8:373
Lafon, Richard, c/o Nicholas to Francis Lafon	Bond	16 NOV 1756	1731:206
Lafon, Richard, c/o Nicholas, by Francis Lafon	Account	15 NOV 1762	1761:025
Landrum, Mark, by Thomas Pitts	Account	19 OCT 1778	1761:136
Latane, Catharine R., h/o Wm. J.L. Latane	Writing	17 OCT 1825	1825:041
Latane, John L., by James H. Latane	Account	20 MAR 1848	1844:265, 267
Latane, John L., by James H. Latane	Account	19 MAR 1849	1844:339, 342
Latane, John L., by James H. Latane	Account	18 MAR 1850	1844:409, 413
Latane, John L., by James H. Latane	Account	16 JUN 1851	1844:539
Latane, John L., by James H. Latane	Account	20 DEC 1852	1851:156
Latane, John L., from James H. Latane	Receipt	21 FEB 1853	1851:169
Latane, M.P.W., from Robt. P. Waring, admr. of John Latane	Receipt	19 SEP 1825	1825:008
Latane, Mary, c/o John to Robert P. Waring	Bond	16 SEP 1811	1796:253
Latane, Mary P.W., h/o Wm. J.L. Latane	Writing	17 OCT 1825	1825:041
Latane, Mary Susan, c/o James H. to her father	Bond	20 MAR 1871	1867:155
Latane, Mary Susan, over 14/under 21, c/o James H.	Certificate	20 MAR 1871	1867:154
Latane, Mary Susan now Sale, by James H. Latane	Account	18 NOV 1873	1867:222
Latane, Roberta, c/o John to John Waring	Bond	16 SEP 1811	1796:255
Latane, William, c/o John to Henry W. Latane	Bond	16 SEP 1811	1796:254
Latane, William Catesby, c/o William C. to James H. Latane	Bond	16 NOV 1846	1844:181
Latane, William C., by James H. Latane	Account	20 MAR 1848	1844:265, 266
Latane, William C., by James H. Latane	Account	19 MAR 1849	1844:336, 342
Latane, William C., by James H. Latane	Account	18 MAR 1850	1844:409, 411
Latane, William C., from James H. Latane	Receipt	18 MAR 1850	1844:408

Ward or Subject (and Parent, Guardian or Other)	Record Type	Date	Reference(s)
Latham, Charles, Jr. c/o Henry to his father	Bond	18 MAY 1829	1825:279
Lathom, Henry to Marinda B. Mothershead	Marriage Ref.	20 FEB 1838	1838:008
Lathom, Jonathan, from Ephraim Beazley	Receipt	21 MAR 1826	1825:094
Lawson, John to Francis Paget	Bond	16 JAN 1722/3	WB4:011
Leavell, Anna M., c/o Byrd C. to Mary C. Leavell	Bond	16 APR 1860	1857:202
Lee, Frances, c/o Thomas to Isaac Scandrett, Gent.	Bond	18 OCT 1757	1731:212
Lee, George W., uncle of John H. Micou	Estate Ref.	16 APR 1849	1844:360
Lee, Thomas to Thomas Starke	Bond	18 FEB 1734/5	WB5:325
Lee [Ley], Thomas, c/o Thomas to Isaac Scandrett	Bond	19 OCT 1756	1731:204
Lewis, Ann S., c/o Warner to Benj. H. Munday	Bond	17 AUG 1835	1831:326
Lewis, Benjamin, c/o Warner to Benj. H. Munday	Bond	17 AUG 1835	1831:326
Lewis, Charles Augustine Lightfoot, c/o John to Wm. Waring, Jr.	Bond	16 OCT 1797	1796:011
Lewis, Francis Meriwether, c/o Warner to Benj. H. Munday	Bond	17 AUG 1835	1831:326
Lewis, Lulie E. late Temple, by Henry W. Latane	Account	18 NOV 1873	1867:224
Lewis, Robert, c/o Warner to Benj. H. Munday	Bond	17 AUG 1835	1831:326
Lewis, Waring, c/o Warner to Benj. H. Munday	Bond	17 AUG 1835	1831:326
Lewis, Warner to Catharine Butler, c/o Reuben	Marriage Ref.	17 AUG 1835	1831:326
Ley, Frances, c/o Thomas	Guard. Ref.	20 DEC 1757	WB11:028
Ley, Thomas, c/o Thomas	Guard. Ref.	20 DEC 1757	WB11:028
Ley [Lee], Thomas, c/o Thomas to Isaac Scandrett	Bond	19 OCT 1756	1731:204
Longest, Elton, c/o Charles S. to Lewis Carlton	Bond	18 MAY 1846	1844:138
Lorimer, Adelaide, c/o George T.R. to Virginia Lorimer	Bond	16 MAR 1840	1838:075
Lorimer, Virginia G., c/o George T.R. to Virginia Lorimer	Bond	16 MAR 1840	1838:075
Lowry, Ann, c/o John to Sarah Lowry	Bond	16 MAY 1758	1731:223
Lowry, Ann, c/o John, by Ischarner DeGraffenriedt	Account	17 AUG 1762	1761:016
Lowry, Ann, Miss, c/o John, by Saml. Rust	Account	17 SEP 1764	1761:049
Lowry, Ann, Miss, by Samuel Rust	Account	18 NOV 1765	1761:061
Lowry, Ann, Miss, by William Brockenbrough	Account	15 AUG 1768	1761:066
Lowry, Anne, c/o Jno., by I. DeGraffenriedt	Account	17 AUG 1761	1761:005
Lowry, Martha, c/o William to Rebeccah Lowry	Bond	15 OCT 1751	1731:136
Lowry, Martha to William Roane	Bond	16 JAN 1754	1731:177
Lowry, Martha, Sally & Robert, c/o William	Account	18 FEB 1760	1731:248
Lowry, Richard, c/o William to Rebeccah Lowry	Bond	15 OCT 1751	1731:136
Lowry, Richard to William Roane	Bond	16 JAN 1754	1731:177
Lowry, Salley to William Roane	Bond	16 JAN 1754	1731:177
Lowry, Sally, c/o William to Rebeccah Lowry	Bond	15 OCT 1751	1731:136
Lowry, Thomas, c/o William to Rebeccah Lowry	Bond	15 OCT 1751	1731:136
Lowry, Thomas to William Roane	Bond	16 JAN 1754	1731:177
Lowry, Thomas, c/o William to John Upshaw	Bond	17 OCT 1758	1731:235
Lowry, Thomas, c/o William	Account	18 FEB 1760	1731:248
Loyde, Austin S., c/o William to Alice Loyde	Bond	21 JAN 1850	1844:401
Loyde, Austin S., by Alice Loyde	Account	16 AUG 1852	1851:128
Loyde, Austin, by Alice Loyde	Account	18 AUG 1856	1851:375
Loyde, Elizabeth, by Alice Loyde	Account	16 AUG 1852	1851:128
Loyde, Georgiana, c/o William to Alice Loyde	Bond	21 JAN 1850	1844:401
Loyde, Georgiana, by Alice Loyde	Account	16 AUG 1852	1851:128
Loyde, Georgiana, by Alice Loyde	Account	16 JUN 1856	1851:357
Loyde, Sarah E., c/o William to Alice Loyde	Bond	21 JAN 1850	1844:401
Ludlow, Mary E. c/o Richard to William Garnett	Bond	16 JUN 1828	1825:237
Ludlow, Richard John, c/o Richard to William Garnett	Bond	16 JUN 1828	1825:237
Lumpkin, Albert, over 14, c/o Robert to William Campbell	Bond	17 JAN 1876	1867:345

Ward or Subject (and Parent, Guardian or Other)	Record Type	Date	Reference(s)
Lumpkin, John Thomas, c/o Carter to Frances D. Lumpkin	Bond	21 MAY 1838	1838:024
Lumpkin, John Thomas, by Frances D. Lumpkin now Carter	Account	21 OCT 1839	1838:060
Lumpkin, Lewis Richeson, c/o Carter to Frances D. Lumpkin	Bond	21 MAY 1838	1838:024
Lumpkin, Lewis Richardson, by Frances D. Lumpkin now Carter	Account	21 OCT 1839	1838:060
Lumpkin, Lewis R., c/o Carter to Zebulon M.P. Carter	Bond	18 DEC 1843	1838:301
Lumpkin, Lewis R., by Zebulon M.P. Carter	Account	17 MAR 1845	1844:018
Lumpkin, Lewis R., by Zebulon M.P. Carter	Account	19 APR 1847	1844:194
Lumpkin, Lewis R., by Zebulon M.P. Carter	Account	21 MAY 1849	1844:374
Lumpkin, Lewis R., by Zebulon M.P. Carter	Account	17 JUN 1850	1844:460
Lumpkin, Lewis R., by Zebulon M.P. Carter	Account	18 MAR 1851	1844:509
Lumpkin, Robert, by Frances D. Lumpkin now Carter	Account	21 OCT 1839	1838:062
Lumpkin, Robert M., c/o Carter to Zebulon M.P. Carter	Bond	18 DEC 1843	1838:301
Lumpkin, Robert M., by Zebulon M.P. Carter	Account	17 MAR 1845	1844:020
Lumpkin, Robert, by Zebulon M.P. Carter	Account	19 APR 1847	1844:196
Lumpkin, Robert M., by Zebulon M.P. Carter	Account	21 MAY 1849	1844:376
Lumpkin, Robert M., by Zebulon M.P. Carter	Account	17 JUN 1850	1844:462
Lumpkin, Robert M., by Zebulon M.P. Carter	Account	18 MAR 1851	1844:509
Lumpkin, Robert, c/o Carter to Joseph T. Tompkins	Bond	15 NOV 1852	1851:153
Lumpkin, Robert M., by Joseph T. Tompkins	Account	17 JUN 1854	1851:243
Lumpkin, Robt. Manning, c/o Carter to Frances D. Lumpkin	Bond	21 MAY 1838	1838:024
Lumpkin, Sarah Ann Carter, by Zebulon M.P. Carter	Account	17 MAR 1845	1844:024
Lumpkin, Susan Ann Carter, c/o Carter to Frances D. Lumpkin	Bond	21 MAY 1838	1838:024
Lumpkin, Susan Ann, by Frances D. Lumpkin now Carter	Account	21 OCT 1839	1838:060
Lumpkin, Susan A.C., c/o Carter to Zebulon M.P. Carter	Bond	18 DEC 1843	1838:301
Lumpkin, Susan Ann Carter, by Zebulon M.P. Carter	Account	19 APR 1847	1844:194
Lumpkin, Susan Ann Carter, by Zebulon M.P. Carter	Account	21 MAY 1849	1844:378
Lumpkin, Susan Ann Carter, by Zebulon M.P. Carter	Account	17 JUN 1850	1844:460
Lumpkin, Susan Ann Carter, by Zebulon M.P. Carter	Account	18 MAR 1851	1844:511
Lumpkin, Susan A.E., c/o Carter to Joseph T. Tompkins	Bond	15 NOV 1852	1851:153
Lumpkin, Susan A.C., by Joseph T. Tompkins	Account	17 JUN 1854	1851:245
Lyons, William Thomas, over 14, to Edward P. Watts	Bond	16 JAN 1882	1867:481

M

Mann, Ann, c/o Augustine to John Trible	Bond	21 JAN 1793	1761:189
Mann, Elizabeth, c/o Philip to Richard H. Mitchell	Bond	21 NOV 1831	1831:078
Mann, Frances, c/o Augustine to Thomas Miller	Bond	21 JAN 1793	1761:188
Mann, Judith A., c/o Thomas to Richard L. Covington	Bond	16 APR 1827	1825:162
Mann, Julia A., by Sarah Sowell	Account	17 OCT 1836	1831:442
Mann, Julia A., by Sarah Sowell	Account	16 MAY 1842	1838:200
Mann, Julia Isabella, c/o William G. to Augustine Crump	Bond	16 FEB 1852	1851:042
Mann, Margaret S., by Sarah Sowell	Account	17 OCT 1836	1831:446
Mann, Margaret S., from Mrs. Sarah Sowell	Receipt	17 MAR 1845	1844:007
Mann, Margaret S., c/o William G. to Augustine Crump	Bond	16 FEB 1852	1851:042
Mann, Margarett S., by Sarah Sowell	Account	16 MAY 1842	1838:196
Mann, Martha G., c/o Philip to Larkin Hundley	Bond	20 MAR 1826	1825:091
Mann, William G., by Sarah Sowell	Account	17 OCT 1836	1831:439
Manning, Henry C., c/o Sandy to Thomas R.B. Wright	Bond	18 OCT 1881	1867:457
Mathews, Rachel to William Williamson	Bond	15 JAN 1744/5	WB7:240
Mathews, Rachell, by William Williamson	Account	21 OCT 1746	1731:100
Matthews, Baldwin, c/o John, Sr. to John Matthews	Bond	19 JAN 1801	1796:084
Matthews, Baldwin Smith Lee, c/o John to Thomas Matthews	Bond	21 JUL 1806	1796:179

Ward or Subject (and Parent, Guardian or Other)	Record Type	Date	Reference(s)
Matthews, Baldwin S.L., by John B. Matthews	Account	16 JUN 1828	1825:208
Matthews, James M., c/o William B. to Reuben M. Garnett	Bond	16 MAY 1836	1831:426
Matthews, James M., from Reuben M. Garnett	Receipt	20 APR 1846	1844:137
Matthews, John Ryburn, c/o John to Thomas Matthews	Bond	21 JUL 1806	1796:179
Matthews, Lucinda E., d/o William B. to her father	Bond	16 OCT 1815	1811:103
Matthews, Lucy W., by Frances A. Temple	Account	16 NOV 1835	1831:382
Matthews, Lucy W. now Temple, by Frances A. Temple	Account	22 NOV 1836	1831:451
Matthews, Maria Louisa, by Frances A. Temple	Account	16 NOV 1835	1831:392
Matthews, Maria L., by Frances A. Temple	Account	22 NOV 1836	1831:454
Matthews, Philip T., by Frances A. Temple	Account	16 NOV 1835	1831:386
Matthews, Philip T., by Frances A. Temple	Account	22 NOV 1836	1831:452
Matthews, Thomas, c/o Rev. John to John Matthews	Bond	16 FEB 1801	1796:086
Matthews, William Baynham, c/o John, Sr. to John Matthews	Bond	19 JAN 1801	1796:084
Matthews, William Baynham, c/o John, Sr. to John P. Lee	Bond	21 APR 1806	1796:173
Matthews, William Baynman, from, to John P. Lee	Receipt	21 AUG 1809	1796:217
McCarty, Sally, c/o Joseph to John Games	Bond	18 APR 1808	1796:200
McCarty, Sally wife of John Harrison, by John Games	Report	19 SEP 1825	1825:020
McDonald, Catharine to Daniel Farguson	Bond	21 OCT 1746	WB7:484
McDonald, Catharine to Nathaniel Conduit	Bond	19 JUL 1748	WB8:070
McDonald, Daniel to Daniel Farguson	Bond	21 OCT 1746	WB7:484
McDonald, Daniel to Nathaniel Conduit	Bond	19 JUL 1748	WB8:070
McDonald, William to Daniel Farguson	Bond	21 OCT 1746	WB7:484
McDonald, William to Nathaniel Conduit	Bond	19 JUL 1748	WB8:070
McFarland, James, c/o Wm., by William L. Lewis, dec.	Account	15 SEP 1851	1851:014
McFarland, James, by Thomas W. Lewis	Account	19 SEP 1853	1851:187
McFarland, Joseph, c/o Wm., by William L. Lewis, dec.	Account	15 SEP 1851	1851:016
McFarland, Joseph, by Thomas W. Lewis	Account	19 SEP 1853	1851:189
McFarlane, James, c/o William to William L. Lewis	Bond	17 MAR 1845	1844:007
McFarlane, James, by William L. Lewis, dec.	Account	20 MAY 1850	1844:452
McFarlane, Joseph, c/o William to William L. Lewis	Bond	17 MAR 1845	1844:007
McFarlane, Joseph, by William L. Lewis, dec.	Account	20 MAY 1850	1844:450
McGuire, Emily P., c/o John P. to her father	Bond	20 NOV 1843	1838:295
McGuire, Grace F.H., c/o John P. to her father	Bond	20 NOV 1843	1838:295
McGuire, James M.G., c/o John P. to his father	Bond	20 NOV 1843	1838:295
McGuire, John P., c/o John P. to his father	Bond	20 NOV 1843	1838:295
McGuire, Maria M., c/o John P. to her father	Bond	20 NOV 1843	1838:295
McGuire, Mary S.M., c/o John P. to her father	Bond	20 NOV 1843	1838:295
McKendrie, Dora, under 14, c/o Thomas N. to G.W. Rice	Bond	19 FEB 1883	1867:502
McKendrie, Flora, over 14, c/o Thomas N. to G.W. Rice	Bond	19 FEB 1883	1867:502
McKendrie, Flora, over 14, to George W. Rice	Certificate	19 FEB 1883	1867:502
McTire, Mary E., c/o George to Ennice Shackelford	Bond	15 FEB 1858	1857:054
Meador, Catherine, c/o Vincent to William L. Waring	Bond	21 FEB 1820	1811:207
Meador, Frances, c/o Vincent to William L. Waring	Bond	21 FEB 1820	1811:207
Meador, James, c/o Vincent to William L. Waring	Bond	21 FEB 1820	1811:207
Meadows, Catharine, c/o Vincent, by Wm. L. Waring	Settlement	19 SEP 1825	1825:011
Meadows, Frances, c/o Vincent, by Wm. L. Waring	Settlement	19 SEP 1825	1825:011
Meadows, James, c/o Vincent, by Wm. L. Waring	Settlement	19 SEP 1825	1825:011
Meggs, Joel to Bersheba Lyall	Bond	17 JUL 1753	1731:162
Meggs, Joell to Gerrard Loyall	Bond	19 FEB 1752	1731:143
Mercer, Isaac, c/o John to Larkin Hundley	Bond	15 JUN 1835	1831:319
Mercer, Isaac, by Larkin Hundley	Account	19 JUN 1837	1831:478

Ward or Subject (and Parent, Guardian or Other)	Record Type	Date	Reference(s)
Mercer, Isaac, by Larkin Hundley	Account	15 APR 1839	1838:052
Mercer, Isaac, by Larkin Hundley	Account	18 AUG 1840	1838:096
Mercer, Isaac, by Larkin Hundley	Account	20 JUN 1842	1838:214
Mercer, Isaac I., by Larkin Hundley	Account	17 NOV 1845	1844:070
Mercer, Isaac I., by Larkin Hundley	Account	15 JUN 1846	1844:149
Mercer, Margaret Ann, c/o John to John Owen	Bond	18 MAY 1835	1831:293
Mercer, Virginia, c/o John to Larkin Hundley	Bond	15 JUN 1835	1831:319
Mercer, Virginia, by Larkin Hundley	Account	19 JUN 1837	1831:477
Mercer, Virginia, by Larkin Hundley	Account	15 APR 1839	1838:052
Mercer, Virginia, by Larkin Hundley	Account	18 AUG 1840	1838:096
Mercer, Virginia J., by Larkin Hundley	Account	17 JAN 1842	1838:172
Mercer, Zezoruh, c/o John to George Thomas	Bond	19 JAN 1835	1831:283
Michell, Jane to James Webb and wife Ann	Bond	18 JUL 1716	D&W14:626
Michell, Peter to James Webb and wife Ann	Bond	18 JUL 1716	D&W14:626
Michell, Sarah to James Webb and wife Ann	Bond	18 JUL 1716	D&W14:626
Micou, Albert Roy, c/o Albert to Susan S. Micou	Bond	18 NOV 1850	1844:478
Micou, Albert Roy, by Susan S. Micou	Account	17 SEP 1855	1851:319
Micou, Christian G., c/o John H. to Catharine C. Micou	Bond	18 DEC 1843	1838:302
Micou, Christian G., by Catharine C. Micou	Account	18 MAY 1846	1844:139
Micou, Edgar Roy, c/o John H. to Catharine C. Micou	Bond	18 DEC 1843	1838:302
Micou, Edgar Roy, by Catharine C. Micou	Account	18 MAY 1846	1844:139
Micou, John, c/o William F. to John Micou, Jr.	Bond	18 APR 1831	1831:061
Micou, John, s/o Wm. F., by John Micou, Jr.	Account	18 NOV 1833	1831:210
Micou, John, infant of Wm. F., by John Micou, Jr.	Account	16 NOV 1835	1831:376
Micou, John, by John Micou, Jr.	Account	17 JUL 1843	1838:280
Micou, John H., s/o Col. Paul & Mary Micou, dec.	Estate Ref.	16 APR 1849	1844:360
Micou, Margaret Ingles, by John Micou, Jr.	Account	18 NOV 1833	1831:196
Micou, Margaret J., by John Micou, Jr.	Account	17 JUL 1843	1838:272
Micou, Margarette J., by John Micou, Jr.	Account	16 NOV 1835	1831:372
Micou, Mary Frances, by Susan S. Micou	Account	20 AUG 1832	1831:130
Micou, Mary Frances, by Susan S. Micou	Account	18 NOV 1833	1831:214
Micou, Mary Frances, c/o Paul, Jr. to James Roy Micou, Jr.	Bond	19 MAY 1834	1831:264
Micou, Mary F., from James Roy Micou, Exor. of John H.	Receipt	16 APR 1849	1844:358
Micou, Mary F., Miss, by James Roy Micou	Account	16 APR 1849	1844:355
Micou, Olimpia C., c/o John H. to Catharine C. Micou	Bond	18 DEC 1843	1838:302
Micou, Olympia C., by Catharine C. Micou	Account	18 MAY 1846	1844:140
Micou, Paul, Jr., dec. by Admr. John H. Micou	Estate Ref.	16 APR 1849	1844:359
Micou, Stela M., by Susan S. Micou	Account	18 NOV 1833	1831:214
Micou, Stella M., by Susan S. Micou	Account	20 AUG 1832	1831:128
Micou, Susan Lee, c/o William F. to John Micou, Jr.	Bond	18 APR 1831	1831:061
Micou, Susan Lee, by John Micou, Jr.	Account	18 NOV 1833	1831:198
Micou, Susan Lee, by John Micou, Jr.	Account	16 NOV 1835	1831:368
Micou, Susan Lee now Keese, by John Micou, Jr.	Account	17 JUL 1843	1838:270
Micou, Thomas Brockenbrough, by John Micou, Jr.	Account	18 NOV 1833	1831:206
Micou, Thomas B., by John Micou, Jr.	Account	16 NOV 1835	1831:378
Micou, Thomas B., by John Micou, Jr.	Account	17 JUL 1843	1838:276
Micou, Thos. Brockenbrough, c/o Wm. F. to John Micou, Jr.	Bond	18 APR 1831	1831:061
Micou, William Denholm, c/o William F. to John Micou, Jr.	Bond	18 APR 1831	1831:061
Micou, William Denholm, by John Micou, Jr.	Account	18 NOV 1833	1831:202
Micou, William D., by John Micou, Jr.	Account	16 NOV 1835	1831:374
Micou, William D., by John Micou, Jr.	Account	17 OCT 1842	1838:235

Ward or Subject (and Parent, Guardian or Other)	Record Type	Date	Reference(s)
Micou, William F., legatees of, by John Micou, Jr.	Account	17 JUL 1843	1838:286
Micou, William B., c/o Albert to Susan S. Micou	Bond	18 NOV 1850	1844:478
Micou, William B., by Susan S. Micou	Account	17 SEP 1855	1851:323
Miller, Achilles, above 14, c/o Lewis to Alfred H. Garnett	Bond	19 JUL 1875	1867:325
Miller, Benjamin to John Miller	Bond	20 NOV 1744	WB7:217
Miller, Benjamin, by John Miller	Account	22 JAN 1745/6	1731:094
Miller, Benjamin, by Simon Miller	Account	17 FEB 1746/7	1731:106
Miller, Benjamin, by Simon Miller, Gent.	Account	17 NOV 1747	1731:112
Miller, John Elfanzo, c/o John to Richard Miller	Bond	22 MAR 1810	1796:226
Miller, John A., c/o John to Thomas Miller	Bond	21 DEC 1813	1811:051
Miller, John A., c/o John, by Richard Miller	Account	19 DEC 1825	1825:074
Miller, Simon, c/o Simon to Robert Baylor	Bond	16 OCT 1797	1796:010
Miller, Simon, by Robert Baylor	Account	21 SEP 1801	1796:100
Miller, Thomas to Simon Miller	Bond	20 NOV 1744	WB7:219
Miller, Thomas, c/o John to Edward Miller	Bond	15 FEB 1808	1796:199
Miller, Thomas, c/o John to George W. Banks	Bond	20 MAR 1810	1796:225
Miller, Thomas, by George W. Banks	Account	15 MAY 1820	1811:212
Miller, Thomas, from George W. Banks	Receipt	15 MAY 1820	1811:212
Miller, William, c/o William to Andrew Boulware	Bond	20 JAN 1800	1796:053
Miller, William, c/o John to Richard Miller	Bond	22 MAR 1810	1796:226
Miller, William, c/o John to Thomas Miller	Bond	21 DEC 1813	1811:051
Miller, William R., c/o John, by Richard Miller	Account	19 DEC 1825	1825:074
Mills, John, c/o John to James Mills	Bond	16 JUL 1754	1731:179
Minor, Benjamin, c/o Hubbard T. to his father	Bond	17 SEP 1832	1831:141
Minor, Edward, over 14, c/o Reuben to Malissa J. Minor	Bond	15 APR 1878	1867:384
Minor, Ella J., over 14, c/o Reuben & Malissa J. Minor	Certificate	15 APR 1878	1867:385
Minor, Ella, over 14, c/o Reuben to Malissa J. Minor	Bond	15 APR 1878	1867:384
Minor, Philip, under 14, c/o Reuben to Malissa J. Minor	Bond	15 APR 1878	1867:384
Minor, Reuben & wife Melissa Jane Moody, c/o Hundley	Receipt	21 FEB 1848	1844:255
Minor, Robert, under 14, c/o Reuben to Malissa J. Minor	Bond	15 APR 1878	1867:384
Minter, James to Josiah Minter	Bond	19 MAR 1744/5	WB7:285
Minter, Joseph to John Phillips	Bond	21 AUG 1744	WB7:181
Minter, Lucy to Frances Minter	Bond	15 MAY 1744	WB7:149
Minter, Lucy, c/o John, by Frances Minter	Account	21 OCT 1746	1731:101
Minter, Lucy, c/o John, by Frances Minter	Account	19 APR 1748	1731:118
Minter, Philip to John Phillips	Bond	21 AUG 1744	WB7:182
Minter, Philip, by John Phillips	Account	21 JAN 1745/6	1731:093
Minter, Philip, by John Philips	Account	20 JAN 1746/7	1731:105
Minter, Philip, c/o John, by Frances Minter	Account	19 APR 1748	1731:118
Minter, Thomas to Frances Minter	Bond	15 MAY 1744	WB7:147
Minter, Thomas, c/o John, by Frances Minter	Account	21 OCT 1746	1731:102
Minter, Thomas, c/o John, by Frances Minter	Account	19 APR 1748	1731:119
Minter, William to John Phillips	Bond	16 MAR 1747/8	WB8:039
Mitchell, Isaac to Thomas Johnson	Bond	16 NOV 1731	WB5:062
Mitchell, John, dec. by Jeremiah Sheaperd, admr.	Account	26 SEP 1752	1731:148
Mitchell, Sarah to Richard Bush	Bond	22 FEB 1715/6	D&W14:479
Mitchell, Sarah, c/o Thomas to John Mitchell	Bond	18 FEB 1752	1731:143
Mitchell, Sarah A., over 14, c/o Charles R. to her father	Bond	20 SEP 1881	1867:456
Mitchell, William, c/o Isaac to Lewis Smith	Bond	20 SEP 1802	1796:129
Monroe, Alice, above 14, c/o Allen to William Monroe	Bond	18 JUN 1877	1867:368
Montague, Abraham to Lewis Montague	Bond	17 NOV 1747	WB8:028

Ward or Subject (and Parent, Guardian or Other)	Record Type	Date	Reference(s)
Montague, Abraham, c/o Richd. to Philip Montague	Bond	20 DEC 1802	1796:127
Montague, Abraham, c/o John C. to Philip T. Montague	Bond	21 DEC 1807	1796:195
Montague, Aeneas, c/o John to Thomas Street	Bond	16 OCT 1815	1811:105
Montague, Amelia, c/o Samuel to James Montague	Bond	20 AUG 1810	1796:232
Montague, Amelia S., by James Montague	Account	21 SEP 1812	1811:022
Montague, Amelia S., by James Montague	Account	17 OCT 1814	1811:067
Montague, Amelia S., by James Montague	Account	18 SEP 1815	1811:101
Montague, Amelia S., by James Montague	Account	17 JUL 1820	1811:223
Montague, Amelia S., c/o Samuel to Philip Montague	Bond	18 SEP 1820	1811:234
Montague, Catharine to Lewis Montague	Bond	21 JUN 1748	WB8:066
Montague, Catharine, c/o Samuel to James Montague	Bond	20 AUG 1810	1796:232
Montague, Catharine Y., by James Montague	Account	21 SEP 1812	1811:023
Montague, Catharine Y., by James Montague	Account	17 OCT 1814	1811:065
Montague, Catharine Y., by James Montague	Account	18 SEP 1815	1811:102
Montague, Catherine Y., c/o Samuel to Philip Montague	Bond	21 DEC 1818	1811:166
Montague, Catherine Y., now Hoskins, d/o Samuel	Account	17 JUL 1820	1811:225
Montague, Frances to John Clements	Bond	17 NOV 1747	WB8:029
Montague, James, c/o Samuel to William Montague	Bond	16 JUN 1794	1761:211
Montague, John, c/o Samuel to John Montague	Bond	16 JUN 1794	1761:211
Montague, Latane to Lewis Montague	Bond	17 NOV 1747	WB8:028
Montague, Lucy, c/o Samuel to James Montague	Bond	20 AUG 1810	1796:232
Montague, Lucy E., by James Montague	Account	21 SEP 1812	1811:020
Montague, Lucy E., by James Montague	Account	17 OCT 1814	1811:066
Montague, Lucy E., by James Montague	Account	18 SEP 1815	1811:100
Montague, Martha to Lewis Montague	Bond	21 JUN 1748	WB8:066
Montague, Mary Elizabeth, c/o William to Amos Newhall	Bond	17 FEB 1817	1811:131
Montague, Philip H.L. & wife Mary Susan Coleman, c/o Rich.	Receipt	19 JUL 1847	1844:218
Montague, Samuel, c/o Samuel to Thomas Waring	Bond	15 OCT 1792	1761:187
Montague, Samuel, by James Montague	Account	21 SEP 1812	1811:024
Montague, Sophronia, c/o John to William T. Evans	Bond	18 MAY 1812	1811:010
Montague, Victura, c/o John to Mary Montague	Bond	21 OCT 1811	1796:259
Montague, Virginia F., c/o William to Andrew Hundley	Bond	15 JAN 1827	1825:126
Montague, William, s/o Samuel to Thomas Jesse, Jr.	Bond	17 APR 1820	1811:211
Moody, Anderson E. for wife Milly A. Owen, fr. Wm. A. Wright	Receipt	21 NOV 1853	1851:219
Moody, Dolly, c/o Hundley to Sthreshley Dunn	Bond	20 AUG 1838	1838:033
Moody, Dorothy, by Sthreshly Dunn	Account	17 MAR 1845	1844:012
Moody, George, c/o Lewis [A.] to Larkin Moody	Bond	17 OCT 1814	1811:068
Moody, Melissa Jane, c/o Hundley to Sthreshley Dunn	Bond	20 AUG 1838	1838:033
Moody, Melissa Jane, by Sthreshley Dunn	Account	21 DEC 1846	1844:182
Moody, Melissa Jane, by Sthreshley Dunn	Account	17 JAN 1848	1844:251
Moody, Melissa Jane now Minor, c/o Hundley	Receipt	21 FEB 1848	1844:255
Moore, Gregory to Zorobabell Billups	Bond	19 MAR 1744/5	WB7:271
Moore, Katharine to Argyle Blaxton	Bond	19 MAR 1744/5	WB7:272
Morgan, Ann to Thomas Thorp and wife Grace	Bond	20 SEP 1737	WB6:088
Morgan, Ann to John Barbee	Bond	19 JUL 1737	WB6:087
Morgan, Ann to William Boulware	Bond	17 NOV 1741	WB6:350
Morgan, Ann, by William Boulware	Account	21 SEP 1742	1731:049
Morgan, Ann [Morgin], by William Boulware	Account	16 OCT 1744	1731:081
Morgan, Ann, by William Boulware	Account	17 SEP 1745	1731:086
Morgan, Ann, by William Boulware	Account	17 SEP 1746	1731:098
Morgan, Ann, by William Boulware	Account	17 NOV 1747	1731:113

Ward or Subject (and Parent, Guardian or Other)	Record Type	Date	Reference(s)
Morris, John to John Bagge	Bond	15 JAN 1722/3	WB4:011
Moseley, Benjamin, c/o Robert to Martha Moss	Bond	20 SEP 1715	D&W14:416
Moseley, Edward, c/o Robert to Martha Moss	Bond	20 SEP 1715	D&W14:416
Moss, Robert to Thomas Ayres	Bond	10 FEB 1714/5	D&W14:341
Moss, William to Robert Jones	Bond	12 NOV 1714	D&W14:328
Mothershead, Eliza, by Marinda B. Mothershead	Account	18 MAY 1835	1831:302
Mothershead, Eliza, by Marinda B. Mothershead	Account	17 MAY 1836	1831:412
Mothershead, Eliza, c/o Nathaniel J. to Miranda B. Mothershead	Bond	18 JAN 1836	1831:402
Mothershead, Eliza, by Marinda B. Lathom late Mothershead	Account	20 FEB 1838	1838:006
Mothershead, Eliza, by Miranda B. Latham late Mothershead	Account	19 OCT 1840	1838:120
Mothershead, Eliza, by Miranda B. Latham formerly Mothershead	Account	20 MAY 1844	1838:330, 332
Mothershead, Jane, by Marinda B. Mothershead	Account	18 MAY 1835	1831:300
Mothershead, Jane, by Marinda B. Mothershead	Account	17 MAY 1836	1831:410
Mothershead, Jane, by Marinda B. Lathom late Mothershead	Account	20 FEB 1838	1838:008
Mothershead, Jane, by Miranda B. Latham late Mothershead	Account	19 OCT 1840	1838:110
Mothershead, Jane, by Miranda B. Latham formerly Mothershead	Account	20 MAY 1844	1838:344, 348
Mothershead, Mary Ann, by Marinda B. Mothershead	Account	18 MAY 1835	1831:304
Mothershead, Mary Jane, c/o Nathaniel J. to Miranda B. Mothershead	Bond	18 JAN 1836	1831:402
Mothershead, Mary Ann, by Marinda B. Mothershead	Account	17 MAY 1836	1831:414
Mothershead, Mary Ann, by Marinda B. Lathom late Mothershead	Account	20 FEB 1838	1838:012
Mothershead, Mary Ann, by Miranda B. Latham late Mothershead	Account	19 OCT 1840	1838:116
Mothershead, Mary Ann, by Miranda B. Latham form. Mothershead	Account	20 MAY 1844	1838:336, 340
Motley, Betty to Henry Motley	Bond	19 MAR 1754	1731:178
Motley, William to William Thomas	Bond	17 JUN 1752	1731:145
Mullins, Benjamin, c/o William to Edward Ware	Bond	19 NOV 1792	1761:187
Mullins, Benjamin, c/o Wm., by Edwd. Ware	Account	21 DEC 1795	1761:215
Mullins, Benjamin, c/o William by Edward Ware	Account	19 DEC 1796	1796:001
Mullins, Fanny, c/o Peter to William Taylor	Bond	17 MAR 1800	1796:055
Mullins, Jane, c/o William to Edward Ware	Bond	16 JUL 1792	1761:183
Mullins, Samuel, c/o William to Edward Ware	Bond	18 JUN 1792	1761:179
Munday, Albert R., over 14, c/o Henry to Robert H. Pratt	Bond	21 FEB 1876	1867:347
Munday, Angelina Cath., c/o Meriday to Susan H. Munday	Bond	21 MAR 1859	1857:137
Munday, Catharine, c/o Edmund to Albert G. O'Neale	Bond	18 FEB 1850	1844:407
Munday, Charles to John Munday	Bond	14 JUN 1711	D&W13:419
Munday, Crittenden to Jane Munday	Bond	16 SEP 1747	WB8:022
Munday, James M., c/o Meriday to Albert P. Gouldman	Bond	21 FEB 1859	1857:133
Munday, John to John Dix	Bond	21 FEB 1748/9	WB8:167
Munday, Mary E., c/o Benjamin H., Jr. to Benjamin H. Munday	Bond	20 AUG 1838	1838:032
Munday, Rebecca Jane, c/o Meriday to Susan H. Munday	Bond	21 MAR 1859	1857:137
Munday, Stephen to Francis Waring, Gent.	Bond	14 MAY 1753	1731:160
Munday, Susanna to Jane Munday	Bond	16 SEP 1747	WB8:022
Munday, Tabitha to Richard Covington	Bond	19 JUN 1745	WB7:343
Mundie, James Addie, over 14, c/o James to James H. Mundie	Bond	15 DEC 1879	1867:416
Mundie, James Addie, over 14, c/o James to J. Henry Mundie	Certificate	15 DEC 1879	1867:415
Muse, Ann B. now Bell, from Peter S. Trible	Receipt	20 MAR 1854	1851:227
Muse, Anna B., c/o Samuel to Peter S. Trible	Bond	20 AUG 1849	1844:385
Muse, Anna B., by Peter S. Trible	Account	16 JUN 1851	1844:519
Muse, Bettie to Joshua Robinson	Certificate	15 MAR 1875	1867:296
Muse, Bettie to Joshua Robinson	Bond	15 MAR 1875	1867:297
Muse, James & wife Mary W. Coleman, d/o Anne	Report	17 OCT 1825	1825:040
Muse, Lawrence, Jr., c/o James to John W. Robinson	Bond	21 MAY 1827	1825:166

Ward or Subject (and Parent, Guardian or Other)	Record Type	Date	Reference(s)
Muse, Lawrence, Jr., by mother Mrs. Mary M. Muse	Account	15 JUN 1829	1825:282
Muse, Lawrence, c/o James, by John W. Robinson	Account	18 JUL 1831	1831:065
Muse, Lawrence, by John W. Robinson	Account	15 OCT 1832	1831:143
Muse, Lawrence, by John W. Robinson	Account	20 JUL 1835	1831:320
Muse, Lucinda, c/o Charles to Lawrence Muse	Bond	20 AUG 1827	1825:169
Muse, Samuel & wife Sarah Coates, from James Durham	Receipt	18 JAN 1858	1857:054
Muse, Sarah Jane late Coates, by James Durham	Account	18 JAN 1858	1857:053

N

Nalle, Nathan to John Nalle	Bond	21 MAY 1734	WB5:263
Nalle, Richard to John Nalle	Bond	21 MAY 1734	WB5:260
Neal, Ralph to Richard Bush	Bond	20 DEC 1737	WB6:102
Neal, Ralph, by Richard Bush	Account	15 SEP 1741	1731:042a
Neal, Ralph, by Richard Bush	Account	15 SEP 1741	1731:042a
Neal, Ralph, by Richard Bush	Account	21 DEC 1742	1731:053
Neal, Stephen to Richard Bush	Bond	17 JAN 1737/8	WB6:108
Neal, Stephen, by Richard Bush	Account	21 DEC 1742	1731:054
Neal, William to Richard Beale	Bond	21 SEP 1737	WB6:092
New, Edward, c/o Robert to R.T. Cauthorn	Bond	23 APR 1886	1867:571
New, James, c/o Robert to R.T. Cauthorn	Bond	23 APR 1886	1867:571
New, Mason, c/o Robert to R.T. Cauthorn	Bond	23 APR 1886	1867:571
New, Taylor, c/o Robert to R.T. Cauthorn	Bond	23 APR 1886	1867:571
New, Thomas, c/o Robert to R.T. Cauthorn	Bond	23 APR 1886	1867:571
New, Virginia, c/o Robert to R.T. Cauthorn	Bond	23 APR 1886	1867:571
Newbill, Bettie Christopher, c/o Christopher to B.F. Newbill	Bond	15 NOV 1880	1867:448
Newbill, Bettie C., by Bettie F. Newbill	Account	19 AUG 1882	1867:495
Newbill, Dandridge Mason, c/o Christopher to B.F. Newbill	Bond	15 NOV 1880	1867:448
Newbill, Dandridge M., by Bettie F. Newbill	Account	19 AUG 1882	1867:495
Newbill, George to George Newbill	Bond	18 MAR 1746/7	WB7:513
Newbill, Leonard Broocks, c/o Nathaniel to Samuel Broocke	Bond	18 DEC 1815	1811:108
Newbill, Lilly Smith, c/o Nathaniel to Samuel Broocke	Bond	18 DEC 1815	1811:108
Newbill, Lucy Etta, c/o Christopher to B.F. Newbill	Bond	15 NOV 1880	1867:448
Newbill, Lucy E., by Bettie F. Newbill	Account	19 AUG 1882	1867:495
Newbill, Polly, c/o Nathaniel to Samuel Broocke	Bond	18 DEC 1815	1811:108
Newbill, Polly, c/o William to Thomas Newbill	Bond	18 SEP 1815	1811:098
Newbill, Richard, c/o William to Thomas Newbill	Bond	18 SEP 1815	1811:099
Newman, Alexander to Thomas Newman	Bond	22 NOV 1752	1731:154
Newman, George to Henry Motley	Bond	15 OCT 1751	1731:134
Newman, George, c/o Elias to Thomas Newman	Bond	19 NOV 1759	1731:247
Newman, Mary Ann to Henry Motley	Bond	15 OCT 1751	1731:134
Newman, William to Henry Motley	Bond	15 OCT 1751	1731:134
Newman, William, c/o Elias to Thomas Newman	Bond	19 NOV 1759	1731:247
Newton, Martha to Henry Newton	Bond	18 MAR 1728/9	WB4:286
Noel, Achilles, Jr., fr. Jas. Andrews, admr. of Thos. Andrews	Receipt	17 OCT 1825	1825:057
Noel, Catharine, c/o Muscoe G., by John J. Wright	Account	21 JAN 1845	1844:004
Noel, Edmund, c/o Edmund to William Fisher	Bond	18 MAY 1812	1811:009
Noel, Emily F., c/o Muscoe G. to John J. Wright	Bond	20 FEB 1843	1838:241
Noel, Emily, c/o Muscoe G., by John J. Wright	Account	21 JAN 1845	1844:002
Noel, Emily, c/o Muscoe G., by John J. Wright	Account	15 SEP 1851	1851:008
Noel, Frances, c/o Theoderick to Theoderick Noel	Bond	18 DEC 1815	1811:106
Noel, Franklin, c/o Alexander to Thomas Vaughan	Bond	20 SEP 1841	1838:153

Ward or Subject (and Parent, Guardian or Other)	Record Type	Date	Reference(s)
Noel, Hannah S., c/o William to Larkin Noel	Bond	19 OCT 1818	1811:162
Noel, Harriet a.k.a. Faulconer to Wm. H. Faulconer	Bond	17 OCT 1808	1796:203
Noel, James, c/o Barnard to Thomas Leeman	Bond	20 AUG 1755	1731:195
Noel, James H., by Thomas Wright, Jr. & wife Ann W. Noel	Account	16 NOV 1835	1831:358, 362
Noel, James H., by Thomas Wright	Account	20 JUL 1846	1844:154, 164
Noel, John, by Owen Carter	Account	15 AUG 1763	1761:031
Noel, John, by Owen Carter	Account	20 AUG 1764	1761:044
Noel, John G., c/o William to Larkin Noel	Bond	19 OCT 1818	1811:162
Noel, John G., from brother Achilles Noel, Jr.	Receipt	19 DEC 1831	1831:082
Noel, Larkin & wife Maria J.	Suit Ref.	21 NOV 1832	1831:153
Noel, Richard, c/o William to Polly Noel	Bond	19 JUN 1815	1811:083
Noel, Richard, c/o William to Larkin Noel	Bond	19 OCT 1818	1811:162
Noel, Richard, c/o Lewis to Albert Micou	Bond	19 FEB 1844	1838:304
Noel, Richard [L.], by Albert Micou	Account	20 OCT 1851	1851:022
Noel, Robert, c/o Theoderick to Theoderick Noel	Bond	18 DEC 1815	1811:106
Noel, Robert N., c/o Andrian to Henry W. Daingerfield	Bond	19 APR 1858	1857:057
Noel, Sally, c/o Ellison to Spencer Noel	Bond	19 SEP 1809	1796:217
Noel, Sally N., c/o Ellison, Jr. to Saml. C. Parker	Bond	19 JUN 1815	1811:081
Noel, Selina, c/o Alexander to Thomas Vaughan	Bond	20 SEP 1841	1838:153
Noel, Susannah, c/o William to Larkin Noel	Bond	19 OCT 1818	1811:162
Noel, Theodorick A., by Thomas Wright, Jr. & wife Ann W. Noel	Account	16 NOV 1835	1831:358
Noell, John, c/o Barnard to John Noell	Bond	16 MAR 1756	1731:198
Noell, John, c/o Bernard, by Berriman Brann	Account	20 SEP 1768	1761:067
Noell, Margaret, c/o Barnald to John Noell	Bond	16 MAR 1756	1731:198
Noell, William to John Boulware	Bond	19 JUN 1753	1731:161
Noell, Zeoriah, c/o Barnard to Thomas Newman	Bond	15 MAR 1757	1731:209
Norris, Adolphus, by Mary Ann Norris	Account	17 JAN 1859	1857:129
Norris, Adolpus, c/o Lowry to Mary Ann Norris	Bond	21 MAR 1853	1851:169
Norris, Altera, c/o Lowry to Mary Ann Norris	Bond	21 MAR 1853	1851:169
Norris, Atway P., by Mary Ann Norris	Account	17 JAN 1859	1857:125
North, Anthony to John Mills, Jr.	Bond	14 FEB 1711	D&W14:016

O

Oliver, Ann, c/o Austin to James Lee	Bond	19 MAY 1856	1851:342
Oliver, Benjamin F., c/o William to George C. Nunn	Bond	20 JUL 1846	1844:150
Oliver, Benjamin F., by George C. Nunn	Account	17 JUL 1848	1844:284
Oliver, Benjamin F., by George C. Nunn	Account	17 SEP 1849	1844:387
Oliver, Benjamin F., by George C. Nunn	Account	16 DEC 1850	1844:492
Oliver, Benjamin F., by George C. Nunn	Account	17 MAY 1852	1851:086
Oliver, Benjamin F., by George C. Nunn	Account	19 SEP 1853	1851:200
Oliver, Benjamin F., by George C. Nunn	Account	21 MAR 1853	1851:172
Oliver, Benjamin F., by George C. Nunn	Account	20 NOV 1854	1851:277
Oliver, Benjamin F., by George C. Nunn	Account	19 NOV 1855	1851:329
Oliver, Benjamin F., by George C. Nunn	Account	18 AUG 1856	1851:365
Oliver, Benjamin F., by George C. Nunn	Account	19 OCT 1857	1857:029
Oliver, Benjamin F., by George C. Nunn	Account	18 JUL 1859	1857:149
Oliver, Leah A., c/o William to George C. Nunn	Bond	20 JUL 1846	1844:150
Oliver, William, children of: Leah A., Wm., Benj. F.	List Slaves	21 SEP 1846	1844:180, 246
Oliver, William A., c/o William to George C. Nunn	Bond	20 JUL 1846	1844:150
Oliver, William, by George C. Nunn	Account	17 JUL 1848	1844:281
Oliver, William, by George C. Nunn	Account	17 SEP 1849	1844:389

Ward or Subject (and Parent, Guardian or Other)	Record Type	Date	Reference(s)
Oliver, William, by George C. Nunn	Account	16 DEC 1850	1844:490
Oliver, William A., by George C. Nunn	Account	17 MAY 1852	1851:086
Oliver, William A., by George C. Nunn	Account	21 MAR 1853	1851:170
Oliver, William A., by George C. Nunn	Account	19 SEP 1853	1851:202
Oliver, William A., by George C. Nunn	Account	20 NOV 1854	1851:275
Oliver, William A., by George C. Nunn	Account	19 NOV 1855	1851:331
Oliver, William A., by George C. Nunn	Account	18 AUG 1856	1851:363
Oliver, William, c/o Austin to James Lee	Bond	19 MAY 1856	1851:342
Oliver, William A., from George C. Nunn	Receipt	20 JUL 1857	1851:437
Oliver, William A., by George C. Nunn	Account	20 JUL 1857	1851:437
Onbee, Thomas to James Williamson	Bond	15 FEB 1742/3	WB6:414a
Oneale, John to Arthur Donelly	Bond	17 JUL 1716	D&W14:619
Oneale, Katherine to Arthur Donelly	Bond	17 JUL 1716	D&W14:619
Owen, Arthur, for wife Cordelia A., from William A. Wright	Receipt	19 AUG 1850	1844:470
Owen, Cordelia A., c/o James & Mary, by William A. Wright	Account	15 JUN 1846	1844:142
Owen, Cordelia A., by William A. Wright, trustee	Account	19 AUG 1850	1844:468
Owen, James and his late wife Mary, children of	Account	15 JUN 1846	1844:142
Owen, Mary C., c/o James & Mary, by William A. Wright	Account	15 JUN 1846	1844:142
Owen, Milly A. now Moody, from William A. Wright	Receipt	21 NOV 1853	1851:219
Owen, Willey A., c/o James & Mary, by William A. Wright	Account	15 JUN 1846	1844:142
Owens, Cordelia A., c/o James & Mary, by William A. Wright	Account	19 MAR 1849	1844:330
Owens, Mary C., c/o James & Mary, by William A. Wright	Account	19 MAR 1849	1844:330
Owens, Willey A., c/o James & Mary, by William A. Wright	Account	19 MAR 1849	1844:330

P

Ward or Subject (and Parent, Guardian or Other)	Record Type	Date	Reference(s)
Pagett, Ephraim to Thomas Waring	Bond	16 DEC 1740	WB6:280
Pagett, Ephraim, by Thomas Waring, Gent.	Account	17 NOV 1742	1731:053
Pagett, Francis to Henry Tandy	Bond	18 FEB 1734/5	WB5:324
Pamplin, James, c/o Nicholas to Sarah Pamplin	Bond	18 JAN 1757	1731:208
Pamplin, Nicholas, orphans of, by Thomas Roane	Account	21 MAR 1774	1761:110, 111
Pamplin, Robert	Account	21 MAR 1774	WB12:581
Pamplin, Thomas, c/o Nicholas to Sarah Pamplin	Bond	18 JAN 1757	1731:208
Parker, Joseph, c/o Thomas to John G. Bentley	Bond	15 JUL 1844	1838:356
Parker, Josephine, c/o Thomas, by John G. Bentley	Account	15 FEB 1847	1844:192
Parker, Josephine, c/o Thomas, by John G. Bentley	Account	15 JUL 1850	1844:464
Parker, Martha, c/o Samuel C., by Robert Hill	Account	21 NOV 1825	1825:054
Parker, Nancy, c/o Thomas to John Saunders	Bond	19 AUG 1844	1838:359
Parker, Nancy, c/o Thomas to John Saunders	Guard.	19 AUG 1844	1838:359
Parker, Philip, c/o Robert to Robert Parker	Bond	20 JAN 1794	1761:200
Parker, Robert to Elizabeth Pley	Bond	22 MAY 1717	D&W15:049
Parker, Sarah, c/o Alexander to Achilles Noel, Jr.	Bond	16 OCT 1826	1825:121
Parker, Susan, c/o Alexander to Achilles Noel, Jr.	Bond	16 OCT 1826	1825:121
Parron, Elizabeth, c/o Thomas to Zachariah Street	Bond	18 DEC 1848	1844:296
Parron, Elizabeth, by Zachariah Street	Account	20 MAY 1850	1844:448
Parron, Elizabeth, by Zachariah Street	Account	16 JUN 1851	1844:529
Parron, Elizabeth, c/o Thomas, by Zachariah Street	Account	21 JUN 1852	1851:106, 110
Parron, Elizabeth, by Zachariah Street	Account	19 SEP 1853	1851:211, 212
Parron, Elizabeth, by Zachariah Street	Account	15 MAY 1854	1851:235
Parron, Elizabeth, c/o Thomas, by Zachariah Street	Account	18 JUN 1855	WB27:528
Parron, Elizabeth, by Zachariah Street	Account	18 JUN 1855	1851:305
Parron, James W., c/o Thomas to Zachariah Street	Bond	18 DEC 1848	1844:296

Ward or Subject (and Parent, Guardian or Other)	Record Type	Date	Reference(s)
Parron, James W., by Zachariah Street	Account	20 MAY 1850	1844:446
Parron, James W., by Zachariah Street	Account	16 JUN 1851	1844:529
Parron, James W., c/o Thomas, by Zachariah Street	Account	21 JUN 1852	1851:106, 108
Parron, James W., by Zachariah Street	Account	19 SEP 1853	1851:211, 212
Parron, James W., by Zachariah Street	Account	15 MAY 1854	1851:235
Parron, James W., by Zachariah Street	Account	18 JUN 1855	1851:305
Parron, James W., c/o Thomas, by Zachariah Street	Account	18 JUN 1855	WB27:528
Parron, Polly C., c/o Thomas to Zachariah Street	Bond	18 DEC 1848	1844:296
Parron, Polly C., by Zachariah Street	Account	20 MAY 1850	1844:446
Parron, Polly C., by Zachariah Street	Account	16 JUN 1851	1844:529
Parron, Polly C., c/o Thomas, by Zachariah Street	Account	21 JUN 1852	1851:106, 108
Parron, Polly C., by Zachariah Street	Account	19 SEP 1853	1851:211, 212
Parron, Polly C., by Zachariah Street	Account	15 MAY 1854	1851:235
Parron, Polly C., c/o Thomas, by Zachariah Street	Account	18 JUN 1855	WB27:528
Parron, Polly C., by Zachariah Street	Account	18 JUN 1855	1851:305
Parron, Thomas E., c/o Thomas to Zachariah Street	Bond	18 DEC 1848	1844:296
Parron, Thomas E., by Zachariah Street	Account	20 MAY 1850	1844:448
Parron, Thomas, by Zachariah Street	Account	16 JUN 1851	1844:529
Parron, Thomas E., c/o Thomas, by Zachariah Street	Account	21 JUN 1852	1851:106, 108
Parron, Thomas E., by Zachariah Street	Account	19 SEP 1853	1851:211, 212
Parron, Thomas C., by Zachariah Street	Account	15 MAY 1854	1851:235
Parron, Thomas C., by Zachariah Street	Account	18 JUN 1855	1851:305
Parron, Thomas C., c/o Thomas, by Zachariah Street	Account	18 JUN 1855	WB27:528
Patterson, Mary Coleman, by Vincent Williamson	Account	15 OCT 1787	1761:156
Patterson, Mary, c/o Jno., by Vincent Williamson	Account	15 SEP 1788	1761:160
Patterson, Mary, c/o John, by Vincent Williamson	Account	21 SEP 1789	1761:161
Patterson, Mary, c/o Jno., by Vincent Williamson	Account	20 SEP 1790	1761:171
Patterson, Mary, c/o John to Thomas Johnson	Bond	17 JUN 1793	1761:195
Patterson, Mary, by Vincent Williamson	Account	22 SEP 1795	1761:213
Payne, Sarah, c/o Thomas, by Reubin Bush	Account	18 OCT 1773	1761:101
Pearson, Theodora Gatewood, c/o Matthew to Wm. Gatewood	Bond	16 OCT 1797	1796:014
Perkins, Ann to Griffin Perkins	Bond	17 FEB 1740/1	WB6:283
Perkins, Sarah to Cary Perkins	Bond	17 FEB 1740/1	WB6:283
Perry, Rachell to Philip Stockdell	Bond	22 JUN 1726	WB4:152
Philips, Frances, c/o Richard to Thomas Henley, Sr.	Bond	17 JUL 1815	1811:084
Philips, Frances now wife of Thomas Hundley	Report	15 MAY 1826	1825:106
Phillips, George L., over 14, c/o Geo. W., by R.C. Phillips	Bond	21 FEB 1870	1867:119; OB3:298
Phillips, James L., c/o Leroy to Benjamin Blake	Bond	20 DEC 1847	1844:249
Phillips, John H., c/o Leroy to Benjamin Blake	Bond	20 DEC 1847	1844:249
Phillips, Leroy, c/o Richard to Richard Phillips	Bond	15 FEB 1819	1811:178
Phillips, Martha T., c/o George W., by Robert C. Phillips	Bond	21 FEB 1870	1867:119; OB3:298
Phillips, Martha Todd, by R.C. Phillips	Account	17 JUL 1876	1867:354
Phillips, Mary, c/o John, by James Webb, Jr.	Account	17 AUG 1762	1761:017
Phillips, Mary, c/o John, by James Webb, Junr.	Account	17 AUG 1763	1761:033
Phillips, Richard, by Jno. Dunn	Account	17 AUG 1763	1761:032
Phillips, Sarah, c/o Richard to Alexr. S. Boughton	Bond	18 JAN 1819	1811:170
Phillips, Susanna, by John Corrie	Account	20 SEP 1763	1761:041
Phillips, Susannah, Mrs., by John Corrie	Account	17 JAN 1763	1761:027
Phillips, Susannah, by John Corrie	Account	20 AUG 1764	1761:047
Phillips, William T., c/o Leroy to Benjamin Blake	Bond	20 DEC 1847	1844:249
Pilcher, Elizabeth, by Robert M. Pilcher	Account	20 FEB 1837	1831:464

Ward or Subject (and Parent, Guardian or Other)	Record Type	Date	Reference(s)
Pilcher, Elizabeth, by R.M. Pilcher	Account	16 AUG 1841	1838:148
Pilcher, Mary Ann, c/o Thomas to Robert M. Pilcher	Bond	15 FEB 1836	1831:406
Pilcher, Mary Ann, by Robert M. Pilcher	Account	20 FEB 1837	1831:466
Pilcher, Mary Ann, by R.M. Pilcher	Account	16 AUG 1841	1838:146
Pilcher, Samuel D., c/o Thomas to Elizabeth Pilcher	Bond	15 FEB 1836	1831:407
Pilcher, Samuel Dawson, by Elizabeth Pilcher	Account	20 FEB 1837	1831:470
Pilcher, Susan Elizabeth, c/o Thomas to Robert M. Pilcher	Bond	15 FEB 1836	1831:406
Pilcher, Winter, c/o Thomas to Elizabeth Pilcher	Bond	15 FEB 1836	1831:407
Pilcher, Winter, by Elizabeth Pilcher	Account	20 FEB 1837	1831:470
Pitts, Alexandria Victoria, c/o David to Birkett G. Rennolds	Bond	17 NOV 1851	1851:025
Pitts, Ann E., c/o Benjamin F. to Robert M. Davis	Bond	17 OCT 1842	1838:234
Pitts, Augusta, c/o Philip to Joseph Gatewood	Bond	15 MAY 1826	1825:105
Pitts, B.F., h/o B.F., by Daniel Rennolds	Account	16 SEP 1844	1838:370
Pitts, B.F., heirs of, by Daniel Rennolds	Account	16 SEP 1844	1838:370
Pitts, Benjamin Franklin, c/o Benjamin F. to Lewis Rennolds	Bond	17 JAN 1842	1838:171
Pitts, Benjamin F., c/o Benjamin F. to Daniel Rennolds	Bond	15 MAY 1843	1838:268
Pitts, Benjamin F., c/o Benjamin F. to Paul Spindle	Bond	19 OCT 1857	1857:031, 033
Pitts, Emily, c/o Benjamin F. to Lewis Rennolds	Bond	17 JAN 1842	1838:171
Pitts, Emily, c/o Benjamin F. to Daniel Rennolds	Bond	15 MAY 1843	1838:268
Pitts, Emily, h/o B.F., by Daniel Rennolds	Account	16 SEP 1844	1838:370
Pitts, Emily Ann, c/o David to Birkett G. Rennolds	Bond	17 NOV 1851	1851:025
Pitts, Emily, by Daniel Rennolds	Account	16 MAY 1859	1857:141, 143
Pitts, Emily A., by Birkett G. Rennolds	Account	21 JUL 1862	1857:287
Pitts, Fanny, c/o David to Thomas L. Oneal	Bond	15 DEC 1800	1796:082
Pitts, Mildred Catharine, c/o David to Birkett G. Rennolds	Bond	17 NOV 1851	1851:025
Pitts, Mildred C., by Birkett G. Rennolds	Account	21 JUL 1862	1857:289
Pitts, R.F., by Daniel Rennolds	Account	16 MAY 1859	1857:141
Pitts, Roxanna, c/o Benjamin F. to Lewis Rennolds	Bond	17 JAN 1842	1838:171
Pitts, Roxanna, c/o Benjamin F. to Daniel Rennolds	Bond	15 MAY 1843	1838:268
Pitts, Roxanna, h/o B.F., by Daniel Rennolds	Account	16 SEP 1844	1838:370
Pitts, Roxanna N., c/o Benjamin F. to Paul Spindle	Bond	19 OCT 1857	1857:031, 033
Pitts, Roxanna, by Daniel Rennolds	Account	16 MAY 1859	1857:141
Pitts, Sarah J., c/o Benjamin F. to Robert M. Davis	Bond	17 OCT 1842	1838:234
Pitts, Zela, c/o Benjamin F. to Lewis Rennolds	Bond	17 JAN 1842	1838:171
Pitts, Zela, h/o B.F., by Daniel Rennolds	Account	16 SEP 1844	1838:370
Pitts, Zela E., c/o Benjamin F. to Paul Spindle	Bond	19 OCT 1857	1857:031, 033
Pitts, Zela, by Daniel Rennolds	Account	16 MAY 1859	1857:141
Pitts, Zelar, c/o Benjamin F. to Daniel Rennolds	Bond	15 MAY 1843	1838:268
Powers, Betty J., by Edward Powers	Account	15 APR 1850	1844:442
Powers, Betty J., by Edward Powers	Account	17 MAY 1852	1851:082
Powers, Betty J., by Edward Powers	Account	17 JUL 1854	1851:255
Powers, Betty J., by Edward Powers	Account	20 JUL 1857	1851:449
Powers, Edward W., by Edward Powers	Account	15 APR 1850	1844:436
Powers, Edward, by Edward Powers	Account	17 MAY 1852	1851:076
Powers, Edward W., by Edward Powers	Account	17 JUL 1854	1851:257
Powers, James & wife Matilda B.	Suit Ref.	21 NOV 1832	1831:153
Powers, James, by Edward Powers	Account	15 APR 1850	1844:444
Powers, James, by Edward Powers	Account	17 MAY 1852	1851:082
Powers, James, by Edward Powers	Account	17 JUL 1854	1851:257
Powers, James, by Edward Powers	Account	20 JUL 1857	1851:445
Powers, James L., by Edward Powers	Account	16 JAN 1865	1857:357

Ward or Subject (and Parent, Guardian or Other)	Record Type	Date	Reference(s)
Powers, Lucy Ann, by Edward Powers	Account	15 APR 1850	1844:438
Powers, Lucy Ann, by Edward Powers	Account	17 MAY 1852	1851:078
Powers, Lucy Ann, by Edward Powers	Account	17 JUL 1854	1851:253
Powers, Lucy Ann, by Edward Powers	Account	20 JUL 1857	1851:447
Powers, Mary Susan, by Edward Powers	Account	15 APR 1850	1844:438
Powers, Mary Susan, by Edward Powers	Account	17 MAY 1852	1851:076
Powers, Mary Susan, by Edward Powers	Account	17 JUL 1854	1851:253
Powers, Matilda B., by Edward Powers	Account	15 APR 1850	1844:440
Powers, Matilda B., by Edward Powers	Account	17 MAY 1852	1851:080
Powers, Matilda B., by Edward Powers	Account	17 JUL 1854	1851:255
Powers, Matilda B., by Edward Powers	Account	20 JUL 1857	1851:447
Powers, Willia Ann, by Edward Powers	Account	15 APR 1850	1844:440
Powers, William (C), under 14, to A.W. Broaddus	Bond	16 JAN 1882	1867:482
Powers, Willie Ann, by Edward Powers	Account	17 MAY 1852	1851:080
Powers, Willie Ann, by Edward Powers	Account	17 JUL 1854	1851:255
Powers, Willieann, by Edward Powers	Account	20 JUL 1857	1851:449
Priddy, William for wife Lucy B. Dix, from Achilles Lumpkin	Receipt	19 JUN 1843	1838:269
Pruitt, Sarah Elizabeth, by Josiah to Peggy Croxton	Bond	21 APR 1845	1844:032
Puller, John B.M., c/o John W. to Thomas H. Simcoe	Bond	20 OCT 1867	1867:017
Puller, Matthew M., c/o John W. to Thomas H. Simcoe	Bond	20 OCT 1867	1867:017
Purkins, Cary, c/o Henry to Gabriel Purkins	Bond	22 SEP 1795	1761:214
Purkins, Mary, c/o Gabriel, Jr. to Winter Bray	Bond	16 DEC 1817	1811:140
Purkins, Mary, by Winter Bray	Account	18 MAY 1835	1831:308
Purkins, Sarah, by Cary Purkins	Account	18 SEP 1744	1731:076
Purkins, Sarah, by Cary Purkins	Account	17 FEB 1746/7	1731:107
Purkins, Sarah, Mrs., by Cary Purkins	Account	17 FEB 1746/7	1731:107
Purkins, Sarah, Mrs., by Cary Purkins	Account	20 OCT 1747	1731:111
Purkins, Sarah, c/o Geo. to Mace Clements	Bond	19 NOV 1827	1825:195
Purkins, Sary, by Cary Purkins	Account	19 OCT 1742	1731:051
Purkins, Young Dimach, c/o Henry to Philemon Purkins	Bond	22 SEP 1795	1761:215
Putman, Mary to Thomas Duling	Bond	20 DEC 1748	WB8:115

Q

Quarles, Ann Eliza., c/o Francis to John Daingerfield	Bond	16 SEP 1811	1796:256
Quarles, Francis Edward, c/o Francis to John Daingerfield	Bond	16 SEP 1811	1796:256
Quarles, Henry West, c/o Francis to John Daingerfield	Bond	16 SEP 1811	1796:256
Quarles, James H., under 14, c/o James H. to Ludy S. Hodges	Bond	15 OCT 1877	1867:375
Quarles, Lucy Daingerfield, c/o Francis to John Daingerfield	Bond	16 SEP 1811	1796:256
Quarles, Sarah Jane, c/o Francis to John Daingerfield	Bond	16 SEP 1811	1796:256
Quarles, Susanna Fauntleroy, c/o Francis to John Daingerfield	Bond	16 SEP 1811	1796:256
Quesenberry, Lucy A.D., c/o John S. to her father	Bond	16 NOV 1835	1831:342

R

Ramsay, Spencer, c/o Francis to Edward Gouldman	Bond	19 DEC 1796	1796:002
Ramsay, Vincent, c/o Francis to Edward Gouldman	Bond	19 DEC 1796	1796:002
Reeves, Elizabeth, c/o Henry to Joseph Pollard	Bond	17 JAN 1748/9	WB8:132
Reeves, Elizabeth, c/o Henry, by Joseph Pollard	Account	20 AUG 1751	1731:133
Reeves, Elizabeth, c/o Henry, by Joseph Pollard, Gent.	Account	21 AUG 1753	1731:165
Reeves, Elizabeth, c/o Henry, by Joseph Pollard, Gent.	Account	17 SEP 1754	1731:184
Reeves, Elizabeth, c/o Henry to William Rennolds	Bond	17 DEC 1754	1731:186
Reeves, Elizabeth, c/o Henry, by Joseph Pollard	Account	15 NOV 1757	WB11:026

Ward or Subject (and Parent, Guardian or Other)	Record Type	Date	Reference(s)
Reeves, Elizabeth, c/o Henry, by William Rennolds	Account	19 SEP 1758	1731:232
Reeves, Elizabeth, c/o Henry to Nicholas Pamplin	Bond	18 JAN 1758	1731:218
Reeves, John, c/o Henry to Joseph Pollard	Bond	17 JAN 1748/9	WB8:132
Reeves, John, c/o Henry, by Joseph Pollard	Account	20 AUG 1751	1731:130
Reeves, John, c/o Henry, by Joseph Pollard, Gent.	Account	21 AUG 1753	1731:163
Reeves, John, c/o Henry, by Joseph Pollard, Gent.	Account	17 SEP 1754	1731:182
Reeves, John, c/o Henry to William Rennolds	Bond	17 DEC 1754	1731:186
Reeves, John, c/o Henry, by Joseph Pollard	Account	15 NOV 1757	WB11:025
Reeves, Susannah to William Daingerfield	Bond	17 SEP 1745	WB7:369
Rennolds, Albert, from Thomas Wright, Jr.	Receipt	16 APR 1827	1825:163
Rennolds, Albert to Louisa Rennolds, for land sale	Debt	21 NOV 1831	1831:079
Rennolds, Albert, c/o Otway to his father	Bond	16 MAR 1857	1851:414
Rennolds, Albert C., c/o Albert to his father	Bond	18 MAY 1886	1867:572
Rennolds, Arthur, by Edmund F. Noel	Account	15 JAN 1827	1825:128, 132, 140
Rennolds, Arthur, by Edmund F. Noel	Account	18 AUG 1828	1825:248
Rennolds, Arthur, by Edmund F. Noel	Account	20 JUL 1829	1825:302
Rennolds, Arthur F., from Edmund F. Noel	Receipt	20 MAR 1832	1831:110
Rennolds, Benjamin to Nicholas Davis	Bond	19 JAN 1724/5	WB4:092
Rennolds, Benjamin C., c/o Albert to his father	Bond	18 MAY 1886	1867:572
Rennolds, Betty, c/o Otway to her father	Bond	16 MAR 1857	1851:414
Rennolds, Catharine Malvina, c/o Otway to her father	Bond	16 MAR 1857	1851:414
Rennolds, Daniel Lewis, c/o John to Andrew Rennolds	Bond	21 JUL 1806	1796:183
Rennolds, Daniel and wife, from Barbee Spindle	Receipt	19 SEP 1825	1825:017
Rennolds, Daniel, from Andrew Rennolds	Receipt	19 SEP 1825	1825:017
Rennolds, E. Rosalie, c/o Albert to his father	Bond	18 MAY 1886	1867:572
Rennolds, Emily, by Thomas M. Henley	Account	19 JUN 1826	1825:108
Rennolds, Emily, Miss, by Thomas M. Henley	Account	19 FEB 1828	1825:224
Rennolds, Emily, by Thomas M. Henley	Account	18 APR 1831	1831:049, 057, 059
Rennolds, Emily, by Thomas M. Henley	Account	16 DEC 1833	1831:228, 230
Rennolds, Emily, by Thomas M. Henley	Account	18 NOV 1833	1831:226
Rennolds, Emily, c/o Sthreshly to Robert B. Rennolds	Bond	21 SEP 1835	1831:328
Rennolds, Emily, by Thomas M. Henley	Account	16 MAY 1836	1831:422
Rennolds, Emily, by Robert B. Rennolds	Account	19 FEB 1838	1838:016
Rennolds, Henry S., from Maj. George Wright	Receipt	19 DEC 1827	1825:186
Rennolds, Henry S., by George Wright	Account	19 DEC 1827	1825:182
Rennolds, John T., c/o Albert to his father	Bond	18 MAY 1886	1867:572
Rennolds, Lewis, from Andrew Rennolds	Receipt	19 SEP 1825	1825:018
Rennolds, Louisa, by Thomas M. Henley	Account	19 JUN 1826	1825:106
Rennolds, Louisa, Miss, by Thomas M. Henley	Account	19 FEB 1828	1825:222
Rennolds, Louisa, by Thomas M. Henley	Account	18 APR 1831	1831:041, 043, 045
Rennolds, Louisa, by Thomas M. Henley	Account	16 DEC 1833	1831:234, 236, 238
Rennolds, Louisa, by Thomas M. Henley	Account	16 MAR 1835	1831:288
Rennolds, Lucy L., c/o James to Rufus S. Rennolds	Bond	16 DEC 1850	1844:480
Rennolds, Nancy, c/o John to Andrew Rennolds	Bond	21 JUL 1806	1796:184
Rennolds, Otway, by Edmond F. Noel	Account	15 JAN 1827	1825:128, 130, 138
Rennolds, Otway, by Edmund F. Noel	Account	18 AUG 1828	1825:246
Rennolds, Otway, by Edmund F. Noel	Account	18 AUG 1828	1825:246
Rennolds, Otway, by Edmund F. Noel	Account	15 JUN 1829	1825:314
Rennolds, Otway, from Edmund F. Noel	Receipt	22 MAY 1832	1831:111
Rennolds, Philip, c/o Philip to Andrew Rennolds	Bond	17 JUL 1815	1811:085
Rennolds, Philip, from Andrew Rennolds	Receipt	19 SEP 1825	1825:018

Ward or Subject (and Parent, Guardian or Other)	Record Type	Date	Reference(s)
Rennolds, Robert, by Edmond F. Noel	Account	15 JAN 1827	1825:128, 134, 142
Rennolds, Robert, by Edmund F. Noel	Account	20 JUL 1829	1825:305
Rennolds, Robert, by Edmund F. Noel	Account	18 APR 1831	1831:011
Rennolds, Robert B., by Edmund F. Noel	Account	19 MAR 1832	1831:105
Rennolds, Robert B., from Edmund F. Noel	Receipt	16 SEP 1833	1831:195
Rennolds, Sidney, c/o John to Andrew Rennolds	Bond	21 JUL 1806	1796:183
Rennolds, Sidney, from Andrew Rennolds	Receipt	19 SEP 1825	1825:018
Rennolds, Susan, by Thomas M. Henley	Account	19 JUN 1826	1825:110
Rennolds, Susan, Miss, by Thomas M. Henley	Account	19 FEB 1828	1825:226
Rennolds, Susan, by Thomas M. Henley	Account	18 APR 1831	1831:047, 053, 055
Rennolds, Susan, by Thomas M. Henley	Account	16 JAN 1832	1831:087
Rennolds, William G., c/o Albert to his father	Bond	18 MAY 1886	1867:572
Rice, Evan, c/o Evan to Winter Bray	Bond	20 MAY 1839	1838:047
Rice, Evan, by Winter Bray	Account	19 JUL 1841	1838:141
Rice, Evan, by Winter Bray	Account	18 DEC 1848	1844:318
Rice, Thomas E., over 14, c/o Evan to William P. Robinson	Bond	16 OCT 1876	1867:357
Richardson, Edwin, c/o John [Richeson] to his father	Bond	18 DEC 1809	1796:223
Richardson, Henry, c/o John [Richeson] to his father	Bond	18 DEC 1809	1796:223
Richardson, Lucy, c/o John [Richeson] to her father	Bond	18 DEC 1809	1796:223
Richardson, Margaret, d/o John to William Andrews	Bond	15 OCT 1792	1761:184
Richerson, Giles, by Edmund F. Noel	Account	19 DEC 1836	1831:460
Richerson, Julia E., from E.F. Noel	Receipt	21 AUG 1837	1831:499
Richeson, Betsy, c/o John to Edmund F. Noel	Bond	19 FEB 1821	1811:247
Richeson, Chaney, c/o John to Edmund F. Noel	Bond	19 FEB 1821	1811:247
Richeson, Delia, by Edmund F. Noel	Account	19 MAR 1832	1831:103
Richeson, Delia, from Edmund F. Noel	Receipt	20 MAR 1832	1831:110
Richeson, Delila, c/o John to Edmund F. Noel	Bond	19 FEB 1821	1811:247
Richeson, Delilah, by Edmund F. Noel	Account	18 APR 1831	1831:007
Richeson, Giles, c/o John to Edmund F. Noel	Bond	19 FEB 1821	1811:247
Richeson, Giles, by Edmund F. Noel	Account	18 APR 1831	1831:009
Richeson, Giles, by Edmund F. Noel	Account	19 MAR 1832	1831:103
Richeson, Giles, by Edmond F. Noel	Account	17 APR 1833	1831:171
Richeson, Giles, by Edmund F. Noel	Account	19 MAY 1834	1831:248
Richeson, Giles, by Edmund F. Noel	Account	20 JUL 1835	1831:310
Richeson, Giles N., from Edmund F. Noel	Receipt	15 JUL 1839	1838:059
Richeson, Jane, by Edmund F. Noel	Account	18 APR 1831	1831:007
Richeson, John, c/o John to Edmund F. Noel	Bond	19 FEB 1821	1811:247
Richeson, Julia, c/o John to Edmund F. Noel	Bond	19 FEB 1821	1811:247
Richeson, Julia, by Edmund F. Noel	Account	18 APR 1831	1831:007
Richeson, Julia, by Edmund F. Noel	Account	19 MAR 1832	1831:103
Richeson, Julia, c/o Edmund F. Noel	Account	21 MAR 1833	1831:170
Richeson, Julia [Richerson], by Edmond F. Noel	Account	19 MAY 1834	1831:250
Richeson, Julia, by Edmond F. Noel	Account	20 JUL 1835	1831:312
Roane, Judith, c/o William, by Thomas Roane, Jr.	Account	15 SEP 1788	1761:159
Roane, Sarah, c/o William, by Thomas Roane, Jr.	Account	15 SEP 1788	1761:159
Roane, William, dec.	Account Ref.	18 FEB 1760	1731:248
Robb, Margaret, c/o Robert G. to Henry Waring	Bond	15 OCT 1832	1831:142
Roberson, James F., c/o Maria (C) to James H. Mitchell	Bond	17 JUL 1882	1867:490
Roberson, Ora Belle, c/o Maria (C) to James H. Mitchell	Bond	17 JUL 1882	1867:490
Roberson, Robt. Manley, c/o Maria (C) to James H. Mitchell	Bond	17 JUL 1882	1867:490
Roberts, Daniel to Nicholas Pamplin	Bond	15 FEB 1736/7	WB6:043

Ward or Subject (and Parent, Guardian or Other)	Record Type	Date	Reference(s)
Roberts, Daniel, by Nicholas Pamplin	Account	17 FEB 1740	1731:038
Roberts, Daniel, by Nicholas Pamplin	Account	17 NOV 1741	1731:045
Roberts, Daniel, by Nicholas Pamplin	Account	19 OCT 1742	1731:051
Roberts, Daniel, by Nicholas Pamplin	Account	19 OCT 1743	1731:059
Roberts, Daniel, by Nicholas Pamplin	Account	18 SEP 1744	1731:075
Robinson, Ann to Susanna Robinson	Bond	20 MAY 1729	WB4:289a
Robinson, Harry C., at *Camp Lee*, to bro. Wm. P. Robinson	Certificate	19 DEC 1864	1857:352
Robinson, Harry C., c/o John W. to William P. Robinson	Bond	19 DEC 1864	1857:353
Robinson, James F., c/o Maria to Benjamin Johnson	Bond	21 NOV 1882	1867:501
Robinson, Mattie, c/o Maria to Benjamin Johnson	Bond	21 NOV 1882	1867:501
Robinson, Orabella, c/o Maria to Benjamin Johnson	Bond	21 NOV 1882	1867:501
Robinson, Robt. Manning, c/o Maria to James H. Mitchell	Bond	21 AUG 1882	1867:492
Roddin, Betsy, c/o Peggy to Thomas Marlow	Bond	17 DEC 1832	1831:156
Roddin, Elizabeth, c/o Stephen to Thomas Brizendine	Bond	17 MAR 1828	1825:229
Rogers, John and wife Lucy Gordon, from Mrs. Susannah Gordon	Receipt	19 SEP 1825	1825:014
Rouzee, Elizabeth A., c/o John to Edward Rouzee	Bond	21 JUN 1819	1811:188
Rouzee, Fanny, c/o William to Edward Rouzee & others	Bond	21 DEC 1802	1796:120
Rouzee, Harriett T., c/o John to Edward Rouzee	Bond	21 JUN 1819	1811:188
Rouzee, John, c/o William to Edward Rouzee & others	Bond	21 DEC 1802	1796:120
Rouzee, Sally F., c/o Richard to James Webb	Bond	17 NOV 1803	1796:141
Rouzee, Sarah F., c/o John to Edward Rouzee	Bond	21 JUN 1819	1811:188
Rowzee, Apphia Bushrod, c/o Richard to Apphia Rowzee	Bond	21 SEP 1801	1796:093
Rowzee, Benjamin, by Henry Harman	Account	15 JAN 1744	1731:082
Rowzee, Benjamin, by Henry Harmon	Account	20 NOV 1745	1731:093
Rowzee, Benjamin, by Henry Harmon	Account	18 NOV 1746	1731:104
Rowzee, Eliza., c/o Ralph to Benja. Edmondson	Bond	18 FEB 1755	1731:191
Rowzee, Elizabeth to Thomas Jones	Bond	16 DEC 1735	WB5:385
Rowzee, Elizabeth to Robert Harbin	Bond	21 MAR 1748/9	WB8:193
Rowzee, Elizabeth A., by Edward Rowzee	Account	19 SEP 1825	1825:029
Rowzee, Elizabeth A., c/o John, by Edward Rowzee	Account	19 SEP 1831	1831:071
Rowzee, Emily R., c/o Robert R. to John S. Rowzee, Jr.	Bond	16 MAR 1857	1851:417
Rowzee, Frances, by Edward Rowzee	Account	21 AUG 1820	1811:228
Rowzee, Harriet F.C., c/o John, by Edward Rowzee	Account	19 SEP 1831	1831:071
Rowzee, Harriett F.C., by Edward Rowzee	Account	17 OCT 1825	1825:029
Rowzee, Harriott, c/o Richard to Apphia Rowzee	Bond	21 SEP 1801	1796:093
Rowzee, Henry S.R., c/o Robert R. to John S. Rowzee, Jr.	Bond	16 MAR 1857	1851:417
Rowzee, John to John Motley	Bond	17 JUN 1724	WB4:062
Rowzee, Martha to Benjamin Rowzee	Bond	21 SEP 1725	WB4:113
Rowzee, Martha B., c/o Robert R. to John S. Rowzee, Jr.	Bond	16 MAR 1857	1851:417
Rowzee, Mary to Elizabeth Holloway	Bond	18 AUG 1747	WB8:016
Rowzee, Ralph to Henry Harman	Bond	16 FEB 1742/3	WB6:421
Rowzee, Ralph, dec. [Elizabeth]	Account	19 OCT 1756	1731:202
Rowzee, Robert R., c/o Robert R. to John S. Rowzee, Jr.	Bond	16 MAR 1857	1851:417
Rowzee, Sarah F., by Edward Rowzee	Account	19 SEP 1825	1825:029
Rowzee, Sarah F., c/o John, by Edward Rowzee	Account	19 SEP 1831	1831:071
Rowzee, William D., c/o Robert R. to John S. Rowzee, Jr.	Bond	16 MAR 1857	1851:417
Roy, Ann C., Miss, by Larkin Hundley	Account	21 FEB 1826	1825:083
Roy, Ann C., by Larkin Hundley	Account	19 FEB 1827	1825:153
Roy, Ann C., Miss, by Larkin Hundley	Account	18 MAR 1828	1825:235
Roy, Ann C., by Larkin Hundley	Account	15 JUN 1829	1825:289
Roy, Ann C., by Larkin Hundley	Account	18 APR 1831	1831:051

Ward or Subject (and Parent, Guardian or Other)	Record Type	Date	Reference(s)
Roy, Ann C., by Larkin Hundley	Account	16 MAR 1831	WB22:303
Roy, Ann C., by Larkin Hundley	Account	18 JUL 1831	1831:063
Roy, Ann C. now Dyke, from Larkin Hundley	Receipt	16 APR 1832	1831:111
Roy, James C., s/o James to his father	Bond	20 AUG 1810	1796:231
Roy, James C., s/o James to Hugh Campbell	Bond	16 DEC 1811	1811:002
Roy, James C., s/o James to Richard P. Banks	Bond	19 NOV 1811	1811:001
Roy, James C., by James Roy	Account	21 JUN 1814	1811:060
Roy, Philip S., c/o Thomas S. to James H. Roy	Bond	19 JUL 1869	1867:084
Roy, Richard S., c/o Richard D. to Larkin Hundley	Bond	21 JAN 1828	1825:210
Roy, Richard D., by Larkin Hundley	Account	15 JUN 1829	1825:287
Roy, Richard D., by Larkin Hundley	Account	19 NOV 1832	1831:146
Rust, Alice Lee, c/o Benj., by Lettice Lee Rust	Account	17 SEP 1792	WB14:327
Rust, Alice Lee, c/o Benjamin to Lettice Lee Rust	Bond	16 JUL 1792	1761:182
Rust, Lettice Smith, c/o Benj., by Lettice Lee Rust	Account	17 SEP 1792	WB14:327
Rust, Lettice Smith, c/o Benjamin to Lettice Lee Rust	Bond	16 JUL 1792	1761:182
Rutherford, Dinah, c/o Micajah to Timothy Goode	Bond	21 JAN 1793	1761:189
Rutherford, John, c/o Micajah to Hezekiah Mitchell	Bond	18 AUG 1791	1761:174
Ryden, Nancy, c/o William to William Hodges	Bond	18 JUL 1791	1761:174
Ryland, Sarah, Miss, by Josiah Minter	Account	15 AUG 1774	1761:118, 119
Ryland, Sarah, by Josiah Minter	Account	20 OCT 1777	1761:132
Ryland, Susannah, Miss, by Josiah Minter	Account	20 OCT 1777	1761:133

S

Ward or Subject (and Parent, Guardian or Other)	Record Type	Date	Reference(s)
Sadler, Charles R., by Robert Y. Henley	Account	20 JAN 1873	1867:209
Sadler, Charles R.., by Robert Y. Henley	Account	19 APR 1875	1867:308
Sadler, Charles R., by Robert Y. Henley	Account	18 JUL 1881	1867:452
Sadler, Charles R., from Robert Y. Henley	Receipt	18 JUL 1881	1867:455
Sadler, Fannie E. late Smith, by James F. Harper	Account	18 NOV 1867	1867:018
Sadler, J.F., by Robert Y. Henley	Account	21 OCT 1886	1867:581
Sadler, John F., by Robert Y. Henley	Account	20 JAN 1873	1867:206
Sadler, John F., by Robert Y. Henley	Account	19 APR 1875	1867:307
Sadler, John F., by Robert Y. Henley	Account	22 NOV 1881	1867:470
Sadler, Thos. Evan, c/o Wm. A., under 14, to John H. Boughan	Bond	17 SEP 1884	CCW:149
Sadler, William F., by Robert Y. Henley	Account	19 APR 1875	1867:308
Sadler, William T., by Robert Y. Henley	Account	22 NOV 1881	1867:473
Sadler, Willie T., by Robert Y. Henley	Account	20 JAN 1873	1867:207
Sale, Arriane, c/o William B. to Nancy Sale	Bond	16 SEP 1805	1796:169
Sale, Betty R., by Edward Wright	Account	19 SEP 1853	1851:191
Sale, Betty R., from Edward Wright by Wm. H. Anderson	Receipt	20 OCT 1856	1851:384
Sale, Betty R., by Washington Bayne, from Edward Wright	Receipt	21 JUL 1856	1851:361
Sale, Betty R., by Edward Wright	Account	16 JUN 1856	1851:347
Sale, Fielding, c/o William Brooking Sale to Leonard Sale	Bond	16 SEP 1805	1796:170
Sale, Fielding, c/o William B., by Leonard Sale	Account	21 DEC 1812	1811:034
Sale, Hawkins, c/o William B. to Nancy Sale	Bond	16 SEP 1805	1796:169
Sale, Humphry, by Thomas Sale	Account	18 OCT 1773	1761:100
Sale, James H., c/o Henry T. to Richard P. Banks	Bond	15 JAN 1855	1851:285
Sale, John to Peter Samuell	Bond	20 NOV 1753	1731:172
Sale, Kitty, c/o William B. to Nancy Sale	Bond	16 SEP 1805	1796:169
Sale, Leonard, from Fielding Sale	Receipt	21 DEC 1812	1811:035
Sale, Lewis, c/o Lewis to Susanna Sale	Bond	16 JUN 1806	1796:177
Sale, Lucy Ann, c/o Leonard to Leonard P. Sale	Bond	19 MAR 1832	1831:108

Ward or Subject (and Parent, Guardian or Other)	Record Type	Date	Reference(s)
Sale, Mary L., c/o Leonard to Leonard P. Sale	Bond	21 DEC 1835	1831:355
Sale, Mary L., by Leonard P. Sale	Account	19 JUL 1841	1838:142
Sale, Mary L., by Leonard P. Sale	Account	21 FEB 1842	1838:180
Sale, Mary Susan late Latane, by James H. Latane	Account	18 NOV 1873	1867:222
Sale, Matilda, c/o Wm. B. to John Rowzee	Bond	17 DEC 1804	1796:159
Sale, Nancy, c/o William Brooking Sale to Leonard Sale	Bond	16 SEP 1805	1796:170
Sale, Nancy, c/o William B., by Leonard Sale	Account	21 DEC 1812	1811:030
Sale, Oswald, c/o William B. to Nancy Sale	Bond	16 SEP 1805	1796:169
Sale, Polly, c/o William Brooking Sale to Leonard Sale	Bond	16 SEP 1805	1796:170
Sale, Polly, c/o Lewis to Susanna Sale	Bond	16 JUN 1806	1796:177
Sale, Polly, c/o William B., by Leonard Sale	Account	21 DEC 1812	1811:032
Sale, Sarah C., c/o Henry T. to Richard P. Banks	Bond	15 JAN 1855	1851:285
Sale, Virginia A., by Edward Wright	Account	19 SEP 1853	1851:209
Sale, Virginia A., c/o John C. to Washington Bayne	Bond	15 OCT 1855	1851:328
Sale, Virginia A., by Edward Wright	Account	16 JUN 1856	1851:348
Sale, Virginia S., by Washington Bayne, from Edward Wright	Receipt	21 JUL 1856	1851:361
Sale, Virginia A., by Washington Bayne	Account	17 JAN 1859	1857:127
Sale, Virginia A., by Washington Bayne	Account	21 JAN 1861	1857:246
Samuel, Maria Frances, c/o Reuben to James Smither	Bond	16 SEP 1833	1831:193
Samuel, Phebe, to James Davis	Bond	20 AUG 1751	WB9:084
Samuel, Vanangus A., c/o Philemon to Reuben L. Pitts	Bond	18 JAN 1836	1831:400
Samuel, William, c/o John to Peter Samuel	Bond	16 JAN 1759	1731:238
Samuell, John to James Davis	Bond	20 MAR 1753	1731:157
Samuell, Robert to James Davis	Bond	20 MAR 1753	1731:157
Sanders, Catharine, by L.C. Gatewood	Account	16 NOV 1835	1831:348
Saunders, James T., c/o William H., to William H. Street	Bond	8 APR 1874	CCW:098
Saunders, Robert, by Lineaus C. Gatewood	Account	21 JAN 1833	1831:163
Saunders, Sucky, d/o Betty to Spencer Saunders	Bond	19 NOV 1827	1825:194
Saunders, William, by L.C. Gatewood	Account	16 NOV 1835	1831:344
Scott, Florence, over 14, c/o Mary to Robert Harris	Bond	17 MAY 1886	1867:573
Scott, J.B., by M.S. Scott	Account	21 OCT 1886	1867:579
Scott, Joseph Bernard, under 14, c/o Joseph to Mary S. Scott	Bond	21 JUN 1880	1867:422
Scott, Joseph B., by Mary S. Scott	Account	22 NOV 1881	1867:468
Scott, Joseph B., by Mary S. Scott	Account	19 AUG 1882	1867:493
Scott, Joseph H. to father Rev. A.F. Scott	Certificate	21 MAY 1883	1867:519
Scott, Joseph H., over 14, c/o Azariah F. Scott to his father	Bond	21 MAY 1883	1867:520
Scott, Joseph B., by Mary S. Scott	Account	21 JAN 1884	1867:532
Scott, Licia, c/o Fanny, to Joseph Ritchie	Bond	16 MAR 1881	CCW:117
Scott, Maggie Holt, unsound, c/o Azariah F. to her father	Bond C.	21 MAY 1883	1867:521
Seares, Sally, by Elizabeth Waggener	Account	17 AUG 1761	1761:006
Searle, Covington to James Curtis	Bond	18 JAN 1730/1	WB5:014
Searle, Covington, by James Curtis	Account	21 DEC 1731	1731:005
Seayres, John, c/o John to Robert Seayres	Bond	21 JAN 1755	1731:191
Seayres, John, c/o John, to Thomas Waring	Bond	21 DEC 1756	WB10:113
Seayres, John	Account	18 OCT 1757	WB11:017
Seayres, John, by Francis Waring	Account	17 JAN 1763	WB12:030
Seayres, Sarah, c/o John to Thomas Waring	Bond	17 DEC 1754	1731:189
Segar, John C., c/o John M. to Agnes Segar	Bond	19 SEP 1859	1857:153
Segar, Rosa to Albert Montague	Certificate	20 JAN 1873	1867:187
Segar, Rosa, c/o Abraham to Albert Montague	Bond	20 JAN 1873	1867:188
Semple, Mary H., c/o James to James Semple	Bond	19 FEB 1849	1844:327

Ward or Subject (and Parent, Guardian or Other)	Record Type	Date	Reference(s)
Shearwood, Ann, by Josiah Minter	Account	18 APR 1831	1831:019
Shearwood, Ann C., by Jameson Moody	Account	16 JUN 1834	1831:272
Shearwood, Catharine, c/o John to Jameson Moody	Bond	18 AUG 1828	1825:241
Shearwood, John, by Jameson Moody	Account	16 JUN 1834	1831:272
Shearwood, Jonathan, c/o John to Jameson Moody	Bond	18 AUG 1828	1825:241
Shearwood, Mary, c/o Richard to Thomas Boughan	Bond	15 NOV 1847	1844:247
Shearwood, Nancy, c/o Johnathan to Richard Shearwood	Bond	18 MAR 1805	1796:162
Shearwood, Richard, by Josiah Minter	Account	18 APR 1831	1831:017
Shearwood, Thomas, c/o John to Jameson Moody	Bond	18 AUG 1828	1825:241
Shearwood, Thomas, by Jameson Moody	Account	16 JUN 1834	1831:272
Shearwood, William, c/o John to Jameson Moody	Bond	18 AUG 1828	1825:241
Shelton, John, orphans of, by George P. Young	Account	21 FEB 1826	1825:086
Shelton, Thomas, from Elizabeth Broocks	Receipt	19 SEP 1825	1825:015
Shepard, Ephraim, c/o Jeremiah to Chs. Howerton	Bond	16 OCT 1797	1796:013
Shepard, Jeremiah, dec.	Account	21 SEP 1756	1731:201
Shepard, Jeremiah, by Humphry Davis	Account	19 SEP 1758	1731:232
Shepard, Jeremiah	Account	20 SEP 1762	1761:020
Shepard, Lettice, c/o Jeremiah to Henry Vass	Bond	21 MAR 1758	1731:220
Shepard, Milly, c/o Jeremiah to Chs. Howerton	Bond	16 OCT 1797	1796:013
Shepard, Sally, c/o Jeremiah to John Trible	Bond	16 OCT 1797	1796:012
Shepard, William, c/o Jeremiah to Thomas Broocke	Bond	19 SEP 1758	1731:234
Shepard, William, by Thomas Broocke	Account	20 AUG 1759	1731:243
Shepard, William, by Thomas Brookes	Account	17 AUG 1761	1761:007
Shepard, William, by Thomas Newbill	Account	19 OCT 1761	1761:009
Shepard, William, h/o Jeremiah, by Thomas Newbill	Account	20 SEP 1762	1761:020
Shepard, Wm., by Thomas Newbill	Account	19 SEP 1763	1761:040
Shephard, Wm., c/o Jeremiah, by Thomas Broocke	Account	18 AUG 1760	1731:259
Shepherd, Charles R., c/o Smith Y. to Edward L. Wright	Bond	18 OCT 1852	1851:131
Shepherd, Elizabeth, c/o Jeremiah to William Young	Bond	21 NOV 1758	1731:236
Shepherd, Emily E., by Edward L. Wright	Account	17 OCT 1859	1857:181
Shepherd, Emily E., c/o Smith Y. to John E. Shepherd	Bond	17 SEP 1866	1857:412
Shepherd, James W., by Edward L. Wright	Account	17 OCT 1859	1857:184
Shepherd, John E., by Edward L. Wright	Account	17 OCT 1859	1857:183
Shepherd, John William, of 14, c/o John to Ludy S. Hodges	Bond	17 MAR 1884	1867:538
Shepherd, Mary T., by Edward L. Wright	Account	17 OCT 1859	1857:185
Sheppard, Emily E., under 14, c/o Smith Y. to G.F. Ramsay	Bond	19 NOV 1860	1857:231
Sheppard, Emily E., over 14, to John E. Sheppard	Certificate	17 SEP 1866	1857:411
Sheppard, James W., c/o Smith Y. to George F. Ramsay	Bond	19 NOV 1860	1857:231
Sheppard, James W., c/o Smith Y. to G.F. Ramsay	Certificate	19 NOV 1860	1857:231
Sheppard, John E., c/o Smith Y. to George F. Ramsay	Bond	19 NOV 1860	1857:231
Sheppard, John E., c/o Smith Y. to G.F. Ramsay	Certificate	19 NOV 1860	1857:231
Sheppard, Mary F., c/o Smith Y. to G.F. Ramsay	Certificate	19 NOV 1860	1857:231
Sheppard, Mary F., c/o Smith Y. to George F. Ramsay	Bond	19 NOV 1860	1857:231
Ship, Richard to William Thomas	Bond	20 JUN 1727	WB4:206
Ship, Thomas to James Blassingham	Bond	20 JUN 1727	WB4:203
Simco, Martha A., by Elizabeth Brooks	Account	15 DEC 1834	1831:284
Simco, William, from James Brooks	Receipt	19 SEP 1825	1825:015
Simcoe, Joseph, c/o Reuben to Elizabeth Simcoe	Bond	18 DEC 1815	1811:110
Simcoe, Martha Ann, c/o Reuben to Elizabeth Simcoe	Bond	18 DEC 1815	1811:110
Simcoe, Mary, c/o Reuben to Elizabeth Simcoe	Bond	18 DEC 1815	1811:110
Simcoe, Susan, c/o Reuben to Elizabeth Simcoe	Bond	18 DEC 1815	1811:110

Ward or Subject (and Parent, Guardian or Other)	Record Type	Date	Reference(s)
Simcoe, William, c/o Reuben to Elizabeth Simcoe	Bond	18 DEC 1815	1811:110
Singleton, Isaac [Asaac] to Thomas Waring	Bond	17 JUL 1739	WB6:196
Skelton, Eliza J., c/o George to Thomas N. Clarke	Bond	18 JAN 1847	1844:186
Skelton, Eudora Agnes, c/o George to Thomas N. Clarke	Bond	18 JAN 1847	1844:186
Skelton, Maria L., c/o George to Thomas N. Clarke	Bond	18 JAN 1847	1844:186
Smether, Edmund, c/o Robert to William Howerton	Bond	17 JUN 1811	1796:248
Smith, Alice, c/o William to Francis Smith	Bond	15 DEC 1800	1796:081
Smith, Benjamin, c/o Col. Joseph, by John Tayloe	Account	16 SEP 1740	1731:005
Smith, Benjamin to John Smith	Bond	17 MAR 1740/1	WB6:290
Smith, Benjamin, c/o Col. Joseph, by John Tayloe	Account P.	16 SEP 1740	1731:024
Smith, Benjamin, c/o Col. Joseph, by John Tayloe	Account	17 AUG 1741	1731:040
Smith, Benjamin, c/o Col. Joseph, by John Smith	Account	20 APR 1742	1731:046
Smith, Benjamin to Thomas Plummer	Bond	20 MAR 1743/4	WB7:098
Smith, Benjamin, c/o Col. Joseph, by John Smith	Account	18 SEP 1744	1731:072
Smith, Betsey, d/o Stephen to Benjamin Haile	Bond	17 JUN 1811	1796:249
Smith, Betty to John Tayloe	Bond	17 NOV 1730	WB4:408
Smith, Betty, c/o Col. Joseph, by John Tayloe	Account P.	16 SEP 1740	1731:024
Smith, Betty, gd/o Mrs. Kath. Gwyn	Account P.	16 SEP 1740	1731:028
Smith, Betty, c/o Col. Joseph, by John Tayloe	Account	16 SEP 1740	1731:005
Smith, Betty, c/o Col. Joseph, by John Tayloe	Account	17 AUG 1741	1731:040
Smith, Betty, legacy by her grandmother Mrs. Gwyn	Account	15 SEP 1741	1731:038
Smith, Edward to John Smith	Bond	17 MAR 1740/1	WB6:290
Smith, Edward, c/o Col. Joseph, by John Tayloe	Account	16 SEP 1740	1731:005
Smith, Edward, c/o Col. Joseph, by John Tayloe	Account P.	16 SEP 1740	1731:024
Smith, Edward, c/o Col. Joseph, by John Tayloe	Account	17 AUG 1741	1731:040
Smith, Edward, c/o Col. Joseph, by John Smith	Account	20 APR 1742	1731:046
Smith, Edward, c/o Col. Joseph, by John Smith	Account	18 SEP 1744	1731:072
Smith, Elizabeth, c/o Stephen to John Games	Bond	15 FEB 1819	1811:176
Smith, Elizabeth dau. of late Thos. Collins, by Virginia Lorimer	Account	20 JUN 1842	1838:210
Smith, Emily F., c/o Francis G. to Ethelbert G. Cauthorn	Bond	21 FEB 1853	1851:168
Smith, Emily F., by James F. Harper	Account	18 JUN 1855	1851:307
Smith, Fannie E., by James F. Harper	Account	19 SEP 1859	1857:161
Smith, Fannie E., by James F. Harper	Account	17 SEP 1860	1857:226
Smith, Fannie E., by James F. Harper	Account	21 JUL 1862	1857:286a
Smith, Fannie E. now w/o Cyrus Sadler, by James F. Harper	Account	18 NOV 1867	1867:018
Smith, Frances E., c/o Francis G.W. to James F. Harper	Bond	15 AUG 1853	1851:184
Smith, Frances E., by James F. Harper	Account	19 JUL 1858	1857:067
Smith, Henry to Ann Smith	Bond	16 OCT 1744	WB7:206
Smith, Henry, c/o Robert, by Ann Smith	Account	20 JAN 1746/7	1731:106
Smith, Isaac to William Mountague	Bond	16 JUL 1745	WB7:356
Smith, James, c/o John, by Newman Miskell	Account	16 OCT 1769	1761:079
Smith, James, c/o John, by Samuel Smith	Account	18 FEB 1771	1761:084
Smith, James H., c/o Joseph B. to Gabriel H. Dillard	Bond	16 OCT 1848	1844:295, 298
Smith, Jane to Ann Smith	Bond	16 OCT 1744	WB7:206
Smith, Jane, c/o Robert, by Ann Smith	Account	20 JAN 1746/7	1731:105
Smith, John to John Tayloe of Richmond Co.	Bond	17 NOV 1730	WB4:407
Smith, John, brother of Edward and Benjamin Smith	Receipt	17 AUG 1741	1731:042
Smith, John, orphans of, by Newman Miskell	Account	20 SEP 1762	1761:019
Smith, John, orphans of, by Newman Miskell	Account	16 AUG 1763	1761:032
Smith, John, orphans of, by Newman Miskell	Account	17 SEP 1764	1761:047
Smith, John, orphans of, by Newman Miskell	Account	17 SEP 1765	1761:059

Ward or Subject (and Parent, Guardian or Other)	Record Type	Date	Reference(s)
Smith, John C., c/o George to Constantine B. Smith	Bond	17 MAR 1856	1851:340
Smith, Lettice to William Mountague	Bond	16 JUL 1745	WB7:355
Smith, Maurice to John Wyat	Bond	11 JAN 1708/9	D&W13:172
Smith, Ralph to Ralph Rowzee	Bond	10 FEB 1708/9	D&W13:185
Smith, Reuben to William Mountague	Bond	16 JUL 1745	WB7:356
Smith, Samuel to John Wyat	Bond	11 JAN 1708/9	D&W13:172
Smith, Susanna, c/o Philip, Gent. to Saml. Hipkins	Bond	18 NOV 1755	1731:196
Smith, William to Francis Meriwether	Bond	10 JAN 1708/9	D&W13:170
Smith, William, c/o John, by Newman Miskell	Account	16 OCT 1769	1761:078
Smith, William, c/o John, by Samuel Smith	Account	18 FEB 1771	1761:083
Smith, William Garland, c/o George to William Smith	Bond	21 FEB 1848	1844:257
Smith, William Garland, by William Smith	Account	21 NOV 1853	1851:214
Smith, William Garland, by William Smith	Account	18 JUN 1855	WB27:530
Smith, William Garland, by William Smith	Account	18 JUN 1855	1851:303
Smith, William Garland, by William Smith	Account	18 AUG 1856	1851:369
Smith, William Garland, by William Smith	Account	19 OCT 1857	1857:021
Smith, William Garland, by William Smith	Account	20 DEC 1858	1857:111
Smith, William Garland, by William Smith	Account	19 SEP 1859	1857:159
Smith, William Garland, by William Smith	Account	17 SEP 1860	1857:221
Smith, William G., c/o George to Robert P.W. Fauntleroy	Bond	17 JUN 1861	1857:265
Smith, William Garland, by R.P.W. Fauntleroy	Account	21 FEB 1866	1857:375
Smither, Edmund, c/o William to James Sale	Bond	21 JAN 1799	1796:041
Smither, John H. & wife Patsy Jones, from Nancy Jones	Receipt	16 MAR 1835	1831:291
Smither, John L., over 14, c/o Elizabeth to Wm. B. Smither	Bond	15 SEP 1856	1851:383
Smither, Joseph E., c/o William B. to Edward Wright	Bond	16 JUL 1838	1838:031
Smither, Martha A., c/o William B. to Edward Wright	Bond	16 JUL 1838	1838:031
Southall, Agnes Neilson, c/o Charles T. to James L. Cox	Bond	21 OCT 1816	1811:122
Southall, Agnes, c/o Charles T. to David P. Wright	Bond	15 AUG 1831	1831:068
Southall, Agnes, by James L. Cox	Account	20 MAR 1833	1831:167
Southall, Agnes N., by David P. Wright	Account	20 JAN 1834	1831:243
Southall, Mary Ellen, c/o Charles T. to James L. Cox	Bond	21 OCT 1816	1811:122
Southall, Mary Ellen, c/o Charles T. to David P. Wright	Bond	15 AUG 1831	1831:068
Southall, Mary Ellen, by James L. Cox	Account	20 MAR 1833	1831:167
Southall, Mary E., by David P. Wright	Account	20 JAN 1834	1831:241
Southern, William, by William Simco	Account	19 DEC 1785	1761:147
Southworth, Harrison, from Frances N. Henshall	P. of Atty.	22 DEC 1887	1867:595
Southworth, Sophia, c/o Richard to Woodford Southworth	Bond	17 FEB 1840	1838:072
Spindle, Archibald R., c/o Silas B. to Daniel Rennolds	Bond	18 JUN 1838	1838:030
Spindle, Archibald, h/o Silas B., by Daniel Rennolds	Account	21 SEP 1841	1838:150
Spindle, Archibald R., by Daniel Rennolds	Account	16 SEP 1844	1838:360
Spindle, Archibald R., by Daniel Rennolds	Account	15 FEB 1847	1844:189
Spindle, Archibald R., by Daniel Rennolds	Account	16 DEC 1850	1844:482
Spindle, Barbee, c/o Barbee to Thomas B. Garnett	Bond	20 JAN 1840	1838:070
Spindle, Barbee, by Thomas B. Garnett	Account	18 JUL 1842	1838:224
Spindle, Barbee, by Thomas B. Garnett	Account	17 MAR 1845	1844:010
Spindle, Elizabeth, c/o Barbee to Thomas B. Garnett	Bond	20 JAN 1840	1838:070
Spindle, Elizabeth, by Thomas B. Garnett	Account	18 JUN 1842	1838:226
Spindle, Elizabeth P., by Thomas B. Garnett	Account	19 JUL 1847	1844:226
Spindle, Frances M., c/o Mordecai to Sally Spindle	Bond	17 OCT 1836	1831:450
Spindle, Francis, c/o Barbee to his father	Bond	18 NOV 1811	1811:001
Spindle, John E., c/o Silas B. to Daniel Rennolds	Bond	18 JUN 1838	1838:030

Ward or Subject (and Parent, Guardian or Other)	Record Type	Date	Reference(s)
Spindle, John, h/o Silas B., by Daniel Rennolds	Account	21 SEP 1841	1838:150
Spindle, John E., by Daniel Rennolds	Account	16 SEP 1844	1838:362
Spindle, John, by Daniel Rennolds	Account	15 FEB 1847	1844:187
Spindle, John E., from Daniel Rennolds	Receipt	19 MAR 1849	1844:335
Spindle, John E., by Daniel Rennolds	Account	19 MAR 1849	1844:334
Spindle, Joseph, c/o Barbee to Thomas B. Garnett	Bond	20 JAN 1840	1838:070
Spindle, Joseph, by Thomas B. Garnett	Account	18 JUL 1842	1838:226
Spindle, Joseph, by Thomas B. Garnett	Account	19 JUL 1847	1844:220
Spindle, Juliet, c/o Barbee to her father	Bond	18 NOV 1811	1811:001
Spindle, Martha, c/o Barbee to her father	Bond	18 NOV 1811	1811:001
Spindle, Philip, c/o Leonard to Thomas B. Garnett	Bond	15 JUN 1840	1838:093
Spindle, Philip, by Thomas B. Garnett	Account	15 MAY 1843	1838:258, 265
Spindle, Philip, by Thomas B. Garnett	Account	17 MAR 1845	1844:008
Spindle, Philip, by Thomas B. Garnett	Account	19 JUL 1847	1844:224, 228
Spindle, Philip S., by Daniel Rennolds	Account	19 JUN 1848	1844:273
Spindle, Rebecca S., c/o Silas B. to Daniel Rennolds	Bond	18 JUN 1838	1838:030
Spindle, Rebecca, h/o Silas B., by Daniel Rennolds	Account	21 SEP 1841	1838:150
Spindle, Rebecca S., by Daniel Rennolds	Account	16 SEP 1844	1838:364
Spindle, Rebecca, by Daniel Rennolds	Account	19 JUN 1848	1844:270
Spindle, Silas B. and wife, from Barbee Spindle	Receipt	19 SEP 1825	1825:016
Spindle, Silas B., orphans of, by Daniel Rennolds	Account	20 SEP 1841	WB24:626
Spindle, Silas B., heirs of, by Daniel Rennolds	Account	21 SEP 1841	1838:150
Spindle, Silas Wilton, by Daniel Rennolds	Account	16 SEP 1844	1838:368
Spindle, Silas Wilton, s/o Silas, from Daniel Rennolds	Receipt	15 MAY 1848	1844:269
Spindle, Virginia Marcella, c/o Leonard to Thomas B. Garnett	Bond	15 JUN 1840	1838:093
Spindle, Virginia M., by Thomas B. Garnett	Account	15 MAY 1843	1838:258, 265
Spindle, Virginia M., by Thomas B. Garnett	Account	17 MAR 1845	1844:008
Spindle, Virginia M., by Thomas B. Garnett	Account	19 JUL 1847	1844:224, 228
Spindle, Virginia M., by Daniel Rennolds	Account	19 JUN 1848	1844:272
Spindle, Virginia M., by Thomas B. Garnett, trustee	Account	20 MAY 1850	1844:456
Spindle, William, h/o Silas B., by Daniel Rennolds	Account	21 SEP 1841	1838:150
Spindle, Wilton S., c/o Silas B. to Daniel Rennolds	Bond	18 JUN 1838	1838:030
St. John, Abraham to John Tyler	Bond	20 SEP 1737	WB6:091
St. John, Katherine to William Covington	Bond	16 JUN 1741	WB6:311
St. John, Catherine, by William Covington, Jr.	Account	19 OCT 1742	1731:052
St. John, Richard, c/o William to Richard Gatewood	Bond	15 APR 1755	1731:192
Stephens, Susanah to Robert Leveritt	Bond	17 JAN 1737/8	WB6:110
Stevens, Stanly to Robert Leveritt	Bond	17 JAN 1737/8	WB6:110
Stewart, Patsey, Miss, by William Stewart	Account	19 DEC 1827	1825:181
Stewart, Patsey, by William Stewart	Account	16 FEB 1829	1825:274
Stewart, Patsey, by William Stewart	Account	18 APR 1831	1831:039
Stewart, Patsey, by William Stewart	Account	19 DEC 1831	1831:082
Stewart, Patsy, from William Stewart	Account	17 OCT 1825	1825:047
Stewart, Patsy, Miss, by William Stewart	Account	19 NOV 1827	1825:193
Sthreshley, Susannah to William Sthreshley	Bond	19 JUL 1748	WB8:069
Sthreshley, Thomas, by James Upshaw	Account	17 SEP 1759	1731:245
Sthreshley, Thomas, by James Upshaw	Account	16 AUG 1762	1761:010
Sthreshley, William, by James Upshaw	Account	17 SEP 1759	1731:245
Sthreshly, Thomas, c/o William to James Upshaw	Bond	20 DEC 1757	1731:214
Sthreshly, Thomas, by James Upshaw	Account	19 SEP 1758	1731:230
Sthreshly, Thomas, by James Upshaw	Account	17 AUG 1761	1761:002

Ward or Subject (and Parent, Guardian or Other)	Record Type	Date	Reference(s)
Sthreshly, Thomas, by James Upshaw	Account	19 SEP 1763	1761:034
Sthreshly, William, c/o William to James Upshaw	Bond	20 DEC 1757	1731:214
Sthreshly, William, by James Upshaw	Account	19 SEP 1758	1731:230
Sthreshly, William, by James Upshaw	Account	17 AUG 1761	1761:003
Sthreshly, William, by James Upshaw	Account	16 AUG 1762	1761:011
Sthreshly, William, by James Upshaw	Account	19 SEP 1763	1761:035
Stoakes, Thomas to John Carragan	Bond	17 DEC 1745	WB7:406
Stokes, Thomas, c/o James to Wm. Hill	Bond	21 DEC 1795	1761:220
Streshley, William to William Roane	Bond	20 NOV 1744	WB7:221
Streshly, Mary to Richard Upshaw	Bond	21 AUG 1744	WB7:187

T

Ward or Subject (and Parent, Guardian or Other)	Record Type	Date	Reference(s)
Tandy, Frances to Edward Waller	Bond	19 JAN 1741/2	WB6:360
Tandy, Frances, by Edward Waller	Account	16 OCT 1744	1731:079
Tandy, Frances, Mrs., by Edward Waller	Account	17 SEP 1745	1731:085
Tandy, Frances, by Edward Waller	Account	17 SEP 1746	1731:098
Tandy, Frances, by Edward Waller	Account	20 OCT 1747	1731:110
Tandy, Frances, Mrs., by Edward Waller	Account	18 OCT 1748	1731:125
Tandy, Martha to Henry Crittenden	Bond	15 DEC 1741	WB6:354
Tandy, Martha, by Henry Crittenden	Account	21 JUL 1742	WB6:377
Tate, Arthur, orphans of, by Richard Phillips	Account	18 OCT 1773	1761:100
Tate, Arthur, orphans of, by Richard Phillips	Account	18 SEP 1775	1761:125
Tate, Letitia, c/o Arthur, by Richard Phillips	Account	17 AUG 1772	1761:088
Tate, Lettishe, by Richard Phillips	Account	17 OCT 1774	1761:123
Tate, Lucy, c/o Arthur, by Richard Phillips	Account	17 AUG 1772	1761:088
Tate, Lucy, by Richard Phillips	Account	17 OCT 1774	1761:123
Tate, William & wife Sarah Jeffries, from Thomas Jeffries	Receipt	24 MAY 1832	1831:112
Tate, William, from R.D. Pitts	Receipt	19 OCT 1835	1831:337
Tayloe, John, from Mr. Edmondson	Receipt	13 SEP 1741	1731:039
Taylor, Arthur, c/o Leroy to Polly Taylor	Bond	18 DEC 1843	1838:299
Taylor, Arthur Leroy, by Polly Taylor	Account	21 JUN 1847	1844:214
Taylor, Arthur, c/o Leroy to Thomas Foreacres	Bond	16 APR 1855	1851:296
Taylor, Arthur, from Thomas Foreacres	Receipt	17 JAN 1859	1857:123
Taylor, Betsey, c/o Samuel to Edmund Noel	Bond	21 JUL 1794	1761:202
Taylor, Betsey, c/o Samuel, by Edmund Noel	Account	17 JUN 1805	1796:163
Taylor, Henry R. for wife Emma Brizendine, fr. R.C. Phillips	Receipt	18 JUL 1887	1867:587
Taylor, James, c/o Reuben to Robert M. Davis	Bond	15 FEB 1836	1831:403
Taylor, James H., by R.M. Davis	Account	21 JAN 1839	1838:044
Taylor, James H., by Robert M. Davis	Account	15 MAY 1843	1838:252
Taylor, James Henry, c/o Reuben to Willis Brooks	Bond	17 APR 1843	1838:248
Taylor, James H., c/o Reuben to Muscoe Garnett	Bond	17 NOV 1845	1844:063
Taylor, James H., by Willis Brooks	Account	17 NOV 1845	1844:074
Taylor, James H., by Muscoe Garnett	Account	17 MAY 1852	1851:054
Taylor, Keturah, c/o Major to Geo. W. Shelton	Bond	18 NOV 1833	1831:213
Taylor, Leroy, c/o Leroy to Polly Taylor	Bond	18 DEC 1843	1838:299
Taylor, Lucy, c/o Samuel to Edmund Noel	Bond	17 JUN 1793	1761:196
Taylor, Lucy, c/o Samuel, by Edmund Noel	Account	17 JUN 1805	1796:163
Taylor, Lucy, c/o William to Philip Davis	Bond	20 OCT 1817	1811:136
Taylor, Lucy, from Philip Davis	Receipt	19 SEP 1825	1825:024
Taylor, Maria, c/o Jesse to Benjamin H. Munday	Bond	16 DEC 1816	1811:126
Taylor, Martha, c/o Reuben to Robert M. Davis	Bond	15 FEB 1836	1831:403

Ward or Subject (and Parent, Guardian or Other)	Record Type	Date	Reference(s)
Taylor, Martha E., by R.M. Davis	Account	21 JAN 1839	1838:042
Taylor, Martha E., by Robert M. Davis	Account	15 MAY 1843	1838:255
Taylor, Martha E., c/o Reuben to Willis Brooks	Bond	17 APR 1843	1838:248
Taylor, Martha, by Willis Brooks	Account	17 NOV 1845	1844:074
Taylor, Mary Boulware, c/o James to John Smether	Bond	21 DEC 1801	1796:112
Taylor, Mary, c/o James, by John Smether, Jr.	Account	21 DEC 1807	1796:193
Taylor, Mary Ann, c/o John to John Hodgers [Hodges]	Bond	22 MAR 1836	1831:408
Taylor, Mary, c/o William to her father	Bond	15 MAY 1854	1851:238
Taylor, Mary A. late Dyke, by Elzer Fogg	Account	19 MAR 1855	1851:286
Taylor, Polley, c/o Samuel, by Edmund Noel	Account	17 JUN 1805	1796:163
Taylor, Polly, c/o Samuel to Edmond Noel	Bond	17 JUN 1793	1761:196
Taylor, Polly, c/o James to John Smith	Bond	17 DEC 1804	1796:161
Taylor, Polly B., c/o James, by John Smether, Jr.	Account	16 SEP 1805	1796:167
Taylor, Polly, c/o James to Ambrose Smith	Bond	20 JUL 1807	1796:192
Taylor, Polly B., by Ambrose Smith	Account	15 JUN 1812	1811:013
Taylor, Polly B., c/o James, by Ambrose Smith	Settlement	17 JUL 1815	1811:091
Taylor, Robert Lee, c/o Joseph to Mildred S. Taylor	Bond	16 JUL 1866	1857:395
Taylor, Sally, c/o Samuel to Edmund Noel	Bond	17 JUN 1793	1761:196
Taylor, Sally, c/o Samuel, by Edmund Noel	Account	17 JUN 1805	1796:163
Taylor, Sophronia, c/o Leroy to Polly Taylor	Bond	18 DEC 1843	1838:299
Taylor, Sophronia, by Polly Taylor	Account	21 JUN 1847	1844:214
Taylor, Sthreshley, c/o Samuel to Edmond Noel	Bond	17 JUN 1793	1761:196
Taylor, Sthreshley, c/o Samuel, by Edmund Noel	Account	17 JUN 1805	1796:163
Taylor, Susan Ann, c/o William to Frances Taylor	Bond	20 NOV 1843	1838:294
Taylor, Susan now Croxton, by Frances Taylor	Account	17 MAY 1847	1844:212
Taylor, Susanna Johnson, c/o James to John Smether	Bond	21 DEC 1801	1796:112
Taylor, Susanna P., c/o James, by John Smether, Jr.	Account	21 DEC 1807	1796:193
Taylor, Tamsin, c/o Samuel, by Edmund Noel	Account	17 JUN 1805	1796:163
Taylor, Tamson, c/o Samuel to Edmund Noel	Bond	17 JUN 1793	1761:196
Taylor, Wat. H., from Dr. Austin Brockenbrough	Receipt	20 MAY 1844	1838:322
Taylor, William & wife Frances Durham, c/o Cath. & James	Receipt	19 SEP 1825	1825:019
Temple, Annie W., by Henry W. Latane	Account	19 APR 1875	1867:304
Temple, Annie W., by Henry W. Latane	Account	20 SEP 1875	1867:326
Temple, Annie W., by Henry W. Latane	Account	16 SEP 1877	1867:374
Temple, Annie W., by Henry W. Latane	Account	16 SEP 1878	1867:394
Temple, Arthur, c/o John to Henry W. Latane	Bond	17 JAN 1815	1811:074
Temple, Betsey, c/o Arthur to his father	Bond	19 OCT 1835	1831:336
Temple, Charles H.T., c/o Henry W.L. to his father	Bond	19 DEC 1864	1857:351
Temple, Charles H.T., c/o Henry W.L., to Henry W. Latane	Bond	17 APR 1871	1867:157
Temple, Charles H.T., over 14/under 21, to Henry W. Latane	Certificate	15 APR 1871	1867:157
Temple, Charles H., by Henry W. Latane	Account	18 NOV 1873	1867:224
Temple, Charles H., by Henry W. Latane	Account	19 APR 1875	1867:303
Temple, Charles H., by Henry W. Latane	Account	20 SEP 1875	1867:326
Temple, John, c/o Arthur to his father	Bond	19 OCT 1835	1831:336
Temple, John N., c/o Henry W.L. to his father	Bond	19 DEC 1864	1857:351
Temple, Loulie E., c/o Henry W.L., to Henry W. Latane	Bond	17 APR 1871	1867:157
Temple, Lucy W. late Matthews, by Frances A. Temple	Account	22 NOV 1836	1831:451
Temple, Lucy E., c/o Henry W.L. to her father	Bond	19 DEC 1864	1857:351
Temple, Lucy E., over 14/under 21, to Henry W. Latane	Certificate	15 APR 1871	1867:157
Temple, Lulie E. now Lewis, by Henry W. Latane	Account	18 NOV 1873	1867:224
Temple, Martha E., c/o Arthur to his father	Bond	19 OCT 1835	1831:336

Ward or Subject (and Parent, Guardian or Other)	Record Type	Date	Reference(s)
Temple, Mary L., c/o Arthur to his father	Bond	19 OCT 1835	1831:336
Temple, Mary, c/o Henry W.L. to her father	Bond	19 DEC 1864	1857:351
Temple, Nancy W., c/o Henry W.L. to her father	Bond	19 DEC 1864	1857:351
Temple, Nancy W., c/o Henry W.L., to Henry W. Latane	Bond	17 APR 1871	1867:157
Temple, Nancy W., by Henry W. Latane	Account	18 NOV 1873	1867:224
Temple, Thomas L., c/o Henry W.L. to his father	Bond	19 DEC 1864	1857:351
Temple, Thomas L.L., c/o Henry W.L., to Henry W. Latane	Bond	17 APR 1871	1867:157
Temple, Thomas L.L., by Henry W. Latane	Account	18 NOV 1873	1867:226
Temple, Thomas L.L., by Henry W. Latane	Account	20 SEP 1875	1867:326
Temple, Thomas L.L., by Henry W. Latane	Account	19 APR 1875	1867:304
Temple, Thomas L.L., by Henry W. Latane	Account	18 DEC 1876	1867:359
Temple, Thomas L.L., by Henry W. Latane	Account	16 SEP 1877	1867:373
Temple, William, c/o Henry W.L. to his father	Bond	19 DEC 1864	1857:351
Temple, William, c/o Henry W.L., to Henry W. Latane	Bond	17 APR 1871	1867:157
Temple, William, by Henry W. Latane	Account	18 NOV 1873	1867:226
Temple, William, by Henry W. Latane	Account	19 APR 1875	1867:305
Temple, William, by Henry W. Latane	Account	20 SEP 1875	1867:327
Temple, William, by Henry W. Latane	Account	18 DEC 1876	1867:359
Temple, William, by Henry W. Latane	Account	16 SEP 1877	1867:373
Temple, William, by Henry W. Latane	Account	16 SEP 1878	1867:394
Temple, William, by Henry W. Latane	Account	21 JUL 1879	1867:413
Tena Fogg, by Elzer Fogg	Account	18 SEP 1871	1867:171
Thomas, Edward L., c/o Edward L. to Martha Thomas	Bond	15 JUN 1863	1857:299
Thomas, Lewis H., c/o Robert to Albert Owen	Bond	17 SEP 1832	1831:140
Thomas, Margaret E., c/o Edward L. to Martha Thomas	Bond	15 JUN 1863	1857:299
Thomas, Mark to orphan of John Gaines	Marriage Ref.	16 MAY 1738	WB6:125
Thomas, Martha E., c/o Edward L. to Martha Thomas	Bond	15 JUN 1863	1857:299
Thomas, Mary Susan, c/o Edward L. to Martha Thomas	Bond	15 JUN 1863	1857:299
Thomas, Matilda Ann to William Alexander	Bond	16 JUN 1851	1844:526
Thomas, Polly, c/o Thomas to William Crittenden	Bond	20 NOV 1809	1796:220
Thomas, Rachel, c/o Thomas to William Crittenden	Bond	20 NOV 1809	1796:220
Thomas, Robert, c/o Lewis to Spencer Noel	Bond	20 FEB 1809	1796:210
Thomas, Thomas to Samuel Landrum	Bond	15 MAR 1742/3	WB6:434
Thomas, William	Account	18 AUG 1752	WB9:195
Threshley, Thomas, c/o William to James Upshaw	Bond	20 DEC 1757	1731:214
Threshley, William, c/o William to James Upshaw	Bond	20 DEC 1757	1731:214
Throckmorton, Ann, c/o Wm., by James Webb	Report	19 SEP 1825	1825:007
Throckmorton, Anna, c/o William to James Webb	Bond	21 DEC 1813	1811:050
Throckmorton, Fanny, c/o Gabriel to James Webb	Bond	21 JUN 1796	1761:225
Throckmorton, Sally, c/o Gabriel to James Webb	Bond	15 DEC 1800	1796:082
Tinsbloom, Alice, c/o Wm., age 16, to John Shackleford	Certificate	3 MAR 1877	CCW:106
Tinsbloom, Alice, c/o Wm., to John Shackleford	Bond	10 MAR 1877	CCW:107
Todd, Susanna to Nathaniel Pendleton	Bond	21 JUN 1748	WB8:066
Toombs, Elizabeth, c/o Wm. to William Dishman	Bond	20 OCT 1817	1811:135
Toombs, Gabriella, over 21, lunatic, to William S. Croxton	Bond C.	21 MAY 1883	1867:522
Toombs, Henry, c/o Wm. to William Dishman	Bond	20 OCT 1817	1811:135
Toombs, Nancy, c/o Wm. to William Dishman	Bond	20 OCT 1817	1811:135
Townley, Buckner, c/o John to John Miller	Bond	21 JAN 1793	1761:191
Trible, Emily Margaret, c/o John S. to John W. Faulconer	Bond C.	17 MAY 1880	1867:421
Trible, Emily M., by John W. Faulconer	Account	22 NOV 1881	1867:478
Trible, Emily M., by John W. Faulconer	Account	16 APR 1883	1867:508

Ward or Subject (and Parent, Guardian or Other)	Record Type	Date	Reference(s)
Trible, Emily M., by J.W. Faulconer	Account	15 SEP 1884	1867:544
Trible, Emily M., by John W. Faulconer	Account	24 SEP 1885	1867:567
Trible, George Meredith, c/o John S. to John W. Faulconer	Bond C.	17 MAY 1880	1867:421
Trible, George M., by John W. Faulconer	Account	22 NOV 1881	1867:480
Trible, George W., by John W. Faulconer	Account	16 APR 1883	1867:504
Trible, George M., by J.W. Faulconer	Account	21 JAN 1884	1867:533
Trible, George M., from John W. Faulconer, curator	Receipt	20 JUN 1887	1867:586
Trible, John to John Dean	Bond	15 AUG 1749	WB8:265
Trible, Lowry W., c/o John S. to John W. Faulconer	Bond C.	17 MAY 1880	1867:421
Trible, Lowry W., by John W. Faulconer	Account	22 NOV 1881	1867:477
Trible, Lowry W., by J.W. Faulconer	Account	15 OCT 1883	1867:528
Trible, Lowry W., by John W. Faulconer	Account	16 APR 1883	1867:510
Trible, Mary, c/o William to Charles Breedlove	Bond	18 APR 1749	WB8:212
Trible, Mary E., c/o John S. to her father	Bond	16 AUG 1869	1867:104
Trible, Peter to John Dean	Bond	15 AUG 1749	WB8:265
Trible, Thomas Young, c/o John S. to John W. Faulconer	Bond C.	17 MAY 1880	1867:421
Trible, Thomas Y., by John W. Faulconer	Account	22 NOV 1881	1867:475
Trible, Thomas Y., by John W. Faulconer	Account	16 APR 1883	1867:506
Trible, Thomas S., by J.W. Faulconer	Account	15 OCT 1883	1867:526
Trible, William A., c/o John S. to his father	Bond	16 AUG 1869	1867:104
Trible,Emily M., from J.W. Faulconer	Receipt	15 SEP 1884	1867:544
Triplett, Caroline T., c/o Wm. to William Coghill	Bond	20 JAN 1800	1796:050
Tucker, Charles, by George W. Phillips	Account	17 OCT 1864	1857:350
Tucker, Charles R., by Susan Phillips, Exrx. of George W.	Account	20 JUL 1868	1867:035
Tucker, Charles L., by George W. Phillips	Account	17 JUL 1876	1867:352
Tucker, Elizabeth Dudley, c/o Dudley to Elizabeth Tucker	Bond	17 MAR 1834	1831:245
Tucker, Elizabeth D., c/o Dudley to James Carter	Bond	16 FEB 1852	1851:044
Tune, Henry C., c/o John to Henry Clarke	Bond	17 DEC 1855	1851:335
Tune, John & wife Catharine Davis, by John Griffin	Certificate	19 SEP 1825	1825:025
Tunstall, Mary Ann, over 14, c/o John to Julius Tunstall	Bond	16 APR 1883	1867:512
Tunstall, Mary Ann, over 14, to bro. Julius Tunstall	Certificate	16 APR 1883	1867:511
Tupman, John, c/o William to Alexander Somervaile	Bond	21 FEB 1820	1811:207
Tupman, John, by Alexander Somervail	Report	21 NOV 1826	1825:126
Turner, Austin D., by John Sadler	Account	17 OCT 1825	1825:051
Turner, Major J.B., c/o John to Cary Turner	Bond	16 JUL 1805	1796:166
Turner, Nancy, by John Sadler	Account	17 OCT 1825	1825:051
Turner, Sally, by John Sadler	Account	17 OCT 1825	1825:051
Tyler, Hannah, c/o John to Richard Tyler	Bond	17 OCT 1758	1731:234
Tyler, Mary, c/o John to Richard Tyler	Bond	17 OCT 1758	1731:234

U

Upshaw, Arthur M.M., c/o James to James W. Upshaw	Bond	16 FEB 1807	1796:189
Upshaw, Arthur M.M., c/o James to Lewis G. Upshaw	Bond	18 OCT 1819	1811:194
Upshaw, Cordelia, c/o John to Edwin Upshaw	Bond	19 OCT 1801	1796:105
Upshaw, Cordelia, c/o John to Wm. Upshaw	Bond	20 OCT 1806	1796:187
Upshaw, Eliza. J., c/o James to James W. Upshaw	Bond	16 FEB 1807	1796:189
Upshaw, Louisa J., c/o James to James W. Upshaw	Bond	16 FEB 1807	1796:189
Upshaw, Lucy B., c/o John H. to David P. Wright	Bond	16 MAY 1836	1831:427
Upshaw, Martha, c/o James to John Hawkins	Bond	16 FEB 1807	1796:188
Upshaw, Mary, c/o William, by Tamzin Upshaw	Account	20 SEP 1762	1761:018
Upshaw, Mary, by Tamzin Upshaw	Account	17 OCT 1763	1761:042

Ward or Subject (and Parent, Guardian or Other)	Record Type	Date	Reference(s)
Upshaw, Mason T.B., c/o James to James W. Upshaw	Bond	16 FEB 1807	1796:189
Upshaw, Sally, Miss, by Mrs. T. Upshaw	Account	17 SEP 1764	1761:048
Upshaw, Sally, c/o James to James W. Upshaw	Bond	16 FEB 1807	1796:189
Upshaw, William, c/o John to John Jones	Bond	21 SEP 1801	1796:094
Ursery, Lucy, c/o Thomas to Edmund Dunn	Bond	20 MAR 1826	1825:092
Ursery, Mary A., by Lawrence Muse	Account	19 SEP 1825	1825:032
Ursery, Mary A., by Kemp Gatewood	Account	17 OCT 1825	1825:037
Ursery, Mary E., c/o Jane to James M. Williams	Bond	21 NOV 1853	1851:216
Ursery, Nancy, by Kemp Gatewood	Account	21 AUG 1820	1811:231
Usery, Mary, c/o John to Kemp Gatewood	Bond	17 JUL 1815	1811:086
Usery, Nancy, c/o John to Kemp Gatewood	Bond	17 JUL 1815	1811:086
Usery, Samuel, c/o John to Kemp Gatewood	Bond	17 JUL 1815	1811:086

V

Vaughan, Mary Jane, c/o Thomas to her father	Bond	21 OCT 1844	1838:372
Vaughan, Mildred Ann, c/o Thomas to her father	Bond	21 OCT 1844	1838:372
Vawter, Allamander, c/o Edward to his father	Bond	16 DEC 1805	1796:171
Vawter, Allamander, from Edward Vawter	Receipt	19 SEP 1825	1825:027
Vawter, Irom, c/o Edward to his father	Bond	16 DEC 1805	1796:171
Vawter, Irom, from Edward Vawter	Receipt	19 SEP 1825	1825:027
Vawter, Julius, c/o Bowler to his father	Bond	18 NOV 1833	1831:218
Vawter, Louisa, c/o Bowler to her father	Bond	18 NOV 1833	1831:218
Vergitt, Mary to William Davis	Bond	10 JUL 1712	D&W14:073
Verlander, Betty Frances, c/o James to Elizabeth Verlander	Bond	18 APR 1853	1851:174
Verlander, James, c/o James to Elizabeth Verlander	Bond	18 APR 1853	1851:174
Verlander, John, c/o James to Elizabeth Verlander	Bond	18 APR 1853	1851:174

W

Wade, Austin, c/o William to Thomas Plummer	Bond	21 DEC 1812	1811:028
Wade, Lilly, c/o William to Thomas Plummer	Bond	21 DEC 1812	1811:029
Wade, Matilda, c/o William to Thomas Plummer	Bond	21 DEC 1812	1811:028
Wagener, Sarah, h/o William Seayres to Eliz. Waggoner	Bond	19 SEP 1758	1731:231
Wagener, Sarah Sears, by Elizabeth Waggenor	Account	16 AUG 1762	1761:014
Wagener, Sarah Sears, by Elizabeth Waggoner	Account	15 AUG 1763	1761:030
Wagenor, Temperence to Edward Coleman	Bond	16 JUN 1741	WB6:314
Waggoner, Patsy, c/o Nathan to Joseph Alexander	Bond	18 DEC 1797	1796:025
Walker, William S., c/o William N. to John M. Walker	Bond	15 FEB 1869	1867:080
Ware, E. Macon, by Catharine E. Ware	Account	19 JUL 1869	1867:093
Ware, E. Macon, by Catharine E. Ware	Account	20 JUN 1870	1867:122
Ware, E.M., by Catharine E. Ware	Account	20 NOV 1871	1867:175
Ware, E.M., by C.E. Ware	Account	20 JAN 1873	1867:190
Ware, Edward M., c/o Edward M. to Catharine E. Ware	Bond	18 MAY 1863	1857:299
Ware, Edward M., by C.E. Ware	Account	16 JAN 1865	1857:354
Ware, Edward M., by C.E. Ware	Account	18 JUN 1866	1857:392
Ware, Edward M., by Catharine E. Ware	Account	18 NOV 1867	1867:021
Ware, Edward M., by Catharine E. Ware	Account	21 OCT 1868	1867:045
Ware, Emma C., c/o Edward M. to Catharine E. Ware	Bond	18 MAY 1863	1857:299
Ware, Emma C., by C.E. Ware	Account	16 JAN 1865	1857:356
Ware, Emma C., by C.E. Ware	Account	18 JUN 1866	1857:390
Ware, Frances G. wife of Richard Croxton, from Winter Bray	Receipt	21 NOV 1826	1825:125
Ware, Frances G., c/o Edward to Winter Bray	Bond	21 FEB 1826	1825:085

Ward or Subject (and Parent, Guardian or Other)	Record Type	Date	Reference(s)
Ware, Rachel, grandmother of Frances G. Ware Croxton	Estate Ref.	21 NOV 1826	1825:125
Waring, Charles C., c/o Henry to Lucia S. Waring	Bond	18 FEB 1850	1844:406
Waring, Charles W., by Lucia S. Waring	Account	15 DEC 1851	1851:038
Waring, Charles W., by Lucia S. Waring	Account	18 OCT 1852	1851:144
Waring, Charles W., by Lucia S. Waring	Account	16 JAN 1854	1851:225
Waring, Charles W., by Lucia S. Waring	Account	18 JUN 1855	1851:299
Waring, Charles W., by Lucia S. Waring	Account	17 FEB 1857	1851:409
Waring, Eliz. Gardner, c/o Robert P. to Edwin Upshaw	Bond	21 SEP 1801	1796:095
Waring, Eliz. Gardner, c/o Robert P. to Theodk. Noel	Bond	20 JUL 1801	1796:092
Waring, Eliza S., wid/o Robert P., by Patrick C. Robb	Account	20 SEP 1847	1844:234
Waring, Eliza. G., by Edwin Upshaw	Account	20 FEB 1809	1796:212
Waring, Elizabeth Gardner, c/o Robt. P. Waring to Thos. Bridges	Bond	16 DEC 1799	1796:049
Waring, Elizabeth S., by Robert P. Waring, Exr. of Mary	Account	18 MAR 1844	1838:310
Waring, Elizabeth S., by Robert P. Waring	Account	17 NOV 1845	1844:064
Waring, Elizabeth S. now Faulconer, by Robt. P. Waring	Account	17 AUG 1846	1844:176
Waring, Elizabeth S., wid/o Robert P., Jr., by Patrick C. Robb	Account	18 DEC 1848	1844:300
Waring, Epaphroditus Lawson, c/o Robt. P. Waring to Thos. Bridges	Bond	16 DEC 1799	1796:049
Waring, Epaphroditus Lawson, c/o Robt. P. to Theodk. Noel	Bond	20 JUL 1801	1796:092
Waring, Epaphroditus Lawson, c/o Robert P. to Robert P. Waring	Bond	21 SEP 1801	1796:097
Waring, Francis Gardner, c/o Robert P. to Edwin Upshaw	Bond	21 SEP 1801	1796:095
Waring, Francis G., c/o Robert P. to John H. Upshaw	Bond	15 FEB 1808	1796:196
Waring, Francis G., c/o Robert P. to Wm. L. Waring	Bond	16 MAR 1812	1811:005
Waring, Francis G., c/o Robt. P. to Silas M. Noel	Bond	20 OCT 1817	1811:136
Waring, Francis G., from Wm. L. Waring	Receipt	19 SEP 1825	1825:011
Waring, Francis G., from Robert P. Waring	Receipt	17 DEC 1827	1825:199
Waring, Gilchrist, c/o Henry to Lucia S. Waring	Bond	18 FEB 1850	1844:406
Waring, Gilchrist R., by Lucia S. Waring	Account	15 DEC 1851	1851:036
Waring, Gilchrist R., by Lucia S. Waring	Account	18 OCT 1852	1851:136
Waring, Gilchrist R., by Lucia S. Waring	Account	16 JAN 1854	1851:221
Waring, Gilchrist R., by Lucia S. Waring	Account	18 JUN 1855	1851:297
Waring, Gilchrist R., by Lucia S. Waring	Account	17 FEB 1857	1851:403
Waring, Henry, c/o Henry to Lucia S. Waring	Bond	18 FEB 1850	1844:406
Waring, Henry, by Lucia S. Waring	Account	15 DEC 1851	1851:038
Waring, Henry, by Lucia S. Waring	Account	18 OCT 1852	1851:142
Waring, Henry, by Lucia S. Waring	Account	16 JAN 1854	1851:224
Waring, Henry, by Lucia S. Waring	Account	18 JUN 1855	1851:299
Waring, Henry, by Lucia S. Waring	Account	17 FEB 1857	1851:407
Waring, Horace, c/o Robert P. to Edwin Upshaw	Bond	21 SEP 1801	1796:095
Waring, Horace, c/o Robert P. to John H. Upshaw	Bond	15 FEB 1808	1796:196
Waring, Horace, c/o Robert P. to John Waring	Bond	21 JUN 1813	1811:041
Waring, John, c/o Robert Payne Waring, Sr. to Robt. Payne Waring	Bond	16 SEP 1799	1796:046
Waring, Lourey, c/o Robert P. to Wm. Latane	Bond	18 JUN 1799	1796:045
Waring, Lucy R., c/o Robert P., Jr. to Patrick C. Robb	Bond	19 AUG 1844	1838:357
Waring, Lucy R., c/o Robert P., by Patrick C. Robb	Account	20 SEP 1847	1844:234, 240
Waring, Lucy R., c/o Robert P., Jr., by Patrick C. Robb	Account	18 DEC 1848	1844:300, 305
Waring, Lucy R., c/o Robert P., by P.C. Robb	Account	17 SEP 1849	1844:395
Waring, Lucy G., c/o Henry to Lucia S. Waring	Bond	18 FEB 1850	1844:406
Waring, Lucy R., by P.C. Robb	Account	19 AUG 1850	1844:472
Waring, Lucy G., by Lucia S. Waring	Account	15 DEC 1851	1851:034
Waring, Lucy R., by John P. Robb, Exor. of P.C. Robb	Account	15 DEC 1851	1851:030
Waring, Lucy G., by Lucia S. Waring	Account	18 OCT 1852	1851:134

Ward or Subject (and Parent, Guardian or Other)	Record Type	Date	Reference(s)
Waring, Lucy Gray, by Lucia S. Waring	Account	16 JAN 1854	1851:220
Waring, Lucy Gray, by Lucia S. Waring	Account	18 JUN 1855	1851:297
Waring, Lucy Gray, by Lucia S. Waring	Account	17 FEB 1857	1851:401
Waring, Margaret M., c/o William L., to Robert P. Waring	Bond	10 NOV 1853	CCW:009
Waring, Maria, c/o Robt. P. Waring to Thos. Bridges	Bond	16 DEC 1799	1796:049
Waring, Maria, c/o Robert P. to Edwin Upshaw	Bond	21 SEP 1801	1796:095
Waring, Maria, c/o Robert P. to Theodorick Noel	Bond	20 JUL 1801	1796:092
Waring, Maria, by Edwin Upshaw	Account	20 FEB 1809	1796:213
Waring, Mary E., c/o Henry to Lucia S. Waring	Bond	18 FEB 1850	1844:406
Waring, Mary E., by Lucia S. Waring	Account	15 DEC 1851	1851:034
Waring, Mary E., by Lucia S. Waring	Account	18 OCT 1852	1851:132
Waring, Mary E., by Lucia S. Waring	Account	16 JAN 1854	1851:219a
Waring, Mary E., by Lucia S. Waring	Account	18 JUN 1855	1851:297
Waring, Mary E., by Lucia S. Waring	Account	17 FEB 1857	1851:400
Waring, Mary E., c/o Robert P. to her father	Bond	18 JAN 1858	1857:051
Waring, Patrick, c/o Henry to Lucia S. Waring	Bond	18 FEB 1850	1844:406
Waring, Patrick C., by Lucia S. Waring	Account	15 DEC 1851	1851:036
Waring, Patrick C., by Lucia S. Waring	Account	18 OCT 1852	1851:138
Waring, Patrick C., by Lucia S. Waring	Account	16 JAN 1854	1851:222
Waring, Patrick C., by Lucia S. Waring	Account	18 JUN 1855	1851:299
Waring, Patrick C., by Lucia S. Waring	Account	17 FEB 1857	1851:405
Waring, Robert P., c/o Robert P., Jr. to Patrick C. Robb	Bond	19 AUG 1844	1838:357
Waring, Robert P., c/o Robert P., by Patrick C. Robb	Account	20 SEP 1847	1844:234, 236
Waring, Robert P., c/o Robert P., Jr., by Patrick C. Robb	Account	18 DEC 1848	1844:300, 301
Waring, Robert P., c/o Robert P., by P.C. Robb	Account	17 SEP 1849	1844:391
Waring, Robert Henry, c/o William L., to Thomas L. Waring	Bond	10 NOV 1853	CCW:010
Waring, Thomas L., c/o William L. to Robert P. Waring, Jr.	Bond	20 DEC 1841	1838:168
Waring, Thomas Lawson, by Robert Payne Waring	Account	18 MAR 1844	1838:314
Waring, Thomas R., c/o Robert P., Jr. to Patrick C. Robb	Bond	19 AUG 1844	1838:357
Waring, Thomas L., by Robert P. Waring	Account	17 NOV 1845	1844:066
Waring, Thomas L., by Robert P. Waring	Account	16 MAR 1846	1844:095
Waring, Thomas L., by Robert P. Waring	Account	17 MAY 1847	1844:210
Waring, Thomas R., c/o Robert P., by Patrick C. Robb	Account	20 SEP 1847	1844:234, 242
Waring, Thomas R., c/o Robert P., Jr., by Patrick C. Robb	Account	18 DEC 1848	1844:300, 307
Waring, Thomas R., c/o Robert P., by P.C. Robb	Account	17 SEP 1849	1844:396
Waring, Thomas R., by P.C. Robb	Account	19 AUG 1850	1844:472
Waring, Thomas R., by John P. Robb, Exor. of P.C. Robb	Account	15 DEC 1851	1851:026
Waring, Thomas L., c/o Robert P. to Robert P. Waring, Jr.	Bond	15 SEP 1851	1851:021
Waring, Thomas R., by Robert P. Waring	Account	18 OCT 1852	1851:146
Waring, Thomas Arthur, c/o William L., to Thos. L. Waring	Bond	10 NOV 1853	CCW:010
Waring, Willantina R., by Lucia S. Waring	Account	15 DEC 1851	1851:038
Waring, Willantina R., by Lucia S. Waring	Account	18 OCT 1852	1851:140
Waring, Willantina R., by Lucia S. Waring	Account	18 JUN 1855	1851:299
Waring, Willentina, c/o Henry to Lucia S. Waring	Bond	18 FEB 1850	1844:406
Waring, Willentina R., by Lucia S. Waring	Account	16 JAN 1854	1851:223
Waring, William L., c/o Robert P., Jr. to Patrick C. Robb	Bond	19 AUG 1844	1838:357
Waring, William L., c/o Robert P., by Patrick C. Robb	Account	20 SEP 1847	1844:234, 238
Waring, William L., c/o Robert P., Jr., by Patrick C. Robb	Account	18 DEC 1848	1844:300, 303
Waring, William L., c/o Robert P., by P.C. Robb	Account	17 SEP 1849	1844:392
Waring, William L., by P.C. Robb	Account	19 AUG 1850	1844:472
Waring, William L., c/o William L., to Richard H. Waring	Bond	10 NOV 1853	CCW:009

Ward or Subject (and Parent, Guardian or Other)	Record Type	Date	Reference(s)
Waring, William L., c/o Robert P. to his father	Bond	18 JAN 1858	1857:051
Waring, Williantina R., by Lucia S. Waring	Account	17 FEB 1857	1851:405
Warrington, James H., c/o Lucy to Sambo Smith	Bond	21 FEB 1888	1867:598
Warrington, Kate, c/o Lucy to Sambo Smith	Bond	21 FEB 1888	1867:600
Warrington, Lucy, c/o Lucy to Sambo Smith	Bond	21 FEB 1888	1867:599
Weaver, Benjamin, c/o Henry to Benjamin Williams	Bond	21 DEC 1840	1838:130
Weeks, Benj. Pope, c/o Charles to James Upshaw, Jr.	Bond	16 FEB 1795	1761:208
Weeks, Eliza, c/o Charles to Reuben Garnett	Bond	19 DEC 1796	1796:001
Weeks, Margaret, c/o Charles to Edward Davis	Bond	17 JUN 1793	1761:194
Weeks, Mary Elliott, c/o Charles to Thomas Hill	Bond	18 DEC 1797	1796:027
Whitelaw, Emily R., under 14, c/o Thomas to John S. Rouzie, Jr.	Bond	16 APR 1866	1857:380
Whitelaw, Emily W. and others, land in Union Co., Ill.	Bond	15 MAR 1869	1867:083
Whitelaw, Emily W. to John S. Rowzie, Jr.	Bond	15 MAR 1869	1867:083
Whitelaw, Emily R., c/o Thomas, by John S. Rowzie	Account	20 DEC 1869	1867:114
Whitelaw, Emily R., by John S. Rowzie	Account	17 JAN 1870	1867:118
Whitelaw, George M. and others, land in Union Co., Ill.	Bond	15 MAR 1869	1867:083
Whitelaw, Robert H. and others, land in Union Co., Ill.	Bond	15 MAR 1869	1867:083
Whitlocke, Emily A. late Haile, by Robert G. Haile	Account	15 FEB 1836	1831:404
Whitlocke, Nathaniel I. & wife Emily A. Haile, fr. R.G. Haile	Receipt	15 FEB 1836	1831:404
Wild, Ann Booker, by Lewis Booker	Account	18 JUL 1796	1761:222
Wild, Ann Booker [Wyld], by Lewis Booker	Account	15 OCT 1798	1796:038
Wild, Elizabeth Howlet, by Lewis Booker	Account	18 JUL 1796	1761:222
Williams, Ann, c/o Richard, to Isaac Brooke	Bond	21 DEC 1756	WB10:112
Williams, Anne to Rachel Williams	Bond	17 OCT 1752	1731:149
Williams, Catharine to Rachel Williams	Bond	17 OCT 1752	1731:149
Williams, Edmond to Rachel Williams	Bond	17 OCT 1752	1731:150
Williams, Elizabeth to Rachel Williams	Bond	17 OCT 1752	1731:149
Williams, Mary to James Webb, Gent.	Bond	16 JAN 1753	1731:156
Williamson, David, c/o Samuel to Leonard Clarke	Bond	19 MAY 1834	1831:266
Williamson, David, c/o Samuel to Arthur Barefoot	Bond	19 OCT 1835	1831:335
Williamson, Dice, by William S. Croxton	Account	21 MAY 1838	1838:021
Williamson, Dicy, c/o Samuel to William S. Croxton	Bond	20 AUG 1832	1831:132
Williamson, Dorathy, c/o Samuel to Arthur Barefoot	Bond	19 OCT 1835	1831:335
Williamson, Dorothea, c/o Samuel to Leonard Clarke	Bond	19 MAY 1834	1831:266
Williamson, Emaline, by George Taylor	Account	18 AUG 1834	1831:276
Williamson, Emaline, by George Taylor	Account	16 FEB 1846	1844:090
Williamson, Emeline, c/o Abraham to George Taylor	Account	18 APR 1831	1831:040
Williamson, Emeline, c/o Elijah to Thomas Marlow	Bond	21 FEB 1853	1851:168
Williamson, Emeline, c/o Elijah to Baylor F. Crow	Bond	19 APR 1858	1857:058
Williamson, Emeline, c/o Elijah to Baylor F. Crow	Certificate	19 APR 1858	1857:058
Williamson, Emeline, by Thomas N. Clarke	Account	17 JAN 1859	1857:124
Williamson, Emiline, by Thomas Marlow	Account	16 APR 1855	1851:294
Williamson, George, c/o Samuel to Leonard Clarke	Bond	19 MAY 1834	1831:266
Williamson, George L., c/o Samuel to Arthur Barefoot	Bond	19 OCT 1835	1831:335
Williamson, Henry, c/o Leonard, by John Williamson	Account	18 SEP 1769	1761:071
Williamson, Howard, c/o Abraham to George Taylor	Account	18 APR 1831	1831:040
Williamson, John, c/o William to George W. Phillips	Bond	19 MAY 1856	1851:344
Williamson, John S., by George W. Phillips	Account	18 MAY 1857	1851:435
Williamson, John S., by George W. Phillips	Account	19 APR 1858	1857:059
Williamson, John S., by George W. Phillips	Account	20 JUN 1859	1857:147
Williamson, John S., by George W. Phillips	Account	21 MAY 1860	1857:203

Ward or Subject (and Parent, Guardian or Other)	Record Type	Date	Reference(s)
Williamson, John S., by George W. Phillips	Account	21 OCT 1861	1857:269
Williamson, John S., by George W. Phillips	Account	21 JUL 1862	1857:293
Williamson, John S., by George W. Phillips	Account	17 OCT 1864	1857:349
Williamson, John S., c/o William to Thomas H. Brizendine	Bond	17 SEP 1866	1857:412
Williamson, John S., by George W. Phillips, dec.	Account	20 JUL 1868	1867:033
Williamson, Judith, c/o Leonard, by Isaac Wm'son.	Account	19 OCT 1772	1761:094
Williamson, Leonard, c/o Leonard, by Isaac Wm'son.	Account	19 OCT 1772	1761:094
Williamson, Lettice, c/o Abraham to George Taylor	Account	18 APR 1831	1831:040
Williamson, Letty, by George Taylor	Account	18 AUG 1834	1831:276
Williamson, Martha, by George Taylor	Account	18 AUG 1845	1844:050
Williamson, Mary, c/o John to James Croxton, Jr.	Bond	15 DEC 1845	1844:079
Williamson, Mary E., c/o Elijah to Thomas Boughan	Bond	15 MAY 1854	1851:239
Williamson, Matilda, c/o Abraham to George Taylor	Account	18 APR 1831	1831:040
Williamson, Matilda, by George Taylor	Account	18 AUG 1834	1831:276
Williamson, Reubin, c/o Leonard, by Isaac Wm'son.	Account	19 OCT 1772	1761:094
Williamson, Susan, c/o Abraham to George Taylor	Account	18 APR 1831	1831:040
Williamson, Susan, by George Taylor	Account	18 AUG 1834	1831:276
Williamson, Susan, by George Taylor	Account	18 AUG 1845	1844:046
Williamson, Vincent, c/o Thomas, by Jno. Williamson	Account	19 DEC 1785	WB13:526
Williamson, William, c/o Samuel to Sthreshley Dunn	Bond	22 MAY 1833	1831:183
Williamson, William, by Sthreshley Dunn	Account	20 FEB 1843	1838:244
Williamson, William	Receipt	20 FEB 1843	1838:245
Williamson, William, c/o William to George W. Phillips	Bond	19 MAY 1856	1851:344
Williamson, William F., by George W. Phillips	Account	18 MAY 1857	1851:434
Williamson, William, by George W. Phillips	Account	19 APR 1858	1857:059
Williamson, William F., by George W. Phillips	Account	20 JUN 1859	1857:147
Williamson, William F., by George W. Phillips	Account	21 MAY 1860	1857:203
Williamson, William F., by George W. Phillips	Account	21 OCT 1861	1857:269
Williamson, William F., by George W. Phillips	Account	21 JUL 1862	1857:294
Williamson, William F., by George W. Phillips	Account	17 OCT 1864	1857:348
Williamson, William F., c/o William to Thomas H. Brizendine	Bond	17 SEP 1866	1857:412
Williamson, Zachariah, c/o Leonard, by Isaac Wm'son.	Account	19 OCT 1772	1761:093
Wilson, David Anderson, c/o David to John Thurston	Bond	21 DEC 1807	1796:195
Winslow, Ann to Richard Covington	Bond	16 FEB 1730/1	WB5:015
Wood, Catharine, c/o Thomas to Philip B. Pendleton	Bond	21 OCT 1811	1796:258
Wood, Catharine, c/o Carter to John Jones	Bond	18 SEP 1815	1811:095
Wood, Fountain, c/o William to Sally Wood	Bond	17 FEB 1800	1796:054
Wood, Fountain, c/o William, by Sally Wood	Account	16 AUG 1813	1811:044
Wood, James, c/o William to Sally Wood	Bond	17 FEB 1800	1796:054
Wood, James, c/o William, by Sally Wood	Account	16 AUG 1813	1811:044
Wood, Julia, c/o William to Sally Wood	Bond	17 FEB 1800	1796:054
Wood, Julia, c/o William, by Sally Wood	Account	16 AUG 1813	1811:044
Wood, Maria J.G., c/o Carter to Reuben M. Garnett	Bond	17 JUN 1816	1811:115
Wood, Mary, c/o Fontaine to her father	Bond	19 DEC 1825	1825:072
Wood, Muscoe G., c/o Carter to Reuben M. Garnett	Bond	16 JUL 1827	1825:167
Wood, Norborne, c/o Jos. to Kemp Gatewood	Bond	15 FEB 1819	1811:178
Wood, Polly, c/o Thomas to Thomas E. Dix	Bond	15 OCT 1810	1796:237
Wood, Thomas, c/o Thomas to Philip B. Pendleton	Bond	18 FEB 1811	1796:244
Wood, Thomas, c/o Fontaine to his father	Bond	19 DEC 1825	1825:072
Wood, William, c/o William to Sally Wood	Bond	17 FEB 1800	1796:054
Wood, William, c/o William, by Sally Wood	Account	16 AUG 1813	1811:044

Ward or Subject (and Parent, Guardian or Other)	Record Type	Date	Reference(s)
Wortham, Ann to Margaret Wortham	Bond	18 MAR 1746/7	WB7:509
Wortham, John to Augustine Boughan	Bond	16 OCT 1744	WB7:213
Wortham, John to Francis Waring	Bond	15 OCT 1751	1731:135
Wortham, John, by Thomas Hawkins	Account	19 OCT 1789	1761:162
Wortham, Margaret now Brookshire to Thomas Thorp	Bond	19 APR 1757	1731:211
Wortham, Mary to Margaret Wortham	Bond	18 MAR 1746/7	WB7:509
Wortham, Mary, c/o William to John Retterford	Bond	18 APR 1749	WB8:212
Wortham, Mary to Margaret Wortham	Bond	20 MAR 1753	1731:158
Wortham, Sarah to Margaret Wortham	Bond	18 MAR 1746/7	WB7:509
Wortham, Sarah, c/o William to John Retterford	Bond	18 APR 1749	WB8:212
Wright, Alice, over 14, c/o Edward L. to Mary Ann Wright	Bond	16 DEC 1861	1857:278
Wright, Catharine M., insane, to Benjamin P. Wright	Bond C.	17 MAR 1883	CCW:132
Wright, Charles Z., c/o David P. to David A. Wright	Bond	17 SEP 1855	1851:327
Wright, Edward to Thomas M. Henley	Receipt	21 NOV 1831	1831:079
Wright, Edward L. & wife Mary Ann Jones, from B.F. Jones	Receipt	15 SEP 1845	1844:059
Wright, Edward L., c/o Edward L. to Mary Ann Wright	Bond	16 DEC 1861	1857:278
Wright, Eliza C., under 14, c/o Benj. E. to Lala R. Wright	Bond	15 MAY 1876	1867:349
Wright, Ellen H., c/o Edward L. to Mary Ann Wright	Bond	16 DEC 1861	1857:278
Wright, George, Jr., c/o Edward L. to Mary Ann Wright	Bond	16 DEC 1861	1857:278
Wright, Lala R., Jr., c/o Benj. E. to Lala R. Wright	Bond	19 JUN 1876	1867:351
Wright, Lala R. to her mother Lala R. Wright	Certificate	19 JUN 1876	1867:350
Wright, Laura M., c/o Edward L. to Mary Ann Wright	Bond	16 DEC 1861	1857:278
Wright, Martha H., c/o William A. to William A. Wright	Bond	20 SEP 1858	1857:105
Wright, Martha H., by William A. Wright	Account	19 APR 1875	1867:316
Wright, Mary Susan, c/o George to Mary B. Wright	Bond	17 NOV 1851	1851:024
Wright, Mary Susan, by Mary B. Wright	Account	21 FEB 1853	1851:166
Wright, Mary Susan, by Mary B. Wright	Account	21 AUG 1854	1851:259
Wright, Mary Susan, by Mary B. Wright	Account	17 DEC 1855	1851:334
Wright, Mary Susan, by Mary B. Wright	Account	18 AUG 1856	1851:382
Wright, Mary Susan, by Mary B. Wright	Account	20 DEC 1858	1857:109
Wright, Mary E., under 14, c/o Robt. of LA, to Benj. P. Wright	Bond	16 DEC 1878	1867:388
Wright, Mary E., by B.P. Wright	Account	22 NOV 1881	1867:464
Wright, Mary E., by B.P. Wright	Account	21 MAY 1883	1867:518
Wright, Orlando S., c/o Edward L. to Mary Ann Wright	Bond	16 DEC 1861	1857:278
Wright, Philip S. to George T. Wright	Bond	19 APR 1858	1857:057
Wright, Richard B. to George T. Wright	Bond	19 APR 1858	1857:057
Wright, Richard Edward, c/o William A. to William A. Wright	Bond	20 SEP 1858	1857:105
Wright, Richard B., above 14, c/o George T. to John J. Wright	Bond	17 JUL 1871	1867:159
Wright, Richard E., by William A. Wright	Account	19 APR 1875	1867:311
Wright, Robert, over 14, c/o Edward L. to Mary Ann Wright	Bond	16 DEC 1861	1857:278
Wright, Sarah, c/o Edward to David W. Pitts	Bond	15 FEB 1819	1811:174
Wright, Sarah G., c/o George to Mary P. Wright	Bond	19 MAY 1851	1844:519
Wright, Sarah G., by Mary B. Wright	Account	17 MAY 1852	1851:090
Wright, Selden S., c/o Thomas, Jr. to his father	Bond	23 MAR 1836	1831:409
Wright, Susan M., c/o Edward L. to Mary Ann Wright	Bond	16 DEC 1861	1857:278
Wright, T.R.B., by William A. Wright	Account	19 APR 1875	1867:312
Wright, Thomas S., s/o Thomas, Jr. to his father	Bond	20 OCT 1834	1831:282
Wright, Thomas R.B., c/o William A. to William A. Wright	Bond	20 SEP 1858	1857:105
Wright, W.A. for his wife [Charlotte Barnes], from Archibald Ritchie	Receipt	19 MAR 1827	1825:158
Wright, William E., by B.P. Wright	Account	22 NOV 1881	1867:466
Wright, William E., by B.P. Wright	Account	16 APR 1883	1867:517

Ward or Subject (and Parent, Guardian or Other)	Record Type	Date	Reference(s)
Wright, Wm. E., c/o Robt. late of LA to Benj. P. Wright	Bond	17 DEC 1878	1867:389
Wyld, Ann Booker, d/o Thomas to Lewis Booker	Bond	16 JUN 1794	1761:201
Wyld, Ann B., by Lewis Booker	Account	20 DEC 1802	1796:123
Wyld, Eliz. Howlett, d/o Thomas to Lewis Booker	Bond	16 JUN 1794	1761:201
Wyld, Elizabeth H., by Lewis Booker	Account	20 DEC 1802	1796:123

Y

Yarrington, Elizabeth, c/o Richard to Kemp Gatewood	Bond	21 FEB 1814	1811:055, 059
Yarrington, Elizabeth, by Kemp Gatewood	Settlement	19 JUL 1819	1811:191
Yarrington, Mary, c/o Robert to Richard Miller	Bond	20 FEB 1809	1796:211
Yarrington, Mary, by Richard Miller	Account	20 APR 1812	1811:008
Yarrington, Wm., c/o Robert to Edward Miller	Bond	15 FEB 1808	1796:198
Yerby, Bettie V.L., c/o Addison O. to William G. Smith	Bond	19 FEB 1866	1857:378
Yerby, Thomas G., c/o Addison O. to his father	Bond	19 JUL 1852	1851:122
Yerby, Thomas G., above 14, c/o Addison O. to Wm. G. Smith	Bond	19 FEB 1866	1857:378
Yerby, Virginia L., c/o Addison O. to her father	Bond	19 JUL 1852	1851:122
Young, Ann Rebecca, c/o Henry, to John C. Richards	Bond	21 JUL 1828	WB22:504
Young, Ann Rebecca, c/o Wm. to John Richards	Bond	17 MAR 1828	1825:231
Young, Ann R., by John C. Richards	Account	15 JUN 1829	1825:291
Young, Ann R., c/o Richard H. Harwood	Account	19 NOV 1832	1831:149
Young, Catharine, c/o Henry to John Smith	Bond	16 OCT 1753	1731:171
Young, Fanny to John Smith	Bond	17 JUL 1750	WB8:347
Young, Frances, c/o Henry to John Smith	Bond	16 OCT 1753	1731:171
Young, Frances, c/o John, by John Smith, dec.	Account	17 AUG 1761	1761:007
Young, Frances, by James Jones	Account	16 AUG 1762	1761:015
Young, Frances, by James Jones	Account	15 AUG 1763	1761:028
Young, Frances, by James Jones	Account	20 AUG 1764	1761:044
Young, Frances, by James Jones	Account	16 SEP 1765	1761:056
Young, Godfrey, c/o William to Smith Young	Bond	21 NOV 1791	1761:175
Young, Henry, c/o Henry to John Smith	Bond	16 OCT 1753	1731:171
Young, Henry, c/o Henry, by W. Young	Account	17 AUG 1761	1761:001
Young, Henry, c/o Henry, by W. Young	Account	18 OCT 1762	1761:023
Young, John to John Smith	Bond	17 JUL 1750	WB8:347
Young, John, c/o John to Samuel Smith	Bond	15 MAY 1759	1731:240
Young, John, by S. Smith	Account	17 AUG 1761	1761:004
Young, John, c/o John, by John Smith, dec.	Account	17 AUG 1761	1761:007
Young, John, by Samuel Smith	Account	19 SEP 1763	1761:036, 037
Young, John, by Samuel Smith	Account	19 NOV 1764	1761:050
Young, John, c/o William to Smith Young	Bond	21 NOV 1791	1761:175
Young, Mary to John Smith	Bond	17 JUL 1750	WB8:347
Young, Mary, c/o John to Samuel Smith	Bond	15 MAY 1759	1731:240
Young, Mary, c/o John, by John Smith, dec.	Account	17 AUG 1761	1761:007
Young, Patty, c/o Henry to John Smith	Bond	16 OCT 1753	1731:171
Young, Patty, c/o Henry, by W. Young	Account	17 AUG 1761	1761:001
Young, Patty, c/o Henry, by W. Young	Account	18 OCT 1762	1761:024
Young, Philemon, c/o Henry to John Smith	Bond	16 OCT 1753	1731:171
Young, Philemon, by James Jones	Account	15 AUG 1763	1761:027
Young, Phillemon, by James Jones	Account	16 AUG 1762	1761:015
Young, Phillemon, by James Jones	Account	20 AUG 1764	1761:043
Young, Phillemon, by Alexr. Saunders	Account	16 SEP 1765	1761:056
Young, Rachel, c/o Henry to John Smith	Bond	16 OCT 1753	1731:171

Ward or Subject (and Parent, Guardian or Other)	Record Type	Date	Reference(s)
Young, Rachel, by John Richards	Account	20 SEP 1762	1761:022
Young, Rachel, by John Richards	Account	19 SEP 1763	1761:039
Young, Rachel, by John Richards	Account	20 AUG 1764	1761:046
Young, Rachel, by John Richards	Account	16 SEP 1765	1761:057
Young, Smith, c/o Henry to John Smith	Bond	16 OCT 1753	1731:171
Young, William, c/o William to Williamson Young	Bond	21 NOV 1791	1761:176
Young, Williamson, by George Davis	Account	20 AUG 1764	1761:045
Young, Williamson, by George Davis	Account	16 SEP 1765	1761:058
Younger, Ann to Thomas Younger	Bond	16 JAN 1732/3	WB5:120
Younger, James to Thomas Younger	Bond	19 DEC 1732	WB5:115
Younger, Jannett to Thomas Younger	Bond	19 DEC 1732	WB5:115
Younger, Mary to Thomas Younger	Bond	16 JAN 1732/3	WB5:119
Younger, Susannah to Thomas Younger	Bond	19 DEC 1732	WB5:115

No Surname

[ ], Allen, young negro, the property of Alfred B. Gordon, in March	Death	17 APR 1826	1825:095

BURIED NAME INDEX

A

Acres
James 1
Acrey
Arthur T. 1
Alexander
Aris 1
Joseph 77
William 75
Allen
Andrew 1, 22
Betsey 9
Catharine 3
Caty B. 3
Eliza 1
Erasmus 44
Hannah 1
Henry 1
James 1
James, Jr. 1
John 2, 38, 39
Lewis 31
Philip 1
Richard 36
Robert 1
Silvanus 1
Thomas 1, 3
Anderson
Burton P. 11
Churchill 14
Elizabeth 2
Robert S. 49
William H. 67
Andrews
Ann 2
James 2, 17, 58
Mark 2
Mary J. 2
Thomas 2, 17, 58
William 65
Armstrong
John T. 2
Purkins 36, 37
Richard 2
Arnold
Thomas T. 11
Atkins
Thomas 2
Atkinson
Charles 2
James 2
John 2

Richard H. 2
Attwood
Frances 2
Francis 2
Atwell
Milton 23
Ayres
Samuel 14
Thomas 57

B

Bagge
John 57
Baird
Matthew 3
Ophelia Cauthorn 16
Baldwin
John 3
Ball
Achilles 29
Churchill 3
Curtis 3
Harrison 3
Motta 24
Banks
George W. 55
James 19
Richard P. 67, 68
Tunstall 23
Washington 7
William 3
Barbee
John 56
Barefoot
Arthur 80
Edward 3
Barnes
A.L. 16
Arthur L. 3, 15
Charlotte 82
Mary C. Haile 40
Richard 3
Barton
Thomas 3
Basket
Abraham 3
Battaile
John 3
Bayliss
Betty Ann Coghill 18
S.P. 3
Silas P. 18

Baylor
Alexander T. 3, 4
R.P. 4
Richard 4
Robert 3, 4, 55
Robert P. 4
Bayne
Washington 68
Baynham
William 4, 5
William A. 31, 32
Beale
John 23
John H. 5
Richard 58
Beasley (see Beazley)
James B. 5
Beazley (see Beasley)
Ellis 5
Ellis A. 5
Ephraim 7, 51
Fanny J. 5
James B. 5
John 2, 18, 33, 42, 50
Teresa J. 5
William J. 5
Beazley & Anderson 6
Belfield
David P. 5
John 46
Bell
Ann B. Muse 57
Bentley
John G. 60
William 25
Berryman
Newton 5
Beverley
Carter 5, 6
Harry 42
Robert 5, 6, 42
Bigger
Ann B. Muse 6
Billups
Zorobabell 56
Birch
Lewis P. 44
Bird
Alexander 6
John 6
Sarah J. 6

Heritage Books by Wesley E. Pippenger:

Alexander Family: Migrations from Maryland

Alexandria (Arlington) County, Virginia Death Records, 1853–1896

Alexandria City and Arlington County, Virginia Records Index: Vol. 1

Alexandria City and Arlington County, Virginia Records Index: Vol. 2

Alexandria County, Virginia Marriage Records, 1853–1895

Alexandria Virginia Marriage Index, January 10, 1893 to August 31, 1905

Alexandria, Virginia Marriages, 1870–1892

Alexandria, Virginia Town Lots, 1749–1801
Together with the Proceedings of the Board of Trustees, 1749–1780

Alexandria, Virginia Wills, Administrations and Guardianships, 1786–1800

Alexandria, Virginia 1808 Census (Wards 1, 2, 3, and 4)

Alexandria, Virginia Death Records, 1863–1896

Alexandria, Virginia Hustings Court Orders, Volume 1, 1780–1787

Connections and Separations: Divorce, Name Change and Other
Genealogical Tidbits from the Acts of the Virginia General Assembly

Daily National Intelligencer *Index to Deaths, 1855–1870*

Daily National Intelligencer, *Washington, District of Columbia*
Marriages and Deaths Notices (January 1, 1851 to December 30, 1854)

Dead People on the Move: Reconstruction of the Georgetown Presbyterian
Burying Ground, Holmead's (Western) Burying Ground, and
Other Removals in the District of Columbia

Death Notices from Richmond, Virginia Newspapers, 1841–1853

District of Columbia Ancestors,
A Guide to Records of the District of Columbia

District of Columbia Death Records: August 1, 1874–July 31, 1879

District of Columbia Foreign Deaths, 1888–1923

District of Columbia Guardianship Index, 1802–1928

District of Columbia Interments (Index to Deaths)
January 1, 1855 to July 31, 1874

District of Columbia Marriage Licenses, Register 1: 1811–1858

District of Columbia Marriage Licenses, Register 2: 1858–1870

District of Columbia Marriage Records Index
June 28, 1877 to October 19, 1885: Marriage Record Books 11 to 20
Wesley E. Pippenger and Dorothy S. Provine

District of Columbia Marriage Records Index
October 20, 1885 to January 20, 1892: Marriage Record Books 21 to 30

District of Columbia Marriage Records Index
January 20, 1892 to August 30, 1896: Marriage Record Books 31 to 40

District of Columbia Marriage Records Index
August 31, 1896 to December 17, 1900: Marriage Record Books 41 to 65

District of Columbia Probate Records, 1801–1852

District of Columbia: Original Land Owners, 1791–1800

Early Church Records of Alexandria City and Fairfax County, Virginia

Essex County, Virginia Guardianship and Orphans Records, 1707–1888: A Descriptive Index

Essex County, Virginia Marriage Bonds, 1804–1850, Annotated

Essex County, Virginia Newspaper Notices, 1738–1938

www.ingramcontent.com/pod-product-compliance
Lightning Source LLC
Chambersburg PA
CBHW081157270326
41930CB00014B/3193